- QUALITY FIRST
- GEMBA ORIENTATION
- WASTE ELIMINATION
- VISUAL STANDARDS
- PROCESS + RESULTS
- PULL FLOW THINKING

CONSTANTLY FIGHT FOR THE ELIMINATION OF WASTE, VARIABILITY AND OVERBURDEN.

T RANSFER
I NVENTORY
M OTION

W AITING
O VERPRODUCTION
O VERPROCESSING
D EFECTS
S KILLS

D1001503

Kaizen in Logistics and Supply Chains

About the Author

Euclides A. Coimbra has over 25 years of experience teaching *kaizen* and implementing it across a wide variety of business sectors worldwide. He has served in various global leadership roles within the Kaizen Institute since 1998, including Director and CEO of Global Operations and Founder and Managing Director of the Kaizen Institute Iberia.

Mr. Coimbra has strong experience in quality improvement using total quality management (TQM) and especially design of experiments and Taguchi methods. He received first-hand training in Lean flow and pull-system principles at the Kawasaki Heavy Industries motorcycle plant in Japan. Building on this, as well as many successful just-in-time and Toyota Production System implementations in extended supply chains within Europe, he formalized *kaizen* in logistics and supply chains as a pillar consulting capability of the Kaizen Institute.

Prior to joining the Kaizen Institute, Mr. Coimbra served at Texas Instruments as production engineer in charge of quality improvement projects, as an assistant professor of industrial engineering at the University of Porto (Portugal), and with the Price Waterhouse Manufacturing Consulting Department. He earned a master's degree in industrial engineering from the University of Porto, Faculty of Engineering.

Kaizen in Logistics and Supply Chains

Euclides A. Coimbra

New York   Chicago   San Francisco
Lisbon   London   Madrid   Mexico City
Milan   New Delhi   San Juan
Seoul   Singapore   Sydney   Toronto

Kaizen in Logistics and Supply Chains

1 2 3 4 5 6 7 8 9 0   DOC/DOC   1 9 8 7 6 5 4 3

ISBN   978-0-07-181104-0
MHID   0-07-181104-4

The pages within this book were printed on acid-free paper.

Sponsoring Editor
  Judy Bass

Editorial Supervisor
  Stephen M. Smith

Production Supervisor
  Richard C. Ruzycka

Acquisitions Coordinator
  Bridget L. Thoreson

Project Manager
  Patricia Wallenburg, TypeWriting

Copy Editor
  James Madru

Proofreader
  Paul Tyler

Indexer
  Judy Davis

Art Director, Cover
  Jeff Weeks

Composition
  TypeWriting

CONTENTS

Foreword xiii

Preface xv

Acknowledgments xix

PART ONE

From *Gemba Kaizen* to Supply-Chain Excellence

CHAPTER 1   *Kaizen* **for Pull and Flow Across the Supply Chain** 3

Paradigms 4

Kaizen Principles in the Supply Chain 6

    Quality First 7

    Gemba *Orientation* 7

    Waste Elimination. 8

    People Development 10

    Visual Standards. 11

    Process and Results 11

    Pull-Flow Thinking. 12

Adopting the *Kaizen* Pull-Flow Principles 13

Keeping the System Going. 13

The Structure of *Kaizen* in Logistics and Supply Chains 14

CHAPTER 2   **The Story of Company A: No *Kaizen*, No Pull Flow!** 17

Process Improvement 18

The Supply Chain and Logistic Loops 19

    Logistics Loop 1: Picking and Delivery of Finished Goods 20

    Logistics Loop 2: Assembly of Finished Goods. 21

    Logistics Loop 3: Preassembly and Internal Manufacturing. 23

    Logistics Loop 4: Buying Components from External Suppliers 24

Continuous Improvement, Paradigms,

    and Real Pull-Flow Challenges 24

CHAPTER 3 **The Pulse of High Performance:**
Pull Logistics Loops and Customer _Takt_ 27

Creating Flow Depends on an Emphasis on _Muda_ 28
The Theory of Pull Logistics Loops 31
    Pull Logistics Loop 1: FGs Picking 31
    Pull Logistics Loop 2: FGs Production 33
    Pull Logistics Loop 3: Production Parts Picking 34
The Supply Chain: A Chain of Logistics Loops 34
Creating a Total Pull Flow 35
    Improving Production Flow 38
    Improving Internal Logistics Flow 38
    Improving External Logistics Flow 39
    The Total Flow Management Model 39

PART TWO

The Dynamics of _Kaizen_ in Logistics and Supply Chains

CHAPTER 4 **Creating Change Capability and Basic Reliability** 45

Creating a _Kaizen_ Mindset 46
Identifying the Critical _Muda_ Variables 46
The Four _M_s of Basic Reliability 48
    People Basic Reliability 49
    Standardizing 49
    Machine Basic Reliability 51
    Materials Basic Reliability 53
    Methods Basic Reliability 54
    More People Basic Reliability: Resistance to Change 54

CHAPTER 5 **Production Flow: Introduction and Line and Layout Design** . . 57

Line and Layout Design 58
Border of Line 59
Standard Work 60
Single-Minute Exchange of Dies 60
Low-Cost Automation 61
Line and Layout Design Revisited 62
    Large versus Small Machines and Lines 64

Simple Profiling and Line Balancing for Line and Layout Design . . . 66
Summary of Main Concepts 69
The 20 Important Principles of Layout and Line Design 71

CHAPTER 6   **Production Flow: Border of Line and Standard Work** 73

Border of Line 73
The Concept of the Small Container 73
Advantages of Using Small Containers 74
Two Types of Border of Line 76
Location of Parts and Containers in the Border of Line 77
Flow Containers 79
Arrangement of Parts and Single Feed 81
Defining Small Containers 82
Standard Work 83
The Standard Work Improvement Process 84
The Role of Containers in the Design of Standard Work 88

CHAPTER 7   **Production Flow: SMED Flexibility
and Low-Cost Automation** 95

SMED 95
The Impact of SMED on Capacity, Flexibility, and Flow 96
*The Conflicting Targets of Machine Utilization and
    Creation of Flow* 97
The SMED Process 98
Low-Cost Automation 100
Automation Levels 102
Examples of LCA Devices 104
LCA Design Guidelines 107

CHAPTER 8   **Internal Logistics Flow: Introduction and Supermarkets** 109

Introduction 109
Traditional Supply versus Flow Supply 110
The Logistics Domains 114
Supermarkets 114
The Mizusumashi ("Water Spider") System 115
Synchronization 116
Leveling 117

Production Pull Planning 117
How the Supermarket Concept Works. 118
Types of Flow Supermarkets 120
Deciding Supermarket Size. 124

CHAPTER 9 **Internal Logistics Flow: *Mizusumashi* and Synchronization**. . 127

Mizusumashi 127
Traditional Forklift Supply versus Mizusumashi *Supply*. 128
*Assembly-Line Supply (*Kanban *and* Junjo *Flows)* 131
The Water Spider's Standard Work. 133
Synchronization 136
What Is a Kanban *Replenishment Logistics Loop?* 136
The Six Types of Kanban *Loops* 139
What Is a Junjo *Logistics Loop?* 141
Some Examples of Supermarkets, *Mizusumashi*,
and Synchronization 144
Example 1 144
Example 2 146

CHAPTER 10 **Internal Logistics Flow: Leveling and
Production Pull Planning** 149

Leveling 149
The Process of Leveling 149
Designing the Format 150
The Toyota Definition of Leveling. 150
The Bullwhip Effect. 151
The Steps of Kaizen *for Leveling* 154
Line Sequencing: Sequencing the Production Lines 155
The Standard Leveling Model. 159
Production Pull Planning 162
Steps in the Production Pull Planning Process 162
Dealing with Demand Seasonality. 167
Two Models of Pull Flow. 169

CHAPTER 11 **External Logistics Flow: Introduction and
Storage/Warehouse Design** 171

Introduction 171
Source and Delivery: The Two Parts of External Logistics Flow 173

    Elements of External Logistics Flow 174
  Storage and Warehouse Design 178
    Organization and Availability 178
    Customer Packaging Requirements 179
    Warehouse Paradigms 181
    Warehouse Flow Principles 183
  Toyota's Journey to Lean Distribution 187

CHAPTER 12   **External Logistics Flow: Milk Runs and Source Flows** 189

  Milk Runs 189
    Customer-Service Policies 190
    Types of Milk Runs 192
    Using the Different Types of Milk Runs 196
  Source Flows 197
    Traditional Inbound Operations Flows 198
    Creating Flow in Inbound Supply Logistics 202
    Eliminating Muda *Through Synchronization in the Supply Chain* . . 204
    Elements of a Source-Flow Strategy 206

CHAPTER 13   **External Logistics Flow: Delivery Flows**
                    and Logistics Pull Planning 211

  Delivery Flows 211
    Flow Warehouse Operations 213
    Elements of a Delivery Flow Strategy 218
  Logistics Pull Planning 219
    Goods Ready to Be Sold 220
    Logistics Pull Planning Steps 222
    Order Pull Planning 223

PART THREE

How to Implement *Kaizen* in Logistics and Supply Chains

CHAPTER 14   **Facing the Truth: Analyzing the Current State**
                    of the Supply Chain 229

  Building Teams and Setting Challenges 230
  Preparing the Current-State Analysis 232

Mapping the Current State of the Material Flow 233
Mapping the Current State of the Information Flow 236
Understanding the Current-State Process 237
    Waste Observation and Awareness Exercises 237
Kaizen Reliability Training and Scorecard Audit 238
    Training Step 1: Basic Reliability 238
    Training Step 2: Production Flow 240
    Training Step 3: Internal Logistics 244
    Training Step 4: External Logistics 245
Defining the Main KPIs of the Current State. 249

CHAPTER 15   **Establishing the Vision: Designing the *Kaizen***
Pull-Flow Supply Chain 251

Beginning the Value-Stream Future Map:
   Creating Production Flow 251
Fine-Tuning the Map 253
Identify Clear Internal Logistics Loops. 254
Production Pull Planning 255
Create a Source Flow Strategy 256
Create a Delivery Flow Strategy 258
Finalizing the TFM Supply-Chain Design Strategy 259
    Using Mock-Ups 259
    Defining the Vision 259
    Putting It into Practice 260

CHAPTER 16   **Taking Action: The Power of the *Kaizen* Way** 263

Introducing the *Kaizen* Foundations Approach. 263
The *Gemba Kaizen* Workshop 264
    SMED Workshop 264
    Standard Work Workshop. 266
    Kobetsu *Workshop* 267
    Line Design Workshop 267
Specialized Subprojects 269
    Logistics Implementation 270
    Pull Planning 271
    External Logistics 272
Other Important Implementation Points 272

CHAPTER 17   **The *Kaizen* Pull-Flow Life of Company A** 275

The *Kaizen* Pull-Flow Project Planning Phase 276

Finished Goods Assembly Lines 278

Changes to the Planning System 280

     Finished Goods Pull Planning and Leveling 280

     Supermarkets and Mizusumashi *Lines* 283

     Implementing Other TFM Tools 283

     Summary of the Subprojects 284

Results and Ongoing Strategy 287

PART FOUR

Appendices

APPENDIX A   **Calculations for Transport *Kanban* Loops** 291

Kanban Loop 1: Transport Delivery *Kanban* 291

Kanban Loop 2: Transport Source *Kanban* 294

Order Size Calculations: A Word of Advice 294

Kanban Loop 3: Transport Internal *Kanban* 297

APPENDIX B   **Calculations for Production *Kanban* Loops** 301

Kanban Loop 4: Production Flow *Kanban* 301

Kanban Loop 5: Production Signal *Kanban* 305

Kanban Loop 6: Production Batch *Kanban* 308

APPENDIX C   **Two Types of Pull Planning Algorithms** 313

Logistics Pull Planning Algorithms 313

     Calculating the Logistics Pull Planning Algorithm 313

Production Pull Planning Algorithms 314

     Calculating the Production Pull Planning Algorithm 316

APPENDIX D   **Total Flow Management (TFM) Scorecards** 317

Bibliography 343

Index 345

About the Kaizen Institute 359

Kaizen Institute Worldwide Contact Information 361

FOREWORD

Lean has become one of the most popular management methods for enhancing the competitive strength of manufacturing and logistics companies in the past few decades. Because the introduction of Lean involves all levels of management and employs a number of unfamiliar terms such as *kanban*, *takt time*, *push*, *jidoka*, *mizusumashi*, and *muda*, it has not been easy to understand its full implications.

Consequently, Lean has so far been introduced in bits and pieces in many companies and not as a total supply-chain management system. Although the benefits of Lean are gained only when the web of the total flows has been extended throughout all the supply-chain processes, few companies have realized the full benefit of *kaizen* in logistics and supply chains.

As a result, very few companies so far have succeeded in embracing Lean as a total system across their entire companies.

Euclides Coimbra's book, *Kaizen in Logistics and Supply Chains*, has come at an opportune time, when many companies are going through reexamination of their supply-chain strategies in the aftermath of the financial crisis and the pressures of global competition. Many companies are seeking a road map to enable a quantum leap in improving their supply operations.

Coimbra's book will be a perfect guide both to those who wish to embrace Lean for the first time in their factories, warehouses, supply chains, or planning processes and to those who have begun their journey but have enjoyed only marginal success in embracing Lean.

The gist of the book can be captured in the following quotes:

"For now, forget about the jargon and the acronyms. We only need to concentrate on making a total flow of materials and information and minimize it."

"The information of the flow should come from the customer order and not from a sales forecast."

"By creating and increasing the flow, you can improve quality, reduce cost and inventory, and meet diversified customer requirements in terms of volume and delivery."

"Lean means to employ minimum resources for maximum output. Lean is what you gain as a result of building a Total Flow Management system."

Sound simple? Yes, it is, because we are not talking about high-tech solutions but rather about daily, hands-on contacts with the realities on the shop floor. However, it does require everybody's determination and commitment, which comes from *kaizen*.

Kaizen means ongoing, continual improvement and a mindset that is never satisfied with the status quo. *Kaizen* drives everybody to engage in the never-ending *kaizen* in logistics and supply chains. Coimbra says that you have to change the mindset, then change the *gemba* (shop floor), and then change the mindset again.

This book helps readers to review their activities and total supply chains from the vantage point of the *flow* and provides hands-on instructions for how to build a system based on *kaizen* in logistics and supply chains step by step. This book also includes a successful case study of a company that introduced *kaizen* in logistics and supply chains under the author's guidance.

Sometimes the detailed steps of introducing total flow across the supply chain as outlined in this book may seem to be too complicated and cumbersome, but when you start practicing them, you will find that they work—because *kaizen* also means learning by doing. *Kaizen* in logistics and supply chains is very much an action-oriented program of learning by doing.

I do hope that this timely book will help readers to survive the *Sturm und Drang* period after the financial crisis and build an enterprise of lasting prosperity.

Masaaki Imai
Founder, Kaizen Institute
Tokyo

PREFACE

Since I joined the Kaizen Institute Consulting Group in 1998, I have had the privilege of applying *kaizen* in many corporations worldwide. People's perceptions of *kaizen* have evolved since Masaaki Imai first presented the *kaizen* principles in 1985, and nowadays it is accepted as a fundamental management philosophy.

The meaning of *kaizen* is "change for the better" or "continuous improvement," and more and more companies are adopting continuous-improvement (or CI, as it is more commonly known) management systems. In fact, CI is becoming a company strategy dedicated to the continuous improvement of operations, a truly operational strategy based on *kaizen* principles and tools.

Lean is another way of describing *kaizen* or continuous improvement, and we often hear of companies implementing a Lean management system (sometimes called a *Lean transformation process*). Six Sigma is also very popular. Many consulting companies have recently altered their marketing strategy to Lean Sigma, which is supposedly a combination of Six Sigma and Lean. Regardless of terminology, the goal of all these strategies is the same—the implementation of a sustainable operations strategy that delivers extraordinary results in terms of safety, quality, delivery, cost, and motivation (SQDCM).

This is exactly what happened in Toyota with its well-publicized Toyota Production System (and lesser-known Toyota Operations System). The relentless, step-by-step application of *kaizen* principles changed the company's culture, defined the way of thinking of all its employees, and produced extraordinary results. Today this strategy has contributed to Toyota's undeniable global success and its recognition as a true leader in the field of manufacturing. Toyota is a truly *dantotsu* (meaning "by far the best") company!

Despite the success and popularity of many commercial CI brands offered by consulting companies and adopted by many corporations, it is a fact that few organizations really succeed in changing the company culture to a *kaizen* culture. It is not easy to fully incorporate a company-wide strategy, particularly one that aims to change the thinking and behavior of all employees and stakeholders. It can take years and should be implemented everywhere, every day, and by everybody (using the words of Masaaki Imai, founder of the Kaizen Institute). If such a culture is achieved, it will from its inception deliver significant benefits to the company, and these will be sustained or increased over subsequent years.

Why do many companies only become healthy and Lean for a while or when it suits them and then, sooner or later, go back to their original, unhealthy status?

This is the aim of the Kaizen Institute: to design and implement sustainable CI strategies that can make modern businesses more competitive.

This book is part of that quest.

It has long been known that, together with the *kaizen* spirit and mindset, Toyota has a superior physical operations model (as well as a production model), but that it is highly complex. Toyota never made a secret of this extraordinary model, but at the same time it has never made any effort to describe it in an organized, detailed way. Toyota invented the model and just started applying and deploying it in all its operations, whether manufacturing, distribution, transportation, or offices. Taiichi Ohno was the driving force behind this invention in terms of management methods and tools. Once this wonderful new operations model was established, many people became interested in explaining what was happening.

Consequently, there are many books today about Lean and the Toyota Production System. In my opinion, however, the existing literature on the Toyota Production System and Lean is incomplete, in the sense that there is no one holistic model that explains all of their applications in terms of the supply chain. The "production" (or manufacturing) side of the Lean model is well documented, but the link to logistics is less known. Every time we visit a Toyota plant or warehouse, logistics (whether internal or external) is there in action, but most people cannot see it because they cannot understand it in terms of a sound operations model. The model is indeed very different from the current operations paradigms based on central planning and "functional" optimization techniques, which can be seen in 99 percent of operations worldwide.

So we come to this book, in which we talk about Total Flow Management (TFM) and the holistic application of *kaizen* and Lean to the entire supply chain. Total Flow Management is about incorporating *kaizen* principles with pull-flow principles to streamline the whole supply chain. It uses the Toyota model to create a flow pulled by customer demand across any supply chain. It also explains the well-known Toyota Production System and its connection to sourcing and delivering, which together make worldwide supply chains a reality.

This book sets out a model for implementing the pull-flow principles in all types of operations. It refers to many improvement tools, some well-known and others less so. It is divided into three parts. Part 1, "From *Gemba Kaizen* to Supply-Chain Excellence," begins by explaining the seven main *kaizen* principles and the importance of really believing in them. On numerous occasions during consulting projects I have questioned my customer's degree of commitment to *kaizen* and Lean principles, such as *muda* (the seven Toyota wastes), visual management, or pull-flow thinking. These principles are regarded as golden rules in Toyota, and no one ever questions or doubts them.

This book then describes the story of Company A, a very successful company that for many years applied Lean but with no concept of *kaizen* and no true understanding of pull flow. Part 1 concludes by discussing pull logistics loops and the importance of being aware of their existence in any supply chain. They are there, just waiting to be seen, analyzed, and improved.

Part 2, "The Dynamics of the Total Flow Management Model," is dedicated to an explanation of the TFM model and its underlying four pillars, namely

▲ Basic reliability
▲ Production flow
▲ Internal logistics flow
▲ External logistics flow

Each pillar is composed of five improvement domains that are presented together with some examples and practical applications. Some improvement domains, such as the single-minute exchange of dies (SMED), are very well known, but others, such as *mizusumashi* (the Japanese word for "internal logistics standard work") or pull planning, are less common.

Part 3, "How to Implement *Kaizen* in Logistics and Supply Chains," is dedicated to explaining the fifth pillar of the TFM model, which is supply-chain design. The application of the TFM pillars and domains of improvement may vary a great deal depending on the particular type of supply chain (e.g., automotive, consumer goods, or processes and services), and supply-chain design is the way to customize a solution for any type of supply chain. It is based on application of the value-stream mapping (VSM) tool to the supply chain and includes the steps necessary to design a TFM supply chain, just as an architect would design a house before its construction. Building a *kaizen* pull-flow supply chain is a complex task, and it still amazes me how many companies begin building their "house" with only limited design and planning in place. The part ends by presenting the *kaizen* pull-flow life of Company A, the company introduced in Part 1. The new structure of Company A was designed and implemented following the TFM model.

Kaizen in logistics and supply chains based on the TFM model is a new operations strategy paradigm that has the potential to create a breakthrough in performance for the twenty-first century. The Kaizen Institute is convinced that 100 years from now this will be the prevailing paradigm in the most advanced supply chains. Why 100 years? It may seem a long time, and let us hope it is achieved far sooner, but consider the following: Toyota started its implementation 60 years ago, and some elements of the system have been well known since at least the 1973 oil crisis. History has demonstrated over and over again that it takes time for new ideas to be fully accepted.

The Kaizen Institute will continue the quest for the development of *kaizen* and continuous improvement. We hope that this book can be a trusted contribution to the advancement of operations management and a useful, creative source for implementing *kaizen* and Lean.

Euclides A. Coimbra

ACKNOWLEDGMENTS

Individually, we are one drop. Together, we are an ocean.

—RYUNOSUKE SATORO

This book is the culmination of many discussions over the last 10 years in the Kaizen Institute Consulting Group. Ultimately, the "several drops" created a mature model. It would be impossible to mention everyone who has contributed, so I will mention only those closest to me.

First, I would like to thank my colleagues from the Kaizen Institute of Portugal under the leadership of Alberto Bastos. On countless occasions we have debated the questions, What is *kaizen*? What is Lean? We are still searching for a satisfactory answer. My fellow consultants António Costa, João Castro, Tiago Sanchez, Rui Tenreiro, Tiago Costa, and José Pires have readily reflected on this with me and continue to be an endless source of ideas and inspiration.

Other friends from the Kaizen Institute Consulting Group, namely, Carlo Ratto, Ruy Cortez, Vinod Grover, and Udo Reimer, also have made invaluable contributions to furthering the development of *kaizen* in logistics and supply chains know-how. A special acknowledgment must be made to Danie Vermeulen and Richard Steel from the Kaizen Institute of New Zealand for their extraordinary support in reviewing my manuscript in terms of both its English and the clarity of the concepts covered.

In addition, I would like to thank Masaaki Imai for his boundless energy and enthusiasm when explaining the *kaizen* principles and for stressing the importance of flow, synchronization, and leveling (FSL), the basic principles behind *kaizen* in logistics and supply chains.

This book would not have been possible without the involvement of our customers and the rich experiences they provided to our consulting *gembas*. As I have often commented, the only way to continue learning is to continue doing stressful, difficult jobs. To this end, I would like to thank Mário Pais de Sousa, João Paulo Oliveira, Lázaro Sousa, Patrick de Bruyne, Filipa Pimenta, António Sá Cunha, and Horácio Sousa for the challenging projects they entrusted to us.

Writing a book is never easy, particularly when you are managing a global consulting company at the same time. I have achieved this with the help of my family, so I am indebted to my wife, Luisa, and my daughters, Silvia, Luisa, and Helena, for their unwavering love, support, and encouragement.

PART ONE

From *Gemba Kaizen* to Supply-Chain Excellence

CHAPTER 1

Kaizen for Pull and Flow Across the Supply Chain

The meaning of the word *kaizen* is "change for the better." It is a concept that today is being implemented by more and more people and organizations worldwide. Ever-increasing global competition and the information technology (IT) revolution have resulted in many challenges and stresses. More and more, businesses and individuals see the pursuit and achievement of the *kaizen* principle as a potential solution.

Kaizen is also known as *continuous improvement*. Masaaki Imai, founder and president of the Kaizen Institute and author of the world-famous books *Kaizen: The Key to Japan's Competitive Success* and *Gemba Kaizen: A Commonsense Approach to a Continuous Improvement Strategy*, says that *kaizen* is not simply continuous improvement but is improvement every day, everywhere, for everybody. *Kaizen*, in fact, can embody a way of life for modern corporations so that change for the better becomes a daily habit of continuous improvement.

This is precisely what the Toyota company has developed over the last 60 years in its Toyota way of management, in which continuous improvement is a daily occurrence. Toyota began implementing *kaizen* shortly after World War II. Many stories are told about Japan's relentless efforts to increase its economic competitiveness after World War II, particularly in relation to the high productivity of Germany and the United States. Toyota's aim was to make the rising Japanese automotive industry a success. Today, after more than 60 years of *kaizen*, Toyota is the undisputed leader of the automotive industry worldwide.

> *The Total Flow Management model is based on the creation of pull flow both in manufacturing and in supply-chain operations.*

We can see the *kaizen* spirit behind the ground-breaking discoveries of Taiichi Ohno at Toyota, who developed a new way of organizing manufacturing and logistics—the Toyota Production System (also known as *Lean transformation*), which is based on creating a flow of materials and information. Melding this system with the principle of *kaizen,* or the continuous improvement of operations, has brought about the most powerful operations strategy ever developed, as this book will show.

Based on our experience of implementing *kaizen* and Lean since 1985, we at the Kaizen Institute have developed Total Flow Management (TFM), a detailed model that allows the smooth implementation of the Toyota Production System not only inside manufacturing plants but also across complete supply chains.

We believe that TFM, which has its roots in *kaizen* and is a new way of organizing operations based on the creation of *pull flow* (a new operations system paradigm), is by far the best way of managing the operations of any company.

Before I explain TFM, though, I want you to look at the effects of resistance to change and consider the nature of paradigms.

Paradigms

The Lean system, or Lean transformation, is another name for the Toyota Production System. However, the system is not well described or understood—and therefore not very well established.

Anyone who has ever tried to promote and implement a new idea knows how difficult it can be to get the idea accepted. People simply resist change, and the reason they do so has to do with paradigms. A *paradigm* is a way of thinking (based on our values and beliefs and reinforced by standards, habits, and past results) that influences how we interpret a given situation or problem. When we react to a situation in a habitual way, this is called a *paradigm.* Each person reacts to events according to the particular paradigm he or she has adopted.

I prefer to simplify the concept of paradigms and just say that we all have two types of habits: physical habits and thought habits. And when we are confronted with a new idea, in most cases we react according to our habits. Carol S. Dweck, in her book *Mindset: The New Psychology of Success* (Random House, 2006), says that there are two types of people: those with fixed mindsets and those with growth mindsets.

People with fixed mindsets have rigid habits of behavior and thought that have provided some good results for them in the past. These people have difficulty in changing their habits (and, as a consequence, adopting *kaizen*). They believe that they already know all they need to know, and they find it hard to accept new ideas. They live with inflexible paradigms and are not open to change.

People with growth mindsets are the ones who are more ready to adopt *kaizen* because they are willing to change their habits and take on new, better ones. They are open to accepting new ideas and to learning new things. They live with flexible paradigms and are open to change for the better.

History shows us many examples of resistance to change and resistance to the adoption of new ideas or systems (let's call them *new paradigms*). In his book *Paradigms: The Business of Discovering the Future* (HarperBusiness, 1993), Joel Barker tells many such stories—the resistance Galileo encountered when he presented his theory that the earth revolved around the sun, for instance, or the refusal of the Swiss watch industry to adopt the quartz watch technology invented by a Swiss research laboratory—and other examples where people couldn't see and accept new, emerging ways of doing things, new paradigms that could change their industry and the world.

One of these stories that I like the most is about the change from wind-powered to engine-powered ships. In an effort to improve the speed of sailing ships, people tried to develop an old paradigm and improve it to its absolute limits on the basis of "more of the same." In this instance, the old paradigm, in the fifteenth century, stated that the more sails a ship had, the better its speed and performance would be.

Following this paradigm, for many years ships were built with more and more sails, to the point where a single vessel had a huge number of sails in order to take the fullest possible advantage of the wind. There was, of course, a limit to this. This is called the *limit of the current paradigm.*

While all these super-sail-powered boats were being developed, a new paradigm was emerging: What about a ship without any sails? This type of thinking, where you question the existing solution, is the kind that promotes and opens the mind to the adoption of new paradigms. Our current paradigm, of course, is for ships without sails. The big cruise and cargo ships that cross the oceans are propelled by powerful diesel engines, another new paradigm for powering ships (although no longer so new in the twenty-first century). The time will come when someone invents a commercial ship without a combustion engine. There are already nuclear-powered submarines.

The current paradigm in operations management is the no *kaizen*, no pull-flow paradigm. This tells us that there is no time for improvement and that an operations system that is based on big batches and order forecasts is the way forward. This is the reality on most shop floors, both in manufacturing and in logistics. People do listen to new ideas and are usually open to discussing them, but deep inside, the prevailing paradigm is still the old no *kaizen*, no pull-flow system (we call it the *push system*). This is why it is so difficult to implement the new *kaizen*, Lean, or Toyota Production System ideas, especially those related to supply-chain and logistics systems based on pull flow.

Let's take a closer look at the solutions used in the old paradigm. The old paradigm talks about big batches, so let's talk about unit batches (yes, batches of *one unit of product*). The old paradigm talks about order forecasts, so let's talk about no order forecasts (using only final customer orders). The old paradigm talks about no time for staff to be involved in *kaizen*, so let's talk about involving people, promoting awareness of *muda* (waste), and making *kaizen* a natural way of working.

Let's adopt a growth mindset and look in detail at the new Total Flow Management paradigm for the organization of supply chains. I promise you that it will open up new horizons.

Kaizen Principles in the Supply Chain

The *kaizen* pull-flow paradigm was developed by the Toyota Motor Corporation and applied to all its supply chains. It is a completely new operations model based on creating a *flow* that is *pulled* by real customer orders and on continuously improving this flow.

Creating a flow means creating a movement, both of materials and information, across any supply chain. This movement of materials and information should be driven by real customer orders or real customer consumption.

This means that in a supply-chain environment, movement of materials and information starts with the customer. Consumers buy (pull) products (materials) from the retail stores, the retail stores pull stock from the product distribution centers, the distribution centers pull from the manufacturing companies, and the manufacturing companies pull from their network of suppliers. This describes the flow in a simplified supply chain (a real supply chain probably will have many more elements in the chain both before and after the point of the final manufacturing facility).

Viewing the flow of material and information from the customer end is an important point of difference from other systems.

This is the system Toyota developed and applied in its supply chains, starting with the car dealers and going back to all its suppliers. It's a system whose underlying principles are pull flow (one-piece flow pulled by consumption) and a strong engagement in *kaizen* every day, everywhere, by everybody in the supply chain.

To put such a system into practice, companies need to develop a strong commitment to some *kaizen* pull-flow principles. These principles include

▲ Quality first
▲ *Gemba* orientation
▲ Waste elimination
▲ People development
▲ Visual standards
▲ Process and results
▲ Pull-flow thinking

Let me explain what I mean by these.

Quality First

This is a very important principle—a classic belief in terms of *kaizen*. From the very beginning of the quality movement, led by gurus such as Crosby, Deming, Juran, Ishikawa, and others, quality has been one of the most important factors in *kaizen*. This belief is supported by three concepts:

▲ Market in.
▲ The next operation is the customer.
▲ Upstream improvement.

The principle of *market in* (as opposed to product out) states that it is both possible and necessary to use real factual data to understand customers' quality, cost, and delivery (QCD) needs and to anticipate and understand their unstated wants and needs. In fact, a wonderful example of market in can be seen in Apple and the development of the iPhone. It is said that Steve Jobs, the cofounder of Apple, doesn't believe in market studies and prefers to develop products based on the idea of creating a superior customer experience. This is a type of market in showing that he really anticipated and understood unstated customer wants and needs—and developed a superior mobile phone as a result.

The principle that *the next operation is the customer* is also very important because it transforms the company into a chain of suppliers and customers, with each supplier doing its own market in and delivering zero defects to the customer.

Upstream improvement is the idea that the cause of any problem or defect is usually found at some point earlier in the process. To really find the root cause of any difficulty with the process, you have to dig hard further up the line.

"Quality first" is one of the most venerated beliefs at the Toyota Motor Corporation. Unlike pull-flow thinking, the quality-first belief is now almost universally accepted.

Gemba *Orientation*

Gemba orientation means "go to the *gemba* (the real place, the shop floor, the place to make improvement) and change the working habits of people for the better." There are two ways to change these working habits: Either we immediately change the physical layout so that people have no option but to work differently, or we change a work standard and train people to follow this new standard until it becomes a habit—and, in fact, a new working paradigm.

Gemba orientation is also the belief that *reality is stranger than fiction*. This means that what we *think* is happening in the *gemba* is usually quite different from what is actually taking place.

Taiichi Ohno used to say, "People's ideas are unreliable things, and I would be impressed if we were right even half the time. . . . Very often, after we try, we find that the results are completely opposite to what we expected, and this is because having misconceptions is part of what it means to be human."

This is why the following *gemba* orientation attitudes are so important:

▲ Going to *gemba*, the actual place where things are happening
▲ Thoroughly observing the reality
▲ Checking the *gembutsu* (the real things, the elements of that reality, such as tools, materials, and information)
▲ Speaking from the basis of observed and validated data

Gemba orientation also means that *if you desire to see, learn how to act*. In other words, if you truly want to understand a new idea without misconceptions, the best way is to try it and learn how to do it yourself. The learning process of actually putting the idea into practice will result in a much deeper understanding.

At the Kaizen Institute, we involve people in what we call the *gemba kaizen* workshop. This is an intensive period of work undertaken by a group of people whose aim is to design and implement improvements within a short time frame (usually up to five days). The workshop is preceded by preparation days with a group leader. Afterwards, there are follow-up sessions with the group to reinforce and train the new standards so that strong new habits are established.

Waste Elimination

Waste elimination is the first pull-flow-related *kaizen* principle. *Kaizen* defines seven forms of waste and targets their elimination as a way of achieving competitiveness and excellence. These seven wastes include

1. Defects (internal or external failures of quality)
2. People waiting
3. People moving
4. Too much processing
5. Material waiting
6. Material moving
7. Overproduction

In all the *kaizen* and Lean literature, you will find that these seven types of waste are part of a broader concept—that of the three *M*s: *muda*, *mura*, and *muri*.

Muda, we already know, means "waste." *Mura* means "variability" and is a concept that represents the lack of stability and reliability. Too much *mura* means too many unexpected variations from moment to moment. For example, one moment a machine is under control, and the next it's not. And then it's under control again, even though you did nothing.

> The aim of kaizen *is to constantly fight for the elimination of waste, variability, and overburden.*

Muri means "too difficult" and stands for the concept of time and energy loss. A bad ergonomic position in a workstation that requires the worker to bend is a waste of time (the movement has to cover a greater distance than necessary), a waste of energy, and a risk of injury (because the energy required for the movement can go over the threshold of the individual's capacity).

So the three *M*s consist of the seven types of *muda* (waste), *mura* (variability, or the lack of reliability), and *muri* (loss of time and waste of energy).

Some authors, such as Taguchi, even talk about measuring variability in terms of loss to society. The greater the standard deviation of a quality variable, the deeper is the feeling of loss the user will experience.

One thing I always question is the degree of commitment people have to the seven types of waste. In my experience of working with companies to implement a *world class business management system* and various improvements, people have no problem accepting and believing in wastes one through four. These four kinds of waste are widely accepted. Nobody questions that defects, people waiting, people moving, and too much processing should be eliminated (or at least reduced).

In contrast, wastes five through seven are not so easily accepted. Let's look at each of these wastes one at a time.

Muda 5: Material Waiting

This is more commonly known as *stock* or *inventory*. I prefer to call it the *muda of material waiting* because while material is standing, nothing is happening, the material is not being transformed, and no value is being added. Why don't people accept this as a waste? Because they have learned that inventory has a purpose or is a consequence of the optimization of another variable (such as machine or plant capacity). These may be valid reasons not to believe that inventory is a waste. But what if the same process could be achieved with lower inventory—and what if the machine or plant capacity were independent of the amount of inventory?

Muda 6: Material Moving

This is also known as *transport*. I call it *material moving* to stress the fact that here, too, no value is being added because no transformation is happening. Some types of transport are considered a waste, and people have no difficulty in accepting this. Generally, however, getting people to accept the concept of transport as a waste is difficult. People tend to believe that the number of situations where movement is clearly waste is less than the number of situations where the movement is necessary, and they see no alternative solution. One typical comment is that *all* logistical activities should be considered waste. This thinking rings alarm bells because it indicates that people don't really believe that transport is a waste. We will see later how this type of belief can be changed.

Muda 7: Overproduction

This *muda* refers to the accumulation of inventory through an error in forecasting customer demand and production capacity or an imbalance between machines or for many other reasons. This is a type of inventory, and the same reasoning applies as for waste number five. People have difficulty accepting that too much production is a waste. They tend to feel that at least when a customer order comes, the product is already available, and they don't need to bother making it.

What happens is that wastes five, six, and seven are not easily seen as waste. Most people consider that material waiting, material moving, and overproduction are features of the system that provides the goods to society. They have a hard time accepting that these kinds of waste can be reduced and don't really think that it is possible that they can be eliminated. It is a problem of mindset.

Can you guess which company has demonstrated the strongest dedication to fighting the seven types of waste (muda), variability (mura), and overburden (muri)?

It is Toyota, of course.

By trying to eliminate all *muda*, Toyota invented a new operations system whose fundamental guiding principles are the seven plus two wastes and applied it to all the Toyota supply chains. The results the company has achieved are amazing—and the basis of it all is strong beliefs and a lot of practice and reinforcement.

People Development

This principle places a great deal of emphasis on the involvement of people in the improvement activities. The most important aspect is that working in teams and developing people ultimately result in the development and adoption of new habits of working that improve quality, reduce costs, or improve customer service—or achieve all three.

The first step in changing a habit is to become aware of possible improvements. For example, a product-changeover operation occurs on many machines or lines. The people doing the changeover are not usually aware of the importance of reducing the changeover time or of their way of working because they do it automatically (this, after all, is the definition of a habit). When we involve them in the improvement effort, we show them a film of a changeover. By observing what actually happens during a changeover, they begin to develop an awareness of all the wastes and inefficiencies that take place—which is the first step toward improvement.

> *For each type of improvement or change, there is a habit to alter. For each habit, there is a group of people who will need to drop old habits and adopt better ones.*

For new habits to be adopted, everyone in a company, from top management to the shop floor, needs to be involved. The way to do it is by organizing *kaizen*-focused teams. Developing people through teamwork is one of the strongest principles of *kaizen*.

Visual Standards

The *visual standards* principle embodies the concept that a picture is worth a thousand words and that a standard is the most efficient known way of performing a task. It's as simple as that. First, it is very important to define the most efficient way of performing a task. If the task is not standardized, it is usually prone to variability (a key *kaizen* concept). When several people perform a task, each one probably will have a different way of doing it.

The *visual* aspect of the standard is also important. A standard that is based on pictures, drawings, and creative word pictures is quickly and easily understood, unlike the text-based descriptive standards and instructions we see in many *gembas*.

Standard work is a special type of visual standard. Standard work represents the optimization of the movements of workers (according to a certain cycle time and following some rules for maintaining a good flow of materials). In a standard-work standard, it is easy to observe the movements of a worker, how much time the action takes, and other important information relating to the maintenance of material flow. We will come back to standard work and its important connection to pull flow later.

Process and Results

Process and results is another very important *kaizen* principle. Many managers believe that defining the target is all that is necessary; the method of achieving the result is not important. They say, "I don't care about the method (process)—just deliver the results!"

However, if you are really serious about *kaizen*, you have to look in detail at the process and analyze the ways to improve it. Just imagine that you are a golfer wanting to improve your handicap. What do you do? Do you focus only on the handicap you get, or do you establish a strong connection between the process that you are following and the result that you are achieving?

You will probably think about improving the process in terms of posture (swing), equipment, and even mental preparation. Only by working on process improvement can you achieve good results. It is this focus on improving process details that will bring extraordinary results.

In fact, process-and-results thinking assigns equal importance to the process and the result. The result is also important, in the sense that it is a commonly agreed target for the team or group (the company)—a kind of north star that gives you direction. It also allows you to check whether the process improvement is having the right effect.

Pull-Flow Thinking

Now we come to the really controversial principle. Very few people really believe in pull-flow thinking. *Pull flow* means organizing all your supply chain (or, to simplify and narrow the concept, your internal logistics and manufacturing flows) in terms of an optimal material flow and an optimal information flow. To achieve this, the emphasis must be on eliminating the *muda* of material waiting—in other words, your inventory. The term *pull* means that the material flow should be pulled and initiated by customer consumption or customer orders.

The idea of material flow—ideally, a one-piece flow all across a supply chain—frightens many people. From their school years, people have been told that processing a batch is more economical than producing a single unit. People believe that it makes sense to think in these terms, when, in fact, it simply *looks* more efficient to work in this way. In terms of information flow, too, it seems strange to consider working according to customer consumption or orders because these usually mean a relatively small quantity, and so once again, there is a feeling of inefficiency. Many people are still stuck in the old paradigm of demand forecasts and batch-and-queue flow.

Pull-flow thinking is the essence of the Toyota Production System. In this book we will see why and how it works. For the moment, just remember that for Toyota people, this is the number one principle. The Toyoda family and Taiichi Ohno started thinking in this way and through trial and error invented a radical new method of organizing operations that continues to produce outstanding results. This has become known as the *Toyota Production System*—a more appropriate name for this would be the *Toyota Operations System* or the *Toyota Supply-Chain System*. In this book we describe it as TFM—Total Flow

Management, based on the latest developments of pull systems over the Kaizen Institute's experience of 25 years.

Adopting the *Kaizen* Pull-Flow Principles

Most managers we meet don't have a full understanding of and belief in the seven *kaizen* principles. In many cases, they simply don't understand what these principles mean. Therefore, they can never fully benefit from the indisputable value of applying them. This is why it is so important for managers to make an effort to learn about these principles.

So what is the best way to acquire the *kaizen* pull-flow ethos? It is a process in which you have to change your mindset, then change the *gemba*, and then change your mindset again. I mean that you have to start by trying to change your thinking through reading (in fact, reading this book is a good first step toward acquiring the *kaizen* principles). Being exposed to new ideas and concepts is also important. This could be in the form of, for example, benchmark tours or visits. It is also helpful to talk to a Toyota manager or anyone involved in a pull-flow operation. If you have the opportunity to visit a Toyota plant (or supplier), you probably will see all the principles working on the shop floor.

But there is no substitute for the real thing. To really learn something, you have to do it, experience it. A *kaizen* expression says, "If you desire to see, just learn how to act." If you really want to understand, you have to practice and live the real thing—you have to be exposed to the *gemba* reality.

The best way to demonstrate the value of the system is through a *gemba kaizen* workshop. I talked about these workshops earlier. They involve an intensive implementation session involving key people in the organization who need to identify the waste, eliminate it, and then maintain the new process. There are many types of *kaizen* workshops; later in this book I'll cover which are the most appropriate for building strong pull-flow beliefs. For the moment, just remember that if you want to understand the process, you have to apply it and do it, probably on a limited scale or as a pilot project, and then learn from the experience. Toyota was a pioneer whose ideas are now much easier to implement, but why not be a pioneer and an innovator in your own industry?

Keeping the System Going

Once the system has been established, there is the question of keeping it going. We call this *sustainability*. We hear many stories of companies that have tried this process but were not capable of maintaining it. When this happens, it's because people have gone back to their old beliefs and habits—a case of not being able to adopt the new *kaizen* in logistics and supply chains paradigm of TFM.

One of the reasons this happens is that the implementation focused only on a few points and was not a complete pull model. If you really do a full implementation, you are in fact changing the operations system in its entirety. All its subtle nuances will be altered, and all functions will be involved, from operations planning to purchasing through to product and process design, as well as all the manufacturing functions. Some people call this a Lean transformation, but to be genuinely successful, it has to be a Lean pull-flow transformation.

Many Lean projects and Lean transformations follow the Christopher Columbus model. Winston Churchill rightly pointed out that when Columbus set out across the Atlantic to the Americas, he didn't know where he was going; when he got there, he didn't know where he was; and when he returned, he didn't know where he had been—and he did it all with borrowed capital.

Unfortunately, many Lean transformation projects are done in this way, and only a very limited number have the luck of Christopher Columbus in developing a really sustainable new system that represents a breakthrough in results.

Another factor that works against the success of many Lean transformation projects is the limited scope of the approach. The implementers simply forget to include the customers (the delivery supply chain) and the suppliers (the source supply chain) in the system design.

The Structure of *Kaizen* in Logistics and Supply Chains

The approach to *kaizen* in logistics and supply chains via the TFM system is one that includes the entire supply chain of a given company. The starting point for the design is the point where you are located in the supply chain. Maybe your organization is a manufacturing facility or a product-distribution facility. By applying the model, you will be creating your internal pull-flow system and also considering how you can expand this model, both downstream of your supply chain (what we call the *delivery side* of the supply chain) and upstream (the *source side* of the supply chain).

In fact, we are talking about a TFM model based on the process of creating a flow of materials and information aimed at achieving breakthrough results in terms of quality, cost, and delivery.

The basic TFM model is shown in Figure 1.1. This diagram shows the different supply-chain flows from the perspective of a single manufacturing plant. The delivery of raw materials and components from suppliers to the plant is shown as regular, high-frequency transport loops. Manufacturing is pulled from the retail customer on the basis of continuous real demand requirements (execution orders). Similarly, forecasts are also sent from retail customers, to be used for capacity-planning purposes only—not to drive actual production.

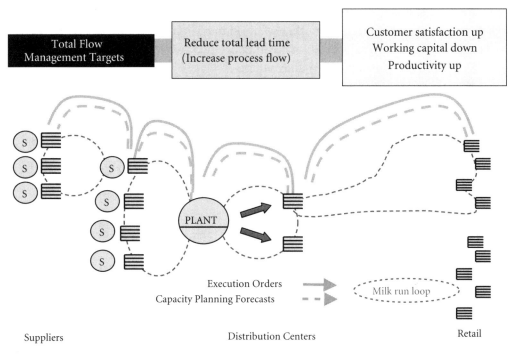

Figure 1.1 The TFM model.

The main target is the reduction of the total lead time in the supply chain. The measure of lead time is the inventory coverage across the entire supply chain (this can be measured in days). It is called *lead time* and not *coverage* because the inventory coverage is usually a good estimate of the time it takes one individual product unit to cross the chain.

Reducing lead time also eliminates the waste of waiting and really means creating a material flow. Rigorous systems, processes, and standards are required to create and maintain this flow and to ensure

▲ Reduced cost
▲ Reduced working capital
▲ Increased productivity
▲ Improved quality
▲ Higher levels of customer service and satisfaction

This is achieved by creating a flow across the entire supply chain, starting with customer consumption—that is, production can be driven by real orders or inventory-replenishment orders. It will be necessary to physically create one-piece flow, one-container flow, and one-pallet flow and to accelerate this flow by redesigning transport routes using the concept of high frequency transport loops (another solution many managers find hard to accept).

Forecasts will no longer be used for creating production or distribution orders; rather, they will be used only for capacity management.

At the same time, the system works to change the company culture to one that is based on the *kaizen* spirit of improvement every day, everywhere, and by everybody.

In the following chapters we will see how this can be achieved.

CHAPTER 2

The Story of Company A: No *Kaizen*, No Pull Flow!

Before providing a detailed presentation of the Total Flow Management (TFM) model, I want to tell you the story of a no *kaizen*, no pull-flow company.

Company A is a very well-respected company belonging to one of the largest corporate groups in the world. The company was founded in 1977 in a small European country and started operating under license from the corporate group. The company was at that time owned by the founding family.

The founding family had high hopes for development of the company, which produced water-heating devices such as water heaters and boilers for the domestic appliances market, and worked hard for many years to achieve this. Between 1977 and 1988, the company became the market leader in the country, with a sound business and a respected trademark. The owners were, however, concerned about quality issues and made quality one of their key areas for improvement. The local university was brought in to build a database of quality defects, and a concerted effort was made to find and eliminate internal and external failures. These methods were very successful and yielded excellent results for many years.

In 1988, the company was bought by the corporate group that had been licensing the brand and providing some of the technology for a number of years. The original CEO from the founding family became the general manager, and the company became the biggest and best plant in the group.

Since its inception, Company A had been a model organization, with a very good social climate in which everyone worked hard for the success of the company. The general manager continued his existing policy of excellence, now reinforced by the values, mission, financial power, and technical and organizational know-how of the corporate group.

Company A had always been very profitable; joining the corporate group created new horizons and new opportunities. Company A quickly became a product-development center for the corporation, exporting to all European markets and soon dominating the European market.

Process Improvement

The story of Company A is clearly that of a very successful and profitable business—In fact, one that was used to increasing productivity by a minimum of 10 percent every year. Why, then, did this company suffer from a lack of *kaizen* and pull flow (as noted in the chapter title)?

After the initial years of strong investment in *quality improvement* (we have to remember that the 1980s were the heyday of Total Quality Management [TQM] and many other quality initiatives), Company A started looking for other ways to increase its performance. At the beginning of the 1990s, the company introduced a *two-bin system* to reduce the stock-outs of components supplied to the assembly lines and began to make some smaller improvements in the *productivity* of the assembly lines.

At the same time, an important project was started in the press section, aimed at cutting the changeover time in the stamping presses by half (from about two hours to one hour).

Some projects to implement *one-piece flow cells* also were initiated and achieved a high level of integration of operations. Some *bending cells* and *subassembly cells* were created, with very good results.

This strategy of improvement continued steadily from the very beginning of the company through to the end of the 1990s. Every year the company saw an overall improvement in productivity of around 10 percent, with continuous improvement in quality and customer service. Meanwhile, a big drive on product development launched many new products and established Company A as the biggest and most profitable plant in the corporation.

By the end of 1999, the main key performance indicators (KPIs) of the plant were as follows:

Total inventory coverage (raw materials plus work in process plus finished goods)	50 days
Internal defects rate	12,000 parts per million (ppm)
Customer service level	91 percent
Achievement of the assembly production schedule	50 percent
Productivity	70 parts per operator
Final assembly-line efficiency	75 percent

All the KPIs showed a good trend until the end of 1999, but from 2000 on, it became more and more difficult to create further improvement, and all the KPIs reached a plateau. It looked as though the initial improvement streak had ended.

By this time, the company was using a lot of Lean tools. The main ones included

▲ Quality problem solving
▲ Single-minute exchange of dies (SMED)
▲ Integration of operations into one-piece flow lines
▲ A two-bin system (full-box/empty-box *kanban*)
▲ Maintenance improvement
▲ A scheduling and synchronization system (I will discuss this system in more detail in due course)

This company had invested considerable efforts to change its approach and develop new initiatives. Why was this not enough to sustain the improvements?

The Supply Chain and Logistic Loops

This is a good place to analyze the supply chain of Company A. As a marketer of consumer goods (i.e., water heaters), the plant has a product distribution center (PDC) on site. This warehouse is divided into two areas: one for distribution direct to customers (product installers and retail stores) and another for in-transit storage to PDCs in other countries. Thus the customers of the plant also can be divided in two groups: direct and final customers nationally and PDCs belonging to the same corporation but sited in other countries. These PDCs receive the goods and store them ready for delivery to customers in their own countries.

Company A has four final assembly lines, three for water heaters and one for boilers. Each line operates on a cycle time of about 30 seconds and assembles about 2,500 products per day. The suppliers of these lines can be divided into three groups:

▲ Parts preassembled (in four preassembly lines)
▲ Parts manufactured internally (the degree of internal manufacturing was relatively high because the main parts were manufactured within the plant)
▲ Parts bought from external suppliers

For the sake of simplicity, let's say that the final assembly lines have the same three types of suppliers: preassembly lines, internal suppliers, and external suppliers. The preassembly lines are supplied from both internal and external suppliers.

The size of the finished product is about 3 feet × 1 foot × 1 foot. The biggest part, the metal cover, is of approximately the same dimensions as the finished product. Other parts inside (e.g., the copper burning chamber) are about one-third the size of the product. The number of finished-goods references (or stock-keeping units [SKUs]) is about 600.

Note: Here I would like to introduce the concept of *logistics loops* (LLs). Pull logistics loops are a conceptualization of several pull-flow operations that are an essential part of any supply chain.

Figure 2.1 shows how Company A's supply chain can be divided into four main types of logistics loops types of logistics loops (LL1 to LL4):

LL1—picking and delivery of finished goods (FGs)
LL2—assembly of FGs
LL3—internal subassembly and manufacture of parts
LL4—buying of parts from external suppliers

Logistics Loop 1: Picking and Delivery of Finished Goods

LL1 for Company A can be defined as

1. The loop starts with the *final customer order* (the final customer here is the retail or product installer who buys the product from the corporation).

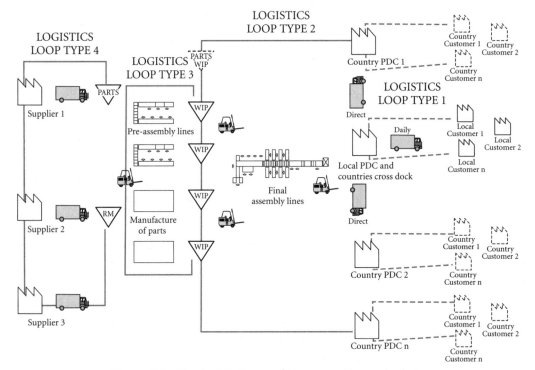

Figure 2.1 The logistic loops of Company A's supply chain.

2. The customer orders on a daily basis and expects to receive the product within the next couple of days from the order. Some customers go to the PDC to pick up the product immediately.

3. Sales orders are then picked and packed in the PDC.

4. The product is dispatched by a third-party transport provider, usually for delivery to the customer on the next working day.

Company A manages this logistic loop directly in the case of the local PDC (the warehouse serving the requirements of local customers). The PDCs in the other countries also manage their own local customer orders. This means that Company A doesn't have complete control over all parts of the complete supply chain. Company A has no information about the inventory and sales-order statistics held by PDCs in other countries, which, despite belonging to the same corporation, are legally independent companies.

The amount of finished goods inventory kept on hand in the local PDC is about 15 days' worth of sales (inventory coverage). Customer service, measured in terms of delivery in full and on time (DIFOT), is about 91 percent.

Here we see the first example of *nonfunctional inventory*: How is it possible to have 15 days' worth of inventory and miss 9 percent of customer orders?

The 91 percent service level was a major problem because it usually resulted in lost sales—customers don't want to wait and will order from a competitor who has the product available. This meant that the company was consistently losing about 9 percent of sales because it did not have the right product available at the right time.

> *Too much inventory and low service levels can be easily explained by having too much of what you don't need and too little (or none) of what you need immediately.*

The DIFOT situation in the PDCs in other countries was probably even worse because there was a delivery lead time to fill their orders (LL2), making the overall lead time even longer. (In addition to assembly, it involved transport by truck, which could take anything up to a week.)

The amount and type of inventory on hand were in fact being determined by the effectiveness of LL2: deciding what to assemble and then implementing this plan. Let's look at this now.

Logistics Loop 2: Assembly of Finished Goods

LL2, the assembly of the finished goods, for Company A can be defined as

1. The finished-goods planning section (belonging to logistics) issues assembly orders.

   2. A weekly plan for final assembly is prepared.
   3. A daily schedule for final assembly is prepared
   4. Parts are collected for assembly.
   5. The product is assembled and delivered to the PDC.

This loop also can be started by assembly orders from the other PDCs in the corporation.

Planning

For the first step of this loop, the finished-goods planners use a centralized planning system based on a very common model, *enterprise resource planning* (ERP). They receive monthly orders from PDCs in other countries and also a monthly order from the local PDC. These monthly orders are prepared by the sales offices in each country. Because of the characteristics of the market (remember, the final customers order on a daily basis), the only way to calculate a monthly order is by making a forecast, which is then sent to the planners. The planners do not know how this forecast is calculated; they simply use this information to start the planning process.

In the case of the local PDC, there is a calculation error in the forecast (generally between −18 percent and +16 percent). This was one of the causes of the 9 percent failure in customer service.

There is always some level of error associated with any method of forecasting because forecasts by nature make assumptions about the future.

As well as the monthly forecast, the PDCs also send a forecast for the next six months. This information is used in two ways: a monthly plan and a weekly plan (the weekly plan is simply the monthly information divided by the number of weeks in the particular month).

The monthly plan is used to discuss and agree on the assembly and manufacturing capacity of the plant. The weekly plan is used to start the assembly. The weekly plan is then frozen each day until 11 a.m., when an assembly schedule is sent to the assembly lines, in the right sequence, and for the amount agreed on for the line capacity.

The degree of fulfillment for this plan was only 50 percent. Why? The reason is that the necessary components were not always available, and adjustments had to be made to the schedule and the plan almost daily. This fact also explained the dysfunctional inventory seen in the finished-goods PDC.

Another hidden problem was the highly stressful weekly planning process. The planners had to redo the plan numerous times within the week and take into account the availability of hundreds of parts. The level of departmental overtime consequently was very high.

The assembly lines had a cycle time of 30 seconds and an efficiency of 75 percent compared with time standards computed using the methods-time measurement (MTM) system. At this time, a line-design expert from corporate headquarters calculated the efficiency-improvement potential of the lines to be only about 3 percent. Management decided that this improvement was too small to justify any investment.

Since the beginning of 2000, improvements in productivity had been very small. Management became worried about the implications of this perceived lack of improvement potential.

Logistics Loop 3: Preassembly and Internal Manufacturing

LL3 for Company A is defined as

1. Preassembly and internal manufacturing orders come from the weekly plan for final assembly.
2. Parts are collected for preassembly or manufacturing.
3. Preassembly and manufacturing are completed.
4. Delivery is made to the final assembly line.

Production in the subassemblies was started by a proprietary production planning system that calculated the required quantity of each preassembly based on the daily schedule of the final assembly lines. The scheduling of the preassembly lines followed the sequence defined in the final assembly line. Because so many adjustments had to be made to this schedule, the supervisors of all the lines had a planning meeting every day from 9 to 11 a.m., during which they tried to find the best schedule to improve synchronization. Often the final assembly lines had to change sequence because of a lack of parts that had to be purchased externally, breakdowns, or quality problems.

The manufacturing sections, which had long setup times, were using the weekly plan to make weekly batches.

Delivery to the final assembly line was made by forklift drivers, who worked according to the instructions of the line and section supervisors. Traffic was very high, but supervisors had very little time to dedicate to improvements because most of their energies were spent trying to synchronize assembly and preassembly.

Surprisingly, the level of work in process (WIP) between the assembly and preassembly lines was relatively small, and the plant was in fact praised for maintaining very low levels of WIP in the group (in fact, it was considered to set a benchmark). For the preassemblies, the level of WIP was about one day. In the case of the manufacturing sections, it was about five days.

Logistics Loop 4: Buying Components from External Suppliers

LL4 for Company A is defined as

1. A buying plan is calculated on a weekly basis, with a six-week horizon.
2. Orders for parts are sent to suppliers.
3. Suppliers manufacture or pick the parts in their facilities.
4. Parts are transported to the plant.
5. Parts are received, checked for quality, and stored in a parts warehouse.

The amount of inventory in the raw materials and parts warehouse was about 30 days' worth, and the DIFOT of the suppliers was about 81 percent. This situation was worse than that in the finished-goods area, with more inventory and worse service to internal customers.

The ordering system was based on the ERP system, with forecasts being sent to suppliers and a weekly call-off schedule based on the first week of the forecast plan. For some remote suppliers, the call-off period was higher and in some cases was achieved only monthly.

The transport consisted of direct deliveries of fully loaded trucks. The inbound process was slow, with the parts left waiting several hours or even days for quality control to process the shipments.

The warehouse was a typical warehouse managed by a system that optimized the space available. The racks allowed storage up to seven meters in height. There was an area for storing small parts, but most of the parts were stored in pallet-sized, nonreturnable containers.

The supply to the production lines was made according to the picking and dispatch orders coming from the internal users, who were using a computer-based ordering system. It was basically the section supervisor who decided what, how much, and when to order. The two-bin system worked in a similar way—the empty bins were used by the supervisors to order the replenishment. Internal transport was organized in one-hour timetables, but the times were unreliable (sometimes it took more than one hour to complete the cycle and sometimes less).

Continuous Improvement, Paradigms, and Real Pull-Flow Challenges

At the start of 2000, corporation headquarters decided to launch a corporate initiative for continuous improvement (CI). A corporate team was set up to develop the CI model. The reason behind this initiative was that all plants applied various improvement tools, but there was no common strategy or common terminology or "language" behind the planning.

Neither was there any system for measuring the degree of development and application of the model.

The first audit applied to Company A showed a score of about 28 percent. This was a surprise to many people inside the plant because they thought that they had used all sorts of improvement tools and couldn't see where further improvements could be made.

One of the existing paradigms in the company was that *gemba* people (the operators and team leaders) did not need to be involved in improvement initiatives. All the improvement activities had been undertaken by project teams and the engineering department.

Another paradigm was that everybody was convinced that they already had a pull system. The production manager in particular argued that the plant was working according to hourly batches in the final assembly. (This was indeed the case because the plant was defining assembly batches that mostly took one hour to assemble. The problem was, however, that the information used to calculate the hourly batches was coming from the forecasts, which is not a pull system driven by customer needs or consumption.) Another argument was that the plant was using the customers' orders to plan the assembly (this was true in the case of the country PDCs, but these orders were in fact forecasts produced by the PDCs, not final supply-chain customer orders).

This paradigm was reinforced by an internally developed synchronization system between the final assembly and the preassemblies (as well as the manufacturing sections). The production manager argued that this system, working according to a central material requirements planning (MRP) algorithm, was pulling to the assembly supplies on an hourly basis.

The problem was that the quality of the synchronization was not effective not only because it depended on the MRP system but also because of the poor synchronization of material movements on the shop floor. The extremely complex logistics of supplying hundreds of components was not being handled very effectively at all.

What was needed was a complete change from a push system to a pull system, with improved flow on the shop floor.

When we observe the system through *kaizen* eyes, we can identify all *muda* (waste), thereby discovering many opportunities for improvement. Basically, all areas of operations can be responsible for *muda* elimination activities. The problem is that it is relatively easy to say that we have too much *muda*, but it is harder to believe that we really can eliminate it. It only becomes reality when this elimination is backed by a strong conceptual model of flow and pull across the supply chain together with experience in implementing it.

> *It became clear that the current system for information and material movement had reached its limit and that a new paradigm had to be implemented if the company wanted to move beyond its current limitation.*

For four years the plant continued to train people and deploy improvement projects in many areas as a result of the corporate CI initiative. By now, it was the end of 2004. However, the push system was not altered, and the flows were never significantly redesigned. As a result, improvement in all the main KPIs was very slow. The plant could no longer show the pace and vitality of improvement that it had in the past.

The time had come to try a system change, with the following targets:

▲ Reduce the finished-goods inventory
▲ Achieve over 98 percent DIFOT in final customer service
▲ Achieve over 98 percent DIFOT in assembly plan fulfillment
▲ Reduce inventory of parts and raw materials
▲ Achieve over 98 percent DIFOT in deliveries from suppliers
▲ Increase overall productivity by a minimum of 10 percent every year
▲ Continue reducing the number of quality defects
▲ Improve the corporate CI audit score from 10 to 20 percentage points every year.

This was the challenge that was finally accepted by Company A. Today, competition in any market is so strong that only the best can survive. Continuous improvement, better defined as improvement every day, everywhere, by everybody, gives a key competitive advantage. Company A was used to being the best in its particular field and couldn't imagine reducing its rate of improvement. A new paradigm had to be implemented. A system change had to be developed and adopted. The old system had reached its limits.

In a later chapter I will show the results Company A achieved by designing and implementing a true model for *kaizen* in logistics and supply chains.

CHAPTER 3

The Pulse of High Performance: Pull Logistics Loops and Customer *Takt*

> All we are doing is looking at the time line from customer order to cash collection . . . and we are reducing that time line by removing the non-value-added wastes.
>
> —TAIICHI OHNO

When Taiichi Ohno was asked what Toyota was doing in terms of improvement strategy, he gave a fine answer. He explained that all the company was doing was creating a flow of materials and a flow of information. The meaning of *flow* is "movement"—the company was trying to create a movement of materials and information by removing the non-value-added waste in the flow timeline. Creating movement means eliminating all the time that materials and information in the system spend waiting. While things are waiting, nothing is happening, so it is non-value-added time.

Ohno was referring to two different flows, the timeline from customer order to order delivery and the timeline from invoicing the customer to collecting the cash. Together these two flows are the essence of operations management. The second flow, of course, is basically an information flow. How can you reduce the timeline from invoicing to cash collection? It involves a lot of waiting and non-value-added operations. However, if the first flow, from order to delivery, is achieved quickly and effectively (i.e., good quality and good service), the chances are that the second flow will go smoothly, too.

Let's go back to the main flow, the one from customer order to delivery of the order. This flow, as Shingo explained very clearly in his seminal book *A Study of the Toyota Production System: From an Industrial Engineering Viewpoint* (Productivity Press, 1989), is made up of many different operations. In fact, Shingo makes a distinction between four types of operation: transport, inspection, waiting, and transformation (value added). He says that a process is a sequence of these four types of operations repeated many times in a supply chain and that improvement is the elimination of all types of operations except the value-added ones. It is only after going through this relentless process redesign that the remaining operations should be improved (point improvement)—for example, doing 5S in a workplace or standard work in an assembly cell.

By using the concepts developed by Ohno and Shingo for the creation of flow by eliminating all *muda* and non-value-adding operations, we can define the system for *kaizen* in logistics and supply chains as *an integrated system for increasing the process flow and pull effectiveness across the entire supply chain.*

We have already seen the meaning of flow. Here I add to it the word *pull. Pull* means that the start signal for production or distribution should be a fixed final customer order. In fact, the flow must be pulled by the *customer takt. Customer takt* is a concept that quantifies the average customer consumption cycle in relation to the manufacturing or distribution facility working time. *Takt* is calculated by dividing the daily working time by the daily quantity consumed (or demanded).

If the facility can operate at the same cycle time (facility cycle time balanced with customer takt time), then theoretically there will be no muda of material waiting or too much output.

I will talk more in the following chapters about customer *takt* and how to create a flow according to the consumption pull cycle. For the moment, it is important to remember that pull means to operate in conjunction with consumption signals.

How to create a pull flow across the whole supply chain is the essence of the Total Flow Management model. The main measure of flow is the *lead time*, which is an estimate of the several timelines existing in a supply chain from order through to delivery.

The more pull flow you create in your supply chain, the more profitable and effective the supply chain will be. This is the new operations management paradigm of the twenty-first century—even if it still has a long way to go before most people accept its feasibility.

Creating Flow Depends on an Emphasis on *Muda*

We have already discussed the seven Toyota types of *muda* (Figure 3.1). We have seen that most people accept four of them but that there are three types that are harder to believe because they contradict all obvious observations. These are the *muda* of material waiting, the *muda* of material movement, and the *muda* of too much production.

All these wastes are related to inventory management, be it production inventory (e.g., work in process) or distribution inventory ready for delivery in product distribution centers (PDCs). The less inventory you have, the better is your flow. But don't forget about customer service—on-time delivery according to customer pull. Applying *kaizen* to logistics

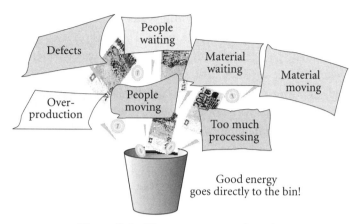

Figure 3.1   The seven types of *muda*.

and supply chains means both reducing material waiting and increasing on-time delivery. It is about simultaneously reducing the working capital and improving customer service.

Why is it so difficult to believe that the elimination of these three types of waste is a major benefit and should be the focus of any effort to redesign or improve the supply chain? It is because for many years we have been told, in university and operations management schools, that inventory has a major role in operations. And it does! But this doesn't mean that it cannot be reduced by the redesign of all the types of processes and operations that exist in the supply chain.

You may be familiar with the work of the graphic artist Maurits Cornelis Escher, who specialized in creating visual paradoxes, showing situations we know to be physically impossible as apparently achievable. Look at one of Escher's best-known illusions, the *Waterfall* lithograph of 1961 (Figure 3.2).

Figure 3.2   Escher's *Waterfall.*

In this image we have the impression that the water is continually flowing from bottom to top, powered by the moving wheel at the bottom. The illusion is created by the design of the canal, which looks to be going down (suggesting a flow of water) when, in fact, the several canals together make us think the water is flowing up. Everybody knows that a simple moving wheel is not enough to power the highly fluid mass of water. So this is a *paradox* (something impossible that looks possible). Most of the concepts we use to do *kaizen* in logistics and supply chains to eliminate the *mudas* of material waiting, too much production, and material moving also look like illusions and paradoxes to most people when they first see them.

We will see later that the most powerful concept for creating a flow of materials is the integration of operations into one-piece flow cells or lines.

"One-piece flow, am I hearing right?" you ask. "Everyone knows that working with a batch of material is better for productivity because the operator always has materials to produce and can achieve greater speed."

One-piece flow looks like a paradox, and so is often dismissed. I have to tell you that when I started studying the Toyota Production System, it took me a long time to accept that this system actually works. Only after many trials and much testing in pilot lines did I fully understand why it is not in fact a paradox.

Let's look at some logistical paradoxes. What about using only small containers (600 mm × 400 mm × 300 mm) to move all parts inside the plant? This immediately seems to be another paradox (because everybody knows that to minimize transport, we should use larger containers) and so is also hard to accept. What about increasing the frequency of transport in order to reduce material waiting time? Surely it's not possible! It is a big paradox because by doing this, we will, of course, increase transportation costs.

> One of the goals of the Total Flow Management (TFM) model is to demystify the words and make what looks like a paradox emerge as a workable concept that will deliver a breakthrough in company performance.

I have just given you three examples of flow paradox. This is why most people who are educated in classic operations management concepts have a really hard time believing in the flow *muda*. They see no way that this can be useful or possible.

Concepts such as one-piece flow, elimination of forklifts, frequent transportation using milk runs, and many others that are integral to *kaizen* in logistics and supply chains are really difficult to accept. At first glance, they look impossible—paradoxes.

One of the goals of the applying *kaizen* to logistics and supply chains is to demystify the words and make what looks like a paradox emerge as a workable concept that will deliver a breakthrough in company performance. This is one of the reasons why we at the Kaizen Institute developed the TFM model—to clarify and bring light to the many paradoxes of total flow.

The Theory of Pull Logistics Loops

As we progress through this book, I will explain why the flow concepts that look like paradoxes are actually very powerful tools to create a pull flow. First, however, I need to introduce the concept of *pull logistics loops.* I began explaining this in Chapter 2 when we looked at the process of Company A.

Pull logistics loops are a conceptualization of several groups of process operations that are ingrained in any supply chain. This conceptualization helps in analyzing the flow and in seeing how and where to create a new one. The loops are simply there, waiting for someone to develop them and gain an incomparable competitive advantage.

Let's consider a simple supply chain that has a supplier and a customer. The supplier is a manufacturing company with a warehouse that stores incoming purchased materials and parts and another warehouse for production and the distribution of finished goods. The customer is a PDC warehouse. The symbols used to depict this simple supply chain are the triangle (for the warehouses or main storage points) and the circle (for operations, the processing of either information or materials).

> *Pull logistics loops are a conceptualization. The loops are simply there, waiting for someone to develop them and gain an incomparable competitive advantage.*

A warehouse, in other words, is an interface point between two loops in a supply chain. The two main groups of operations performed in a warehouse are the *inbound* (e.g., checking, sorting, and binning) and the *outbound* (e.g., picking, checking and sorting).

The three main types of pull logistics loops (Figure 3.3) that can be found in this simple supply chain include

▲ Finished-goods (FGs) picking
▲ FGs production
▲ Production parts picking

Pull Logistics Loop 1: FGs Picking

Let's start by explaining the first logistic loop (LL1), FGs picking. This loop starts with the customer's decision-making process about buying the goods. In this case, the customer is a distribution warehouse, so the decision to buy is probably part of replenishing inventory. When the FGs reach their reorder point, the customer decides to replenish its inventory by reordering the item. The reorder point will have to be calculated in such a way that the quantity remaining will be enough to satisfy demand during the time it takes for replenishment. Or the buying decision could be: Let's order this product because we have

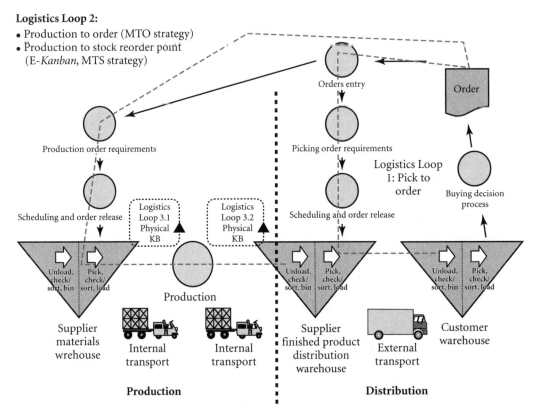

Figure 3.3 Three types of pull logistics loops.

a prospective customer who we know will order or who already has ordered this product. In any case, a decision is made to issue an order for the product.

The order is then forwarded to the supplier, who starts processing this information—entering the order into its sales order system, calculating the picking order (it may be a grouping of several similar products), scheduling the picking order, and releasing the order to the warehouse for processing.

Then we go into the warehouse (FGs inventory) picking process and then the checking, sorting, and packing of the product. Finally, the product is loaded onto transport to be delivered to the customer warehouse. In the customer warehouse, the product then has to go through the inbound system of checking, sorting (possibly to optimize binning), and binning in the appropriate location (or it may be cross-docked immediately to an outbound area).

This is the first logistics loop. The goal for this type of loop, once the buying decision has set it in motion, is to create a flow by eliminating all the stages in which material and information are kept waiting. The main constraints in this loop are usually that the product is not available when needed for picking and the frequency of transport, which implies waiting. We will see later how to improve this flow. For now, it is very important to have a good understanding of the operations in this logistics loop.

Pull Logistics Loop 2: FGs Production

Logistics loop 2 (LL2) is the FGs production loop. The starting point of this loop (the decision to produce the product) can be one of two types: Either the product already exists in the FGs warehouse and the production decision is to replenish its consumption (rather like the customer's buying decision), or the product doesn't yet exist and a decision is made to produce it to order. Usually, any FGs product reference can be classified as *make to stock* (MTS) in the first case or *make to order* (MTO) in the second.

An MTS FG can be made to order if the order is really large. In the case of MTS products, we should allow the order size to be the driver in deciding whether we make it to order or we look at stock replenishment.

After deciding how much to make, we have to go through a sequence of calculations aimed at deciding the production order requirement. We might have a minimum batch size, or perhaps we can group some orders. We need to have a way of calculating the necessary materials or parts according to a bill of materials.

The next type of operation will be the production order scheduling and order release. In this instance, we will have to check the best sequence for the pacemaker lines (the lines or machines that will be scheduled in the first place and that usually define the capacity of the plant).

The information-processing flow can be very time consuming. We need to be certain that we are optimizing our internal productivity in every way. In the meantime, however, the customer is consuming its FGs inventory (the MTS case) or waiting for the order to be completed (the MTO case).

After the order has been processed, the movement of materials can begin. In most cases, the main component will have to be picked from the material store (or the order simply can go directly to the pacemaker line, where all the necessary materials are waiting). Transport and production will have to take place in the right order until the product is finished and enters the FGs warehouse (going through the inbound operations as well).

Once again, there are many opportunities to create a flow. The main ones here are related to the batch size of the production order, the difficulties in production (e.g., defects or availability of machine capacity), the frequency of internal transport, or the unavailability of materials. We will see later how to create a flow in production and how to create a flow in internal logistics.

Pull Logistics Loop 3: Production Parts Picking

The third main type of logistics loop (LL3) is production parts picking. This loop refers to the production parts needed to process the main component, which was picked in LL2, FGs production. Now we need to pick and supply the necessary components in a synchronized way (not an easy task—the number of parts can be in the hundreds or even thousands).

Picking and moving parts to the several points of use (points where the parts are needed for processing or assembly) are usually a process of replenishing to the point of use (or close to point of use). This can be done by using a physical *kanban* or an electronic call-off system that orders the parts from the point of use to the supplying storage points. It is a logistics loop quite similar to the FGs picking loop seen in the first example but with many aspects that are unique to this stage.

The difference between this loop and the previous one (the FGs production loop) is that here the planning and scheduling work is not as difficult (or was partly done in the preceding loop), and we can just pick and move to the correct point of use according to the consumption replenishment signals.

What are the main flow constraints? These are many, the worst being the huge number of different parts that may be required. It is a matter of synchronization: how to synchronize the movement of hundreds of parts so that they are received just in time for the processing or assembly of the main FGs order.

You will see that the TFM model aims to achieve perfect synchronization using replenishment signals and physical devices and standards on the shop floor. It must be a system that is able to react quickly so that when a need is detected, the right actions happen quickly and effectively without the need to stop and plan or make a decision. I will talk a lot more about how to achieve this when I discuss *kanban* (continuous supply), *junjo* (sequenced supply), and standard work in logistics.

The Supply Chain: A Chain of Logistics Loops

The three main types of pull logistics loops form a kind of framework of natural pull information and material flows in the supply chain. Usually, what we see in practice is that companies subvert these flows and build unnatural push-type logistic loops that make it difficult for the information and material to flow. As we have seen, the no *kaizen*, no pull flow of Company A is a good example of overlapping the natural pull logistics flows with artificial systems and processes (usually

Any supply chain (from the raw materials mine to the final consumer) is made up of a series of these three basic pull loops.

modeled in an enterprise resource planning [ERP] system and using a centrally planned material requirements planning [MRP] model that tries to synchronize and control every movement without all the necessary actual shop-floor information).

Any supply chain (from the raw materials mine to the final consumer) is made up of a series of these three basic pull loops. If we represent an extended supply chain, from final consumer to suppliers (as shown in Figure 3.4), it is easy to understand that it is in fact made up in this way.

The supply chain in Figure 3.4 is made up of four FGs picking loops and two FGs production loops (represented in the picture). How many basic production parts picking loops does it have? Two, because there are two manufacturing facilities in this supply chain, and we know that we always have production parts picking loops associated with a main FGs production loop.

When we analyze the supply chain in terms of pull logistics loops, we can see how easy it is to spot where all the complexity lies. In the automotive industry, for example, the complexity is in the FGs production loop (final assembly) and production parts picking loop (parts supply to the assembly line). This is so because there are thousands of parts that need to be synchronized into the assembly of dozens of different FGs (consumers demand a wide variety of cars, the FGs).

Other industries, seen in terms of the pull logistics loops model, have other areas of complexity depending on the particular bill of materials they require (i.e., the number of parts that go into the finished product) and their market distribution flows. It is not the aim of this book to expand the application of the pull logistics loops model to all types of industry but to introduce the model as a simplified concept that will make it easy to design a *kaizen* pull-flow solution for any type of supply chain.

Creating a Total Pull Flow

We can now take all the information and material flows in our pull logistics loops and group them into three main areas of improvement (as shown in Figure 3.5):

▲ Production flow
▲ Internal logistics flow
▲ External logistics flow

These three main areas of improvement are also referred to within the *kaizen* management system as the three TFM pillars. The complete TFM model, based on state-of-the-art *kaizen* pull-flow principles for creating the leanest and most responsive supply chains, is shown in Figure 3.6.

36

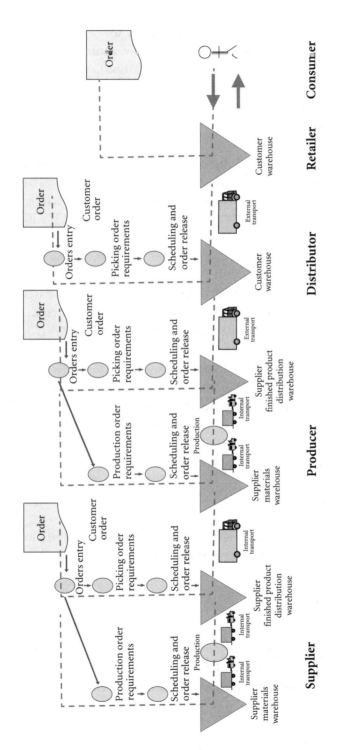

How many main logistics cycles in this supply chain:

- 4 FG picking loops
- 2 FG production loops
- 2 production parts picking loops

Figure 3.4 A chain of logistics loops.

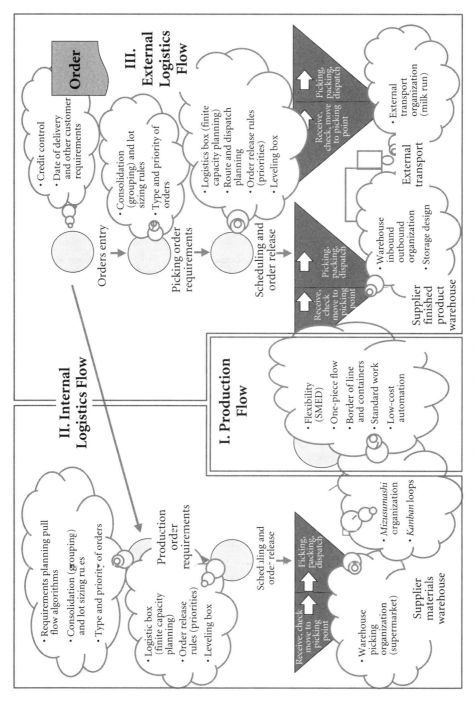

Figure 3.5 The three main pillars of *kaizen* in logistics and supply chains: production flow, internal logistics flow, and external logistics flow.

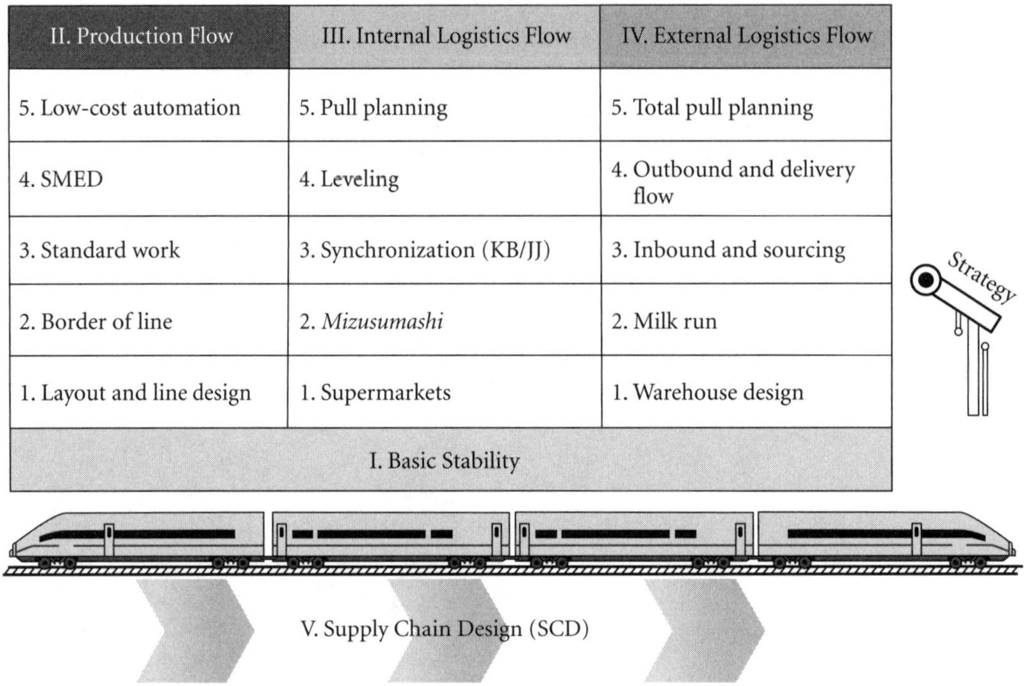

II. Production Flow	III. Internal Logistics Flow	IV. External Logistics Flow
5. Low-cost automation	5. Pull planning	5. Total pull planning
4. SMED	4. Leveling	4. Outbound and delivery flow
3. Standard work	3. Synchronization (KB/JJ)	3. Inbound and sourcing
2. Border of line	2. *Mizusumashi*	2. Milk run
1. Layout and line design	1. Supermarkets	1. Warehouse design
I. Basic Stability		

V. Supply Chain Design (SCD)

Figure 3.6 The TFM model.

Improving Production Flow

The first step in improving production flow is to really implement one-piece flow, achieve flexibility in changeovers, create a flexible and efficient parts supply, and improve operator efficiency. The different types of improvement projects or events for product flow can be grouped into the following categories:

- ▲ *Layout and line design*—to achieve one-piece flow
- ▲ *Border of line*—to achieve flexibility and efficiency in parts production
- ▲ *Standard work*—to achieve efficiency in operators' movements
- ▲ *Single-minute exchange of dies (SMED; quick changeover of line or machine)*—to achieve flexibility in product changeover
- ▲ *Low-cost automation*—to achieve more efficiency in operators' movements and also improve the *muri* (unreasonably difficult task) of operators' work

Improving Internal Logistics Flow

The internal logistics flow includes all movement of small containers inside the production facility, as well as the information flow related to the handling of consumer pull orders (these orders are usually embedded in production planning and scheduling). The different types of improvement areas for internal logistics flow can be grouped into the following categories:

▲ *Supermarkets*—to simplify and increase the efficiency of picking production parts
▲ *Mizusumashi (also known as "water spiders" or internal transportation workers)*—to simplify and increase the efficiency of transporting parts to the points of use
▲ *Synchronization*—to simplify the coordination of parts supply and production between the different links in the production flow
▲ *Leveling*—to schedule the lines and machines efficiently while at the same time diminishing the whiplash effect in the supply chain (this will be explained later)
▲ *Production pull planning*—to calculate the production orders according to consumer pull rules

Improving External Logistics Flow

The external logistics flow includes all external flows of pallets to the production facilities as well as the creation of information flow related to consumer pull in the finished-goods picking loops. The different improvement areas for external logistics flow can be grouped into the following categories:

▲ *Storage and warehouse design*—to produce the most efficient physical infrastructure for warehouses
▲ *Milk run*—to create flow in external transport operations
▲ *Inbound*—to create a physical flow of pallets and small containers in the inbound operations of warehouse facilities (in both plant and distribution warehouses)
▲ *Outbound*—to create a physical flow of small containers and pallets in the outbound operations of warehouse facilities (in both plant and distribution warehouses)
▲ *Logistics pull planning*—to calculate the picking orders according to consumer pull rules

The Total Flow Management Model

At this point, our model for *kaizen* in logistics and supply chains based on pull and flow is almost complete. There are, however, two other pillars (Figure 3.6) that we need to add. These are the pillars of

▲ Basic reliability
▲ Supply-chain design

Basic Reliability

Basic reliability is related to the Toyota concept of *basic stability*, which says that to create flow, you need to achieve a certain level of basic stability in terms of the four *M*s (i.e., manpower, machines, materials, and methods). Contrary to what you would expect, the concept of stability says that if you cannot rely on your manpower (because people are not complying with the timetables or miss work), then you cannot create a material flow because the tightly balanced lines or cells will not work (an example is a car assembly line where the entire line is unable to work if one worker is absent). If the workers are not used to working in teams, you also will have problems in creating a one-piece flow.

The same reasoning applies to machine stability. If the availability of machines is low (normally less than 80 percent), this lack of reliability means that you cannot create a good flow. The same thing happens with material supply if you have serious material shortages or the suppliers are unreliable. It is also true of methods and the effect of bad or variable methods on the quality of products (*bad method* is a synonym for a *lack of reliability*).

Basic reliability is a question of how reliable your manpower, machines, materials, and methods are and how far you can trust your people (operators, maintenance, and suppliers) and processes. Our experience at the Kaizen Institute is that at the beginning of any TFM project, you have to evaluate the level of the basic reliability of your people and processes in order to avoid problems when you start implementing the other flow pillars.

We prefer to start with creating some basic reliability through *gemba kaizen* workshops that clinically target large-scale reliability issues. This pillar is a reminder that there may be some big obstacles in your supply chain and that you should start by finding reliable countermeasures to them. This doesn't mean that you have to wait before starting to create a flow. You will see in the final chapters of this book how to begin implementing changes.

Supply-Chain Design

The fifth pillar is supply-chain design. Many people have heard of and practiced *value-stream mapping* (VSM). This is a good tool for representing material and information flows. In fact, it is better at representing information flows than material flows. In most cases, material flows are better represented by using a layout drawing of the physical flows (usually known as a *spaghetti chart*).

In each case, we need to act as an architect and design the the supply chain based on Total Flow principles. Each company has its own basic reliability problems and its own history and culture. These histories are manifested in many physical elements (e.g., layouts, machines, storage facilities, and transportation) and in many habits (e.g., ways of performing and thinking). It is vital that these factors are taken into account in the initial design of the the supply chain based on Total Flow principles. The *kaizen* pull-flow architect, of course, will use all the flow tools in the TFM model to develop the best solution for the company's supply chain.

A good architect will design a *dantotsu* (the best of the best) house; we aim to design *dantotsu kaizen* pull-flow supply chains. To explain this concept more clearly, and to make the link with the pull logistics loops that exist in any company and in any supply chain, the TFM model shown in Figure 3.6 also can be represented in the way shown in Figure 3.7. In this figure, you can see the three types of pull logistics loops. The diagram also divides the external logistics pillar into two sides: source flows and delivery flows. Within each of these areas there is the need to create flow in storage and warehouse design, milk run, inbound, outbound, and logistics pull planning.

In the chapters that follow I will discuss each one of the five pillars of the TFM model in more detail so that you can understand the dynamics of *kaizen* in logistics and supply chains.

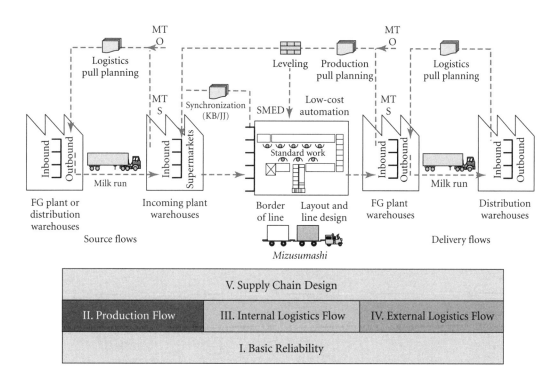

Figure 3.7   An alternative way of depicting the TFM model.

PART TWO

The Dynamics of *Kaizen* in Logistics and Supply Chains

CHAPTER 4

Creating Change Capability and Basic Reliability

The first pillar of our model for *kaizen* in logistics and supply chains is the foundation of basic reliability (Figure 4.1). We have already seen that it consists of developing stability in terms of manpower, machines, materials, and methods—the four *M*s of any operational environment. This stability also can be measured in terms of trust that our basic resources will work reliably when we need them to execute customer orders.

To have sustainable basic reliability, it is also necessary to develop *change capability*. By this I mean that the company must start to develop a culture of change or continuous improvement, one that allows new ideas to be put forward, discussed, and tried out on the shop floor. The company needs to develop a growth mindset in order to become a *learning organization*.

In Part One we discussed the need to be able to accept new ideas even when they look like paradoxes, impossible at first glance. It is therefore very important to start implementing a continuous-improvement culture at the same time as the discussion, design, and implementation of a pull-flow system.

Taiichi Ohno had both a growth mindset and a *gemba* mindset. He believed strongly in the *kaizen* principles. In his book, *Taiichi Ohnos Workplace Management* (McGraw-Hill, 2012), he says that all human beings are prone to having many misconceived ideas about what does and does not work. He explains that in order to arrive at new solutions, one has to develop a *gemba* attitude of willingness to try new ideas without having preconceived ideas about their outcome. If you accept that your ideas may or may not be correct, he says, you will want to try them in order to validate your theories. Doing this will involve your subordinates and colleagues in the project, and they will develop more respect for you when they see that your decisions are based on tested results. This willingness to try out new ideas rather than making decisions based merely on personal opinion or "gut feel" will give your opinions and suggestions more weight.

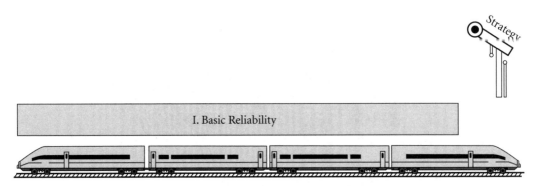

Figure 4.1   Pillar I of the Total Flow Management model.

Another term for this is *learning by doing*. At the Kaizen Institute we say that too much meeting-room discussion is counterproductive because everybody has misconceptions (often based on so-called common sense), and the only real way to know if something works is by trying it out. This is part of developing change capability, and only with change capability can we have reliable processes. This is the type of thinking and environment of acceptance we need to foster if major change projects are to be successful.

Creating a *Kaizen* Mindset

Before attempting to change or improve something, increase your awareness of it through direct observation. This is part of Ohno's *gemba kaizen* spirit.

Many people are so used to performing certain tasks throughout the day that they don't consciously think about what they are actually doing—it has simply become a habit. They are like car drivers just going along on autopilot without noticing what is actually happening, following a protocol deeply ingrained in the neurologic circuitry of their brains by many years of habit. It happens to us all.

This also means that we are often not aware of certain things or variables that are not adding value to our internal or external customers—variables that are important for the competitiveness of the company. Most people who work directly in any operation are not really aware of what I call the *critical muda variables*.

Identifying the Critical *Muda* Variables

The first step in developing change capability is to involve cross-functional focus groups in *muda* awareness exercises to help them understand that they have improvement opportunities. The second step is to give these focus groups *muda* elimination challenges on which to work.

Let's consider, for example, the classic Lean improvement variable of reducing machine changeover (CO) time. Here the critical *muda* variable is the time taken between the last good-quality workpiece from the previous batch to the first good-quality workpiece of the next batch. Traditionally, the total CO time in a given period is reduced by increasing the batch size. The actual CO time was considered to be a fixed parameter for operations management.

Critical muda variables refer to key measurable indicators of the drivers of waste.

Now let's focus on CO time in more detail. You go to the machine, make a video of the changeover, and measure 60 minutes (a common value in many operations). When you look at the video, you see many inefficiencies and opportunities for improvement, which show that CO time is not a fixed parameter but something that can be minimized and improved. Who should be looking at the operation and the video with you? Who should be aware of the CO time and the sequence of tasks? First are the CO operators, the people who actually execute the task; second are the supervisors of these workers; and third are the suppliers of these workers (e.g., the die maintenance operators or their supervisors). This is effectively the focus group (as referred to earlier).

In this way we can define many specific critical *muda* variables that can contribute to improving operations and achieving basic reliability. At the same time, we are starting a change-capability improvement process.

Critical *muda* variables can be the time an operator takes to perform a task (any operator involved in any production, logistics, or administrative task), the number of defective parts, or the amount of inventory (i.e., the amount of materials waiting at a certain point).

What are the critical *muda* variables that are important to creating awareness in terms of pull flow? In production flow, the most important variables to be aware of are those that affect the *work in process* (WIP) between operations and the *machine CO time*. The main flow variable is *lead time*, which can be estimated as the quantity of inventory transformed in a certain number of sales or production days. One of the causes of *muda* is the accumulation of WIP as a result of the absence of one-piece flow. Another cause is batch size because batch size is a major factor affecting lead time. (All these mechanisms will be explained later in this text.)

In terms of logistics flow, the most important variables are the components of the *total lead time within the pull logistics loops*. The key drivers here are the lead time for information flow and the lead time for materials flow. In terms of basic reliability, the critical *muda* variables affecting these are operator absenteeism, machine availability ratios, stock-out ratios (or service level), and defect ratios.

In this section I have defined a certain number of critical awareness variables for pull flow and some other variables critical to acquiring basic reliability. Let's focus for a moment on the critical variables for basic reliability. I will analyze the several critical variables for pull flow in more detail in the following chapters.

The Four *M*s of Basic Reliability

We have already seen that the critical variables for basic reliability can be divided in four groups—the four *M*s (manpower, machines, materials, and methods). Basic reliability consists of analyzing the four *M*s and checking for any major issues that could stop the flow.

Do you know the story of the ship that goes through a canal while below the water level there are rocks of many different sizes? This is a classic Lean metaphor about basic reliability (Figure 4.2). If the water level is lowered, the ship probably will hit one of the larger rocks and sink. These big rocks are the various issues related to the four *M*s.

The exact nature of the rocks in the sea of inventory can vary from company to company. Here we are looking at basic reliability, so we are concerned only with the big rocks that can cause significant problems if they are not addressed right from the beginning.

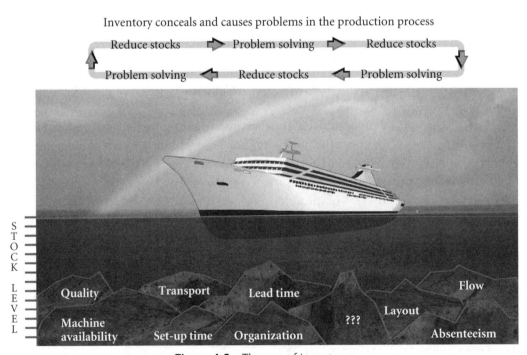

Figure 4.2 The sea of inventory.

The big rocks are related to the following critical variables:

▲ Punctuality and absenteeism
▲ Machine availability ratios
▲ Material stock-out ratios
▲ Quality defect ratios
▲ Great resistance to change

Let's look in more detail at the meaning of each of the four *M*s.

People Basic Reliability

Punctuality and absenteeism are very important basic reliability variables. We need to check these critical variables regularly and be aware of what is happening because poor timekeeping and high absenteeism rates hinder the creation of flow. They may even destroy the functioning of one-piece flow lines or cells designed to create a flow.

In the case of punctuality, it may be that discipline in the workplace is fairly lax, and some operators start 5 or 10 minutes after the beginning of the shift or take longer breaks than they are entitled to. Most important, some workers may not show up for work on a regular basis. All these scenarios cause problems when material is flowing with minimal waiting time. Unexpected absenteeism can completely halt a flow operation, so some basic reliability measures are necessary to prevent this.

The main target groups to involve are the supervisors and human resources (HR) people. They need to understand the root causes of absenteeism, set targets for reducing it, and take measures to achieve the targets.

Standardizing

Standardize, do, check, and act (SDCA) constitute a very important concept and tool for improving manpower basic reliability (Figure 4.3). Basic reliability can be created by starting to standardize or by creating a standard that will solve a particular issue. Next, it is important to do—to implement the standard. Operators (i.e., those who will execute the given standard) need to be informed and trained. "Do" involves a lot of teaching and learning.

Learning itself should be by doing—until a new habit is firmly established. New habits can take time to be fully integrated into the pathways of the brain (our brains literally build connections between neurons), so it is important to reinforce and consolidate them through practice. To be sure that a new standard has fully transformed into a new habit, we have to check to see if it is being implemented in a nonconscious way. In the *gemba*, this is

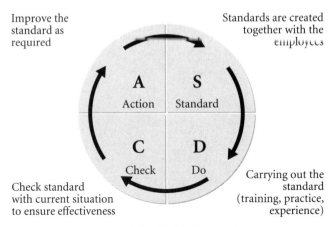

Figure 4.3 The SDCA cycle.

the "check" part of SDCA. The standard needs to be audited at regular intervals. If a deviation is detected, we need to act; that is, we have to provide further instruction and reinforcement of the standard until it is completely assimilated and is employed without too much conscious effort.

It is easy to understand the role of *job instruction* in the implementation of new standards. Job instruction is a method of teaching new jobs or tasks to operators. This method was developed by the Training Within Industry (TWI) training program, a U.S. government program aimed at increasing productive capacity within the armaments industries during World War II. After the war, the same program was introduced in Japan to help the recovery effort. Toyota was one of the first companies to adopt this program and still uses part of it today—the Job Instruction(JI) Module. Training supervisors how to teach operators new tasks or operations is extremely worthwhile. More information about the TWI program is available in *The TWI Workbook: Essential Skills of Supervisors* (Productivity Press, 2006), by Patrick Graupp and Robert J. Wrona.

It is also helpful for managers and supervisors to understand the SDCA cycle (see Figure 4.3). This is a good guide for any improvement agent or coach. It says that when you initially find an issue, you should ask the area supervisor whether there is a standard related to this issue. Obviously, the answer will be yes or no (you may need to ask for clarification to confirm the answer). You then ask the area operators involved if they know of the standard and take note of what they say. Depending on the answers to these questions, you will need to act in one of the following ways:

▲ If the supervisor and operators both answered yes, then you have to change the standard—it is clearly ineffective in solving the issue.

▲ If the supervisor answered yes but the operators said no, then you have to instruct and train the operators (job instruction).

▲ If the supervisor answered no and the operators said yes, then you have to document and apply the standard.

▲ If the supervisor and operators answered no, then you have to make a standard.

Good visual management standards and the SDCA cycle are useful tools for solving many issues related to manpower reliability (Figure 4.4).

Machine Basic Reliability

When the overall equipment effectiveness of key equipment (OEE) is very low or, most of all, very unreliable, issues of *machine basic reliability* may arise. OEE is a key performance indicator that takes into account three groups of losses:

▲ Availability losses
▲ Performance losses
▲ Quality losses

Figure 4.5 shows several elements in the OEE calculation. First, it is necessary to define the *equipment operating time.* This is the time during which the equipment is planned and

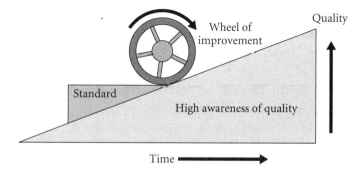

Kaizen Standards: Standard Definition

A standard is the first key to improvement. A standard is the best known way to perform a task.

The best way of having more predictable throughput is to set standards in all departments, measure problems against them and solve them.

Any time improvements are made to a production area, strict adherence to standards is the key to both *maintaining* the performance of the line over time and increasing the performance in the future through continuous improvement systems!

Figure 4.4   The improvement wheel and *kaizen* standards.

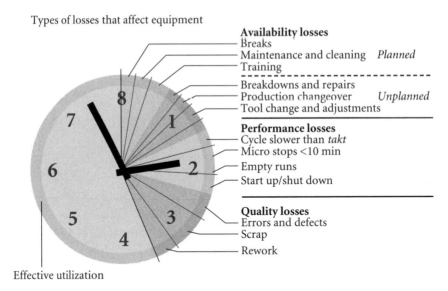

Types of losses that affect equipment

Availability losses
Breaks
Maintenance and cleaning   *Planned*
Training

Breakdowns and repairs
Production changeover   *Unplanned*
Tool change and adjustments

Performance losses
Cycle slower than *takt*
Micro stops <10 min
Empty runs
Start up/shut down

Quality losses
Errors and defects
Scrap
Rework

Effective utilization

Figure 4.5   Overall equipment effectiveness (OEE).

expected to be working in a given day. The *operating time* is also the basis for *takt* time calculations (as we've already seen, *takt* time is the operating time divided by the quantity demanded).

The operating time is then divided into *effective utilization time* and *losses time*. Availability losses are the main issue. If the equipment has many unexpected breakdowns or any unexpected stoppages, this factor can have a major effect on basic flow reliability. An availability index of 80 percent or more is usually considered sufficient to start a flow project. Nevertheless, while an average availability of 80 percent is important, the standard deviation around the average is also important (some people refer to *sigma*, another term for the *mura*). Such excessive variability (standard deviation), as well as unexpected quality or scrap rates, can be a hindrance to the flow.

In most cases, something has to be done to increase the OEE of machines and all types of equipment, especially the *pacemakers*, the equipment that defines the capacity of the whole pull logistics loop and is used to schedule it. An example of a pacemaker is the main assembly line in a car assembly plant or the injection machine in a plant that manufactures plastic parts. Every plant (or, more precisely, pull logistics loop) has a pacemaker group of equipment. This group is easy to identify because it contains the equipment that is carefully scheduled.

One of the key aims of the *gemba kaizen* workshops is to make a list of the top 10 losses for the most problematic machine and start tackling this list from the top down. If the most significant loss is a specific type of breakdown, then the root cause of this breakdown needs to be understood by using the *five whys technique* (by asking "Why?" five times), by making a *cause-and-effect*, or *Ishikawa*, diagram, or by simply understanding the particular mechanism of cause and effect. Once the nature of the breakdown is fully understood, some countermeasures can be designed and implemented. The improvement process follows the plan, do, check, act (PDCA) cycle, using a focus group of people who are aware of the critical-issue variable (*muda* variable) that is involved and who work to solve the issue and achieve an improvement target.

> *How can we improve machine basic reliability? A quick impact can be achieved through focused gemba kaizen workshops.*

For breakdowns, the focus group should have representation from the maintenance department (both operators and supervisors). For defects, the focus group should include the operators and supervisors of the production department and some of its main suppliers (the engineering, maintenance, and quality-control sections). Depending on the type of loss involved, a multifunctional team directly involved in the *gemba* management of the issues may need to be formed to solve the problem.

Materials Basic Reliability

Problems with the basic reliability of materials usually have to do with a lack of parts supply or raw materials necessary to perform an operation. In some cases it may be that an external supplier is unreliable and misses or is late with a delivery. Or there may be delays in internal logistics processes that make a machine stop because the materials are not available in the right place, time, and quantity.

Applying the principle of basic reliability to the situation shows us that the level of stock-outs (or supplier service) is low and that a sufficiently large safety buffer of inventory may need to be built so that the flow of materials is not interrupted. At the beginning of a pull-flow project, the focus is on finding the really big rocks related to lack of materials, and the main improvement technique is a

> *In many cases, only a change of system will solve a chronic problem.*

focused improvement team. The focus-group team for this materials flow problem is the planning and logistics department, the people who order the materials and are responsible for their storage and transportation to the points of use.

Using a top 10 list of materials issues and the same PDCA improvement process, the team will achieve rapid results.

One word of advice: The *kaizen* in logistics and supply-chains system (TFM model) and the creation of flow tools and solutions included in the several pillars of the model will solve most material supply issues, so the value of spending time tackling focused issues is sometimes questionable. It is important to be realistic when assessing whether a given issue of material basic reliability should be attacked in the first place. Our experience at the Kaizen Institute suggests that in most cases it is best to create a systems solution. This will resolve most problems, or they can be solved in parallel. However, it is always good practice to check for any major delivery problems with suppliers or internal or external logistics processes.

Methods Basic Reliability

The principle of methods basic reliability is related to all the other issues that may hinder or stop the flow of materials and information when we remove some of the safety inventories or buffers and start creating a tight flow. How a methods reliability issue can manifest may vary, but usually the problems have to do with quality and time constraints. A serious quality issue can come to light and even worsen if it occurs in a highly variable way (huge variation around the average)—this makes it unexpected, so it can stop a complete line or plant. The problem may not be related to a specific machine (which we could see reflected in the machine's OEE) but will be a random problem that has implications far upstream of the process.

The introduction of a new product needs particularly careful assessment. Usually, starting to produce a new product with new people, machines, materials, and methods is not the best time for a pull-flow project. The reason is that we would be mixing flow solutions with finding the best parameters for the process, and it can take additional time and discussions if we try to do both at once. The best way to start the creation of a pull-flow project is with a process that is stable and reliable in terms of manpower, machines, materials, and methods.

Where no new product is being introduced, or at least none that involves any major change in the current processes, it may be advisable to check the reliability of the current methods before starting a pull-flow project. This can be achieved by looking at any major issues of time, quality, safety, or ergonomics and holding a *gemba kaizen* workshop with a focus group.

More People Basic Reliability: Resistance to Change

Often the biggest problems of basic reliability is a huge resistance to change on the part of everyone involved—operators, middle management, and top management. Maybe the change project or the ideas for improvement are being pushed by someone inside the company or from its headquarters. The result is that people often react against any proposed change by arguing against it and highlighting all the possible obstacles and excuses. Sometimes it seems that their understanding of PDCA is "Please don't change anything!"

In this kind of situation it can be very difficult to make any sustainable change. If the resistance is so strong, its root causes need to be identified and understood. In many cases it is simply the result of many years of doing the same old thing in the same old way. One solution for this type of situation is to start slowly, implementing some changes and involving people in changing some of their deeply ingrained habits.

It may be wise to start in a pilot area and improve a difficult operation in terms of efficiency or start simply by doing the five Ss (5S) well known to every *kaizen* and Lean practitioner— sort out, straighten, scrub, standardize, and sustain. (The Japanese words originally used for these strong improvement concepts are *seiri, seiton, seiso, seiketsu,* and *shitsuke.*)

Doing 5S requires each word to be implemented, in turn, in a given area or workplace. It is a way of introducing people to change. Big teams can be involved in doing this. Usually 5S works best if it is attached to a productivity or time-reduction target to simplify the processes, achieve some time (and efficiency) improvements, and also prevent some errors (by implementing the fourth *S*, standardization).

After a 5S workshop, the working areas look much better organized. People see that a lot has been achieved and feel empowered and positive about the change. 5S can be a necessary foundation step for a pull-flow project. It also will improve the sustainability of new solutions and standards.

I do have a word of caution for companies that are in a difficult financial or competitive situation. They may not have attempted improvements for many years and may now find that rapid improvements are required. However, changing too quickly can be damaging, both to the company and to the morale of the workforce. For example, top managers may be unrealistic in their expectations or may focus purely on results and not have the patience to wait. I will discuss some solutions to this problem in later chapters.

Basic human reliability also can be understood in terms of the degree to which people accept and commit to the seven *kaizen* pull-flow principles presented in the first three chapters (lack of this acceptance is one of the factors contributing to resistance to change). If the degree of acceptance is low or unreliable, then a concerted training effort will be needed.

What else can we do to promote basic reliability and a capacity for change? Basically, anything that involves the discussion and testing of new ideas. We may call this the promotion of innovation and *kaizen* on a company-wide basis.

Some companies call this the promotion of a Lean system or the promotion of Lean thinking. At the Kaizen Institute, we prefer to call it the promotion and implementation of a *kaizen* management system (KMS) that aims to transform the culture of the company from a fixed mindset to a growth mindset—from a "no *kaizen*" to a *kaizen* company.

Many companies also develop a continuous-improvement strategy and model inspired by Toyota with its Toyota Production System (e.g., Valeo with its Valeo Production System or Bosch with the Bosch Production System).

The purpose of this book (this will be left to another book) is not to provide a detailed explanation of how to design and implement a company-wide continuous-improvement system. I will, however, discuss many elements of such systems. By mentioning continuous-improvement systems, I simply wish to show that if the top management of a company has a strong policy on *kaizen*, Lean, or any other type of operational excellence, this will make it much easier to implement a pull-flow system. When faced with new paradigms that seem like paradoxes, people will react more positively if they understand that the new idea relates to a value already nurtured within the company. For example, if one value of the continuous-improvement system is *pull-flow thinking*, and this value is strongly promoted in all communications from top management, then people will have a different mindset when discussing how to put it into practice.

Many companies are now developing what they call a strategy for continuous improvement (which, of course, means the same as the word kaizen).

Before planning any steps for flow improvement in an organization, it is good practice to check the level of human basic reliability and capacity for change and to define some measures for improvement. Score cards for each TFM pillar are provided in Appendix D to help you to make an initial assessment of the situation.

CHAPTER 5

Production Flow: Introduction and Line and Layout Design

The second pillar of the Total Flow Management (TFM) model is *production flow* (Figure 5.1). The targets of this pillar include

▲ Creation of one-piece flow (ideally, one piece at a time, from raw materials to finished product)

▲ Minimization of the waste of operators' movements (border of line and standard work)

▲ Mass customization (flexibility to achieve the efficient production of small lots using single-minute exchange of dies [SMED])

▲ Simplification before automation (automation without flow is automation of *muda*)

Achieving the target of creating one-piece flow means redesigning the layout and equipment in order to manufacture one piece at a time in the right sequence of operations. The aim is to reach a state of continuous movement from raw materials to finished product without any stoppages during the manufacturing process. All the manufacturing resources need to be reorganized to add value-transforming operations and eliminate, through design, all operations that do not add value.

This concept was created by Henry Ford in 1918 when he invented the car assembly conveyor line, where all the operations are aligned in sequence, and the product (the car to be assembled) is continuously moving from one assembly station to the next. Before this, the work was organized by batch—a batch of cars was assembled in a fixed location, with groups of workers moving around the cars to perform various tasks. Taiichi Ohno and his followers took this concept of one-piece flow and applied it with thoroughness to all Toyota manufacturing operations.

> *Achieving the target of creating one-piece flow means redesigning the layout and equipment in order to manufacture one piece at a time in the right sequence of operations.*

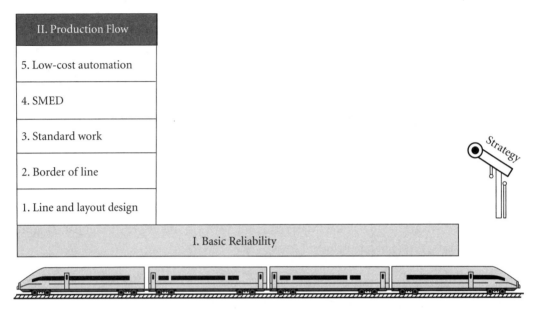

Figure 5.1   Pillars I and II of the Total Flow Management (TFM) model.

The key words here are *continuous material movement*, one of the main goals of *kaizen* in logistics and supply chains.

Along with one-piece flow, we aim to minimize the operators' non-value-adding movements, create a flexible line that can make several different models with zero changeover (CO) time, and, after as much simplification as possible, automate certain operations to improve ergonomics and replace manual work by mechanization.

The *production-flow pillar* has the following five domains of improvement:

▲   Line and layout design
▲   Border of line
▲   Standard work
▲   Single-minute exchange of dies (SMED)
▲   Low-cost automation

Let's look at each of these in more detail.

Line and Layout Design

The first domain of improvement in production flow is *line and layout design*. Here we are interested in analyzing the processes for the several product families and designing manufacturing lines that integrate one-piece flow as much as possible. It is also important to choose the best location for these lines. I would like to remind you of Shingo's definition of process: "A sequence of value-added and non-value-added operations, including transport, quality control, waiting and transportation, necessary to manufacture the product dock to dock." In line and layout design, we aim to eliminate all the non-value-added operations of transport, control, and waiting while focusing on the value-added operations. During the redesign, there may be some value-added operations that can in fact be eliminated by altering the sequence of the process or by improving the effectiveness of certain operations.

> *The aim of one-piece flow is to reach a state of continuous movement from raw materials to finished goods without any stoppages.*

The most important design parameter for one-piece flow lines is *takt* time. This is defined as an estimate of the customer demand cycle and is calculated as the ratio between line operating time and demand quantity for a given period of time (usually one day). The lines will be designed with several workstations working on the same cycle in a balanced way based on the defined *takt* time. The ideal number of products in process (work in process [WIP]) is equal to the number of balanced workstations. If you have 10 work-stations, then the line should always have 10 products being produced simultaneously.

This is waste elimination through design and often involves redesigning or adapting the features of individual pieces of equipment. I will discuss one-piece flow layout and line design in more detail later. For now, keep in mind the idea of a perfect car assembly line. Henry Ford invented the first large-scale one-piece flow assembly line to make the Model T Ford and consequently gained a huge competitive advantage in quality, cost, and delivery service.

Border of Line

The second domain of improvement in production flow is *border of line*. Border of line refers to the design of the location and containerization of all the necessary raw materials and component parts for the entire one-piece flow line. This is part of line design, but it deserves a separate improvement domain because it interfaces with internal logistics. A well-designed border of line has to fulfill four major criteria:

▲ The location of all parts must minimize the picking movement of the line operators.
▲ The location of parts and containers must minimize the movement of the supply logistics workers.
▲ The time needed to change parts from one product to another should be close to zero.
▲ The decision to replenish or resupply should be intuitive and instantaneous.

To fulfill all these criteria, the location of parts, the type of containers, and the container flow in the line (full and empty) need to be carefully designed. Any solution devised at this point must be aligned with the internal logistics system, which also has high efficiency requirements. However, the main focus is on minimizing workers' movements by locating parts as close as possible to their point of use.

Standard Work

The third domain of improvement in Lean production flow is *standard work*. Standard work is commonly defined as the development of standards that represent the best known method of work at that moment. In Toyota, where the term originated, the meaning varies slightly. Many years ago, I accompanied a Japanese industrial engineer trained at Toyota on a plant tour (a plant with lots of *muda*, I might add). He was constantly pointing to the workers (focusing primarily on the workers' movements) and saying, "No standard work, . . . no standard work!" At that time, I didn't fully grasp what he meant. It was only some years later that I began to understand the true meaning of standard work. The workers were moving too much, often far from where the value-added work was being done. Job methods needed improvement.

Standard work at Toyota (and also in our TFM model) means minimizing the movements of workers and is a fundamental form of job improvement that can be achieved for workers in any situation (i.e., manufacturing, logistics, or administrative). Our production-flow pillar aims for operators to be working in one-piece flow lines with an optimized parts border of line while being completely focused on adding value by using the shortest and easiest movements possible. Look at a well-designed one-piece flow line. As you watch the workers' movements, you will have the sense that they are literally glued to the product, making the work with very short, fluid movements without any stress at all. They will be flowing along with the materials.

Single-Minute Exchange of Dies

The fourth domain of improvement in Lean production flow is *single-minute exchange of dies* (SMED). SMED embodies the concept of quick changeover from one product to the next. The person who developed the SMED method was Shigeo Shingo while he was working as a consultant for Toyota. SMED also means to achieve the target of the single minute (this is the single decimal minute—less than 10 minutes). SMED is also a method of improving standard work in changeovers and was developed and applied originally in stamping presses.

The reductions in CO time achieved using the SMED method result in a very powerful domain of improvement that aims to achieve zero-setup lines and machines (or no time lost by setup). The advantages of such flexibility are enormous, and its implications for reducing batch size are one of the main contributors to the creation of flow.

Zero setup, or no setup time, is always the main target in line design. If this can be achieved, a mixed sequence of different products can flow along the line. This is the case in modern car assembly lines, where you can see different models move along the line one after the other. If zero setup is not possible, the target for SMED improvement is the lowest possible time. Of course, a setup time of more than zero involves working with a batch of similar products before changing, or setting up, the next batch. Many machines have higher than zero setup times. Usually, the machine manufacturers do not aim to reduce setup through design (although recently, more and more machine manufacturers have begun to offer zero- or low-setup-time options on their machines). In most cases, the solution is a customized design for each application of the machines, and of course, the CO operator's standard work will need to be improved.

Low-Cost Automation

So we have created one-piece flow layouts and lines, defined the best location and type of container in the border of lines, minimized the workers' movement according to the line *takt* and flow rules, and designed flexibility for the CO of different products. What else can we do? The answer is easy: We can increase mechanization and achieve greater productivity by automating parts of the operation. In fact, the definition of productivity is an output divided by an input, the output being the quantity of product produced and the input being the number of worker-hours required. There are no limits to productivity because if we reduce the denominator (the number of worker-hours required), the ratio becomes nearly infinite.

Of course, automation also can be very costly, and full automation may not provide a sufficient return on investment. One important aspect is that the line must have all the production-flow features developed so far (the first four domains of production flow—line and layout design, border of line, standard work, and SMED) before automation can be implemented.

Why, then, do we call it *low-cost automation*? First, because we are interested in exploring automation that reduces costs and delivers a higher return on investment. The levels of automation, from manual work to full automation, can be defined in a list of seven steps. Going through this list for every operation will reveal many possibilities for low-cost automation.

Good examples of low-cost automation in one-piece flow lines are the lines known as *chaku chaku* lines. *Chaku chaku* in Japanese means "load load lines." These lines were perfected so that the operator has only to pick one piece and load the next operation so that he or she is running along the sequence of machines simply picking and loading. I will discuss this idea in Chapter 6.

For the moment, just remember that low-cost automation as a final improvement stage can bring infinite productivity to our manufacturing facilities.

Line and Layout Design Revisited

There are two different types of layout: the *functional layout* and the *process layout*. In the functional layout, the machines are grouped by function (this layout also can be called a job-shop layout). All the machines that have the same function are grouped together (e.g., in a metalworking shop, all the lathes are together, all the grinding machines are together, and so on). Figure 5.2 shows just such a functional layout, divided into subassembly, assembly, and control. This type of layout is characterized by working with big batches to minimize transportation between machines (usually by forklifts), and of course, the work in process (WIP) is high. The WIP, transformed into an estimate of lead time (WIP quantity divided by daily output will give the lead time in days), is also high. Lead-time figures of more than five days are common in many functionally organized layouts.

The process layout, on the other hand, is organized into sequences of operations and machines along a mechanized conveyor belt (Figure 5.3). In this case, WIP and lead times

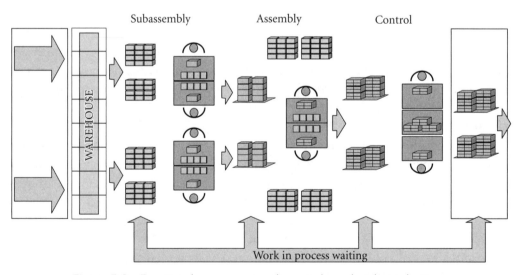

Figure 5.2   Functional versus process layout—large-batch production.

will be reduced substantially. This type of line is not necessarily considered a one-piece flow line. Many people will look at this type of line and think that flow is already created. Closer analysis, however, will reveal that some inventory has accumulated between workstations. This is a symptom of *muda* and may be due to an imbalance between workstation times. It is very important to perform a simple calculation: One-piece flow means one unit of WIP at each workstation, so by counting the number of work stations you will have the optimal WIP. This then can be compared with the actual WIP. There will be a reason for any difference, and understanding it will be very revealing.

The optimal one-piece flow line (or cell), in which the flow is as fast as possible, is sometimes laid out in a U-shaped line. The evolution of layout from a straight line to a U shape has the benefit of increasing flexibility in balancing the workers and allowing the operators to have a better understanding of the flow. The results achieved in this way, by eliminating many different kinds of *muda*, can be phenomenal. A reduction in WIP is the most significant (WIP reductions of 90 percent are common in this type of change).

Another example of transforming a functional layout to a process layout would be the one shown in Figure 5.4. If we have a machine that is separated from the main line (e.g., a

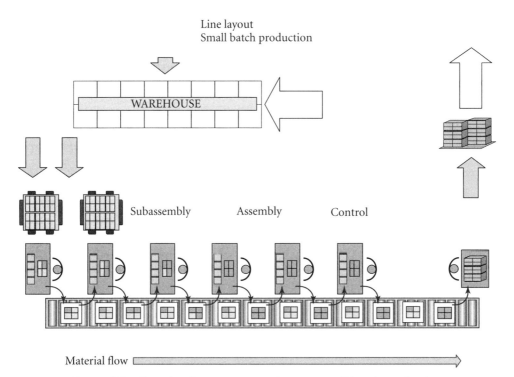

Figure 5.3   Functional versus process layout—small-batch production.

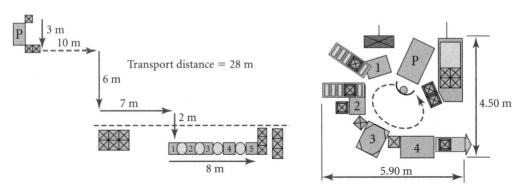

Figure 5.4 One-piece flow lines.

press that is working for many lines), the creation of flow may depend on integrating this machine into the one-piece flow line. Of course, the press would have to be dedicated solely to this flow, and it may then be necessary to invest in another press. The characteristics of the machine that is to be integrated into the one-piece flow line or cell can be adapted to the product family that will be manufactured in these cells. When the machine is integrated, it works only for the assigned product family, with fewer functions and probably a lower investment cost.

One advantage of having several smaller and longer cycle-time lines is that it is extremely easy to balance the line.

When transforming functional layouts into process layouts, in many cases it will be necessary to duplicate several key machines. It is said that a Toyota plant usually has three times as many machines as does a similar functionally designed plant. Toyota developed many machines in-house, specifically for integration into one-piece flow lines. When a company calculates its return on investment (ROI) for additional machines, it often finds it can recover this investment in less than a year.

Large versus Small Machines and Lines

Redesigning a functional layout into a process layout (in other words, redesigning to create material flow) is one of the most rewarding jobs in industrial engineering. Toyota did just this over many years, starting with Taiichi Ohno's trials in the machine shop at the Koromo plant. This kind of redesign can provide a real breakthrough in all the important key performance indicators (KPIs), such as productivity, WIP, lead time, and quality.

When such a redesign to create flow is taking place, one question that generates intense discussion may be whether to substitute large, unique machines for more in-line, smaller ones. However, in-house development often provides numerous solutions.

Another important decision is the number of flow lines required. There are two alternatives: a single, larger multi-staffed line or several smaller lines. In the single line, the line cycle time tends to be short (<25 seconds), and depending on the demand profile, only one or more machines may be needed. Alternatively, we could divide this fast, short cycle-time line into several smaller lines that have a longer cycle time (e.g., a 25-second line could be divided into two 50-second lines or even four 100-second lines).

What are the advantages of having several smaller lines? They become apparent when we consider two challenges: the implications for launching new models and the implications for increased product variety. Let's look at the implications of both solutions on the launch of a new model:

Single Line	Several Smaller Lines
The time required for preparation and training will affect the manufacture of the current product.	The time needed for preparation is reduced, and only one line is affected. There is no impact on other product lines during the initial production period.

The implications of both solutions for increased product variety are as follows:

Single Line	Several Smaller Lines
More COs will mean a bigger loss. The size of the workforce will constantly change. Workers will need to rotate.	The number of COs per line is reduced. The rotation of the workforce is simplified.

One advantage of having several smaller and longer cycle-time lines is that it is extremely easy to balance the line. A line with a cycle time of fewer than 25 seconds normally has a high balancing loss. A smaller, longer cycle time is easier to balance and will have fewer difficulties in accommodating the introduction of a new model and the production of a higher number of models. Instead of automating one large single line to the maximum, it is usually more productive to have several smaller, flexible lines.

Another important feature of small one-piece flow lines is what the Japanese call *shojinka*. *Shojinka* means that the line layout is flexible with regard to the number of workers that can work on the line, and the number of workers will define the cycle time of the line. One operator could work alone on a *shojinka* line, performing all operations from beginning to end. The cycle time is theoretically equal to the sum of all the manufacturing value-added unit times (assuming that the operator has a good work rate with an optimized border of line and an optimized standard work)

Adding more operators reduces the line cycle time and increases the line output. The *shojinka* line is then flexible to volume changes and can be manned according to demand. Capacity is easily adjusted in this type of line.

Of course, *shojinka* lines demand multiskilled operators, and it is the supervisor's responsibility to instruct and train the workers according to a multiskills acquisition plan. This can be achieved with the JI module of the TWI program, which includes the creation of job breakdown sheets and training plans, and following an on-the-job-training method (explained in the discussion of the standard work domain in Chapter 6).

Simple Profiling and Line Balancing for Line and Layout Design

Another important profiling task is the making of process graphs and time estimates. Line and layout design always should start with a product-quantity (PQ) analysis. This is a profiling tool that reveals the quantities sold in one year for each finished-goods reference. The analysis also can be completed using the ABC method—the *A* stands for references classified as high runners (references that represent 80 percent of the quantity sold), the *B* stands for references classified as medium runners (references that represent the next 10 percent of the quantity sold), and the *C* stands for references classified as low runners (representing the final 10 percent of the quantity sold).

> Line and layout design always should start with a product-quantity (PQ) analysis.

Generally speaking, the *A* references are good candidates for automated or semiautomated lines (while always maintaining the principle of one-piece flow). The *B* references are good candidates for manual, less automated one-piece flow lines, whereas the *C* references are good candidates for single-bench or manual lines that give the flexibility to manufacture many different references.

Another important profiling task is the making of process graphs and time estimates. A *process graph* represents a possible order or sequence of the operations necessary for the assembly or production of a product. It is a simple graph, using circles, and shows only value-added operations. The process graph represents the process without most of the *muda* (it is possible, however, that by analyzing the operations, you may decide that you can eliminate or combine some value-added operations).

Initially, the process graph should be done only for the *A* high runners. It provides three types of information (Figure 5.5):

- A process graph represents a possible order of assembly or production
- It shows three types of information:
  - Triangles: components
  - Circles: value-added operations
  - Rectangles: times

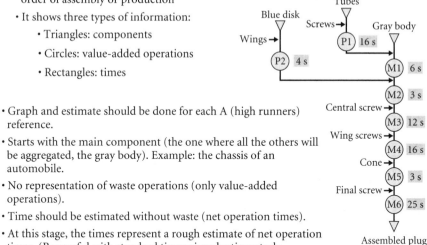

- Graph and estimate should be done for each A (high runners) reference.
- Starts with the main component (the one where all the others will be aggregated, the gray body). Example: the chassis of an automobile.
- No representation of waste operations (only value-added operations).
- Time should be estimated without waste (net operation times).
- At this stage, the times represent a rough estimate of net operation times. (Be careful with standard times given by time study departments. These usually include too much waste.)

Figure 5.5   Process graph and time estimate.

▲   Parts or components
▲   Value-added operations (circles)
▲   An estimate of value-added unit time

When drawing up a graph, you should start with the main component (defined as the one where all the others will be aggregated—the gray body in Figure 5.5). Real examples can be the welded chassis of an automobile or the plastic housing of a headlamp where all components will be assembled.

Whenever possible, the time estimates should be net operation times, without the *muda* or waste that is often included in time estimates. In many cases, standard times include all types of allowances based on the traditional way of calculating standard unit times (i.e., time for changeovers, time for breaks, and time for quality control are common). At this stage, put down only the best rough estimate of net operation times that you have. If no times are available, you will need to collect them by means of a simplified time-study analysis (this will be explained when I discuss standard work in Chapter 6).

Line balancing is a very important part of creating flow lines. It consists of assigning tasks to each workstation so that they become balanced with the line cycle time. Each workstation can have one or more workers, but the assigned workers must finish the workstation task list in the assigned cycle time.

The easiest way to balance a line is by using a *process graph*. This visual guide makes it very easy to group operations (or tasks) in cycle-time-sized chunks (as shown in Figure 5.5).

Start with the first operation performed on the main component. Then go down the graph, adding operation times until you find a branch coming in with a needed subassembly. Go to the beginning of this branch, and start adding the operations until you have reached the balancing cycle time.

After you have completed the process-graph balancing exercise, you can produce a visual balancing chart that represents all the operations (Figure 5.6). This is called a *yamazumi chart* and is a visual method for checking the balancing.

A particular feature of car assembly lines is the balancing of mixed-model lines. The models are mixed in the line according to a scheduling algorithm, so each workstation may receive a different car every cycle. Traditionally balanced lines balance the work in terms of averages, calculating the scheduling of models in such a way that in one hour the average workstation cycle time equals the line cycle time (the line speed). However, the workers on the line are restricted by this averaging (as in the story of the chicken: two men ate on average half a chicken—one ate a whole chicken and the other none). When an easy model comes along, the worker needs less time than the line speed dictates. However, with a more difficult model, the worker has to speed up and work faster than the line speed. This problem affects the stability of standard work because the location of parts to pick varies for each model.

This is solved by *mura balancing*. Using the concept of *mura* ("variability"), we can define two different types of workstations: *mura* and non-*mura*. Non-*mura* workstations are those where a different model does not require a workstation cycle-time change. In *mura* workstations, all the variance is concentrated, so the maximum workstation time can

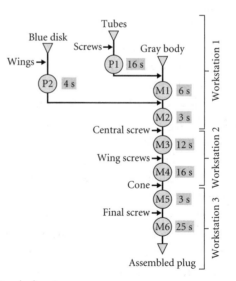

- Balance operations using the process graph:

  - Workstation 1: P1 + M1 + P2 + M2 = 29 seconds

  - Workstation 2: M3 + M4 = 28 seconds

  - Workstation 3: M5 + M6 = 28 seconds

- Start on top of the graph (main component)
- First operation is P1, because this is the first subassembly to go into the main component
- If there are many operations, use balancing charts with magnets (*yamazumi* chart)
- Use Excel worksheets

Figure 5.6 Line balancing.

be more than double that of the cycle time. The length of this station is proportional to the maximum workstation time.

This form of balancing improves the productivity of the line by easing the standard work. Quality also improves because the best workers are assigned to the more difficult *mura* stations, and additional visual standards are employed in these zones.

Having created one-piece flow by integrating value-added operations into flexible lines and cells wherever possible, we must now focus further on workstation design. For this, we have to decide the location and type of containers or cases (this task belongs to the domain of border-of-line design). We also need to design the standard work of the operator, including the location of tools, jigs, and all necessary equipment. This task belongs in the standard-work domain. We will examine border of line and standard work in Chapter 6.

Summary of Main Concepts

The aim of line and layout design is to have an optimized manufacturing facility that works to the highest performance standards:

▲ High efficiency in terms of worker and machine efficiency (equipment OEE)
▲ High flexibility in terms of volume and variations
▲ High quality
▲ The lowest unit value-added cost

Value-added cost is calculated on the basis of the life-cycle time of the product to be manufactured with the equipment. The elements making up value-added cost include the initial cost of the investment, the cost of labor, and other costs associated with the equipment (e.g., space and inventory-handling costs). The unit value-added cost over the product life-cycle time is the ratio of the expected volumes (total quantity of products) divided by the sum of the value-added costs.

Before you decide on line design, it is advisable to look at several different scenarios (ranging from several manual lines to more automated single lines) and calculate their unit value-added cost. You then can make the investment decision on the basis of the lowest cost.

Although I won't discuss it in detail, the following additional important Lean manufacturing line-design features (Figure 5.7) should be considered:

▲ *Daisy line design.* The *daisy* concept refers to islands of automation harmonized with manual work. The petals of the daisy are the automated processes. The petals on the daisy start from the interior of the flower, so the islands of automation should start and end at the same point. The manual work then is organized in a common area with *shojinka* capability.

▲ *Chaku chaku line design.* This has already been discussed and refers to a low-cost automated line in which the operator is doing only the tasks of transport loading.

▲ *Jidoka and autonomous quality control.* The line should be equipped with foolproof quality-control devices (*poka yoke* devices). A quality-control standard needs to be developed so that operators can act in a *poka yoke* way. An *andon*, or light-control system, also should be in place. Such a system includes a way of stopping the line and a visual sign to indicate that the individual workstation that stopped the line needs help to solve a quality problem.

▲ *TPM prepared line.* The line should provide an easy way to control the checking, cleaning, and maintenance points. Visual management should be in place to identify and control these points.

An optimized one-piece flow line has the following features:

▲ One-piece flow
▲ *Mura* balancing
▲ Frontal supply of parts in small cases located at the point of use
▲ *Chaku chaku* line design
▲ Daisy line design
▲ Zero setup
▲ *Shojinka* and standard work
▲ *Jidoka* and autonomous quality control
▲ TPM preparation

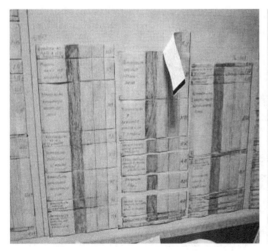

Figure 5.7 Lean line design—line balancing.

After designing the layout and line concept, the best approach is to build a mock-up of the layout or line in order to check and test its main features. A mock-up represents an exact copy of the future line and can be built using plastic tubing, wooden pallets, and cardboard (Figure 5.8). This can be done very quickly (in a week) with a focus team of people including engineers and machine operators. The mock-up can be used to test standard work and even to check manual times. It is a quick way of starting operators' training and of fine-tuning the overall shape of the line.

The 20 Important Principles of Layout and Line Design

1. Design the lines based on the types, volumes, and life cycles of the products.
2. Design a one-piece flow processing line.
3. Design small, in-line equipment that is easy to maneuver.

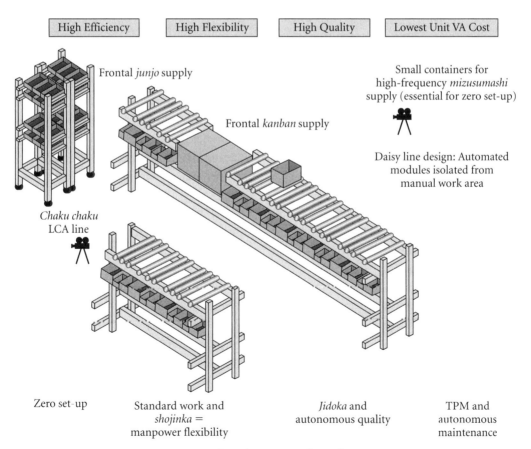

Figure 5.8   Lean line design—cardboard engineering.

4. Take into account the *takt* time of the customers.
5. Say "No" to the *muda* of transportation, and minimize the use of conveyors.
6. Design setup times with a target of zero.
7. Do not allow isolated operator islands (disconnected processes).
8. Separate manual work from machine work.
9. Combine the entrance and exit points of workpieces.
10. Ensure that equipment is narrow.
11. Put only necessary materials within arm's reach.
12. Work should flow from right to left (counterclockwise).
13. Remember that *karakuri* (or subtle maneuverability) is important.
14. Lower the speed as much as possible.
15. Machines should stop when abnormalities occur.
16. A mechanical approach is preferable to an electrical or electronic approach.
17. Do not automate parts supply without careful analysis.
18. Do not work on several parts within a single process at the same time.
19. Simulate new equipment before installing it.
20. Organize layout by process, and keep walls clear.

Finally, I would like to clarify three of these principles. The first is principle 12, that work should flow from right to left (counterclockwise). This is so because most operators are right-handed, and when they move counterclockwise, they are using their bodies more efficiently. The left hand will be withdrawing the work (this movement can even be automated), and the right hand will be doing the loading. The advantages of using the right hand are that generally it is stronger and more precise when loading and positioning a piece of work.

Human space perception is stronger through the left side of our visual field because the hemispheres of the brain control opposite sides of the body. When we move counter-clockwise we have better visibility of space on the left side and are more comfortable, confident, and quick.

The second is principle 13, that *karakuri*, or subtle maneuverability, is important. *Karakuri* is a Japanese word for a toy that uses mechanical devices to perform a lot of movements using the force of gravity. An example of *karakuri* is moving a coin along a table top and into the top of a bottle using only one finger. Try it and you will see what *karakuri* is! It involves using gravity, levers, and other mechanical solutions to simplify and reduce the manual movements of operators.

The final one is principle 16, that a mechanical approach is better than an electrical or electronic one. This is to do with reliability—mechanical devices are generally more reliable than their electrical counterparts. However, the real issue is reliability, not simply the exclusion of electrical or electronic devices.

CHAPTER 6

Production Flow: Border of Line and Standard Work

Border of Line

In this chapter I will talk in more depth about the second and third domains of production flow: border of line and standard work. *Border of line* is the domain of improvement that deals with the appropriate location and physical properties and dimensions of the material-handling containers that need to be available close to the point of use. There is a strong connection between border of line and standard work, in the sense that the suitable placement of the right materials at the right time can minimize the movements of workers and thus improve the standard work (and, of course, considerably improve quality, cost, and delivery).

> *It is the task of internal logistics to supply the right materials, in the right quality, at the right time, at the right location, and with the right method of presentation.*

The border of line is the interface point between the logistics and production processes. It is the task of internal logistics to supply the right material, in the right quality, at the right time, at the right location, and with the right method of presentation. Production should deal only with the correct manufacturing of the product, focusing completely on the quality and time needed for transformation of the materials into the final products. This is the value-added time of production.

The Concept of the Small Container

Border of line includes the concept of the *small container*. But what exactly is a small container? How big should it be? The size of the small container depends on the size of the part that it holds. Generally speaking, a small container is a plastic box that measures around 600 × 400 × 320 mm. This size will allow it to hold many kinds of parts. A typical small container will hold a minimum of four parts. I define a small container in terms of the consumption rate of parts—this is called the *autonomy* of the container. An autonomy of less than 10 minutes is usually considered a small container size. But the next definition is the key factor for understanding the concept of small container.

The concept of a small container depends on the ability of the container to be placed at the optimal point of use to minimize operator picking movements. This ability of a small container to minimize operator picking movement depends on the number of variants of the same part that may be needed at the border of line (e.g., we may need five different variants of a basic airbag component). Since any of the five variants might be needed, they need to be placed at the border of line in such a way as to minimize the amount of movement needed to get them. A small container, therefore, is one that will help to minimize the worker's movement. In the next section you will see that this is a major contribution to standard work.

> I define a small container in terms of the consumption rate of parts. An autonomy of less than 10 minutes is usually considered a small container size.

This brings me to the supply concept that is applied to the border of line. This means that it will be necessary to decide if *all the parts will be available* at the border of line (i.e., all references, including variants of the same type of part, as in the airbag example) or if *some parts will be supplied in the right sequence for production* (i.e., instead of having all airbags standing on the line, we could decide to supply the several airbag variants in sequence based on the production schedule defined for the line). Having all parts available is called *kanban supply* (or *continuous supply*). Having some parts available in the sequence needed for production is called *junjo supply* (or *sequenced supply*).

Clearly, the design of the border of line is one of the most important domains of production flow and the one that will really define the requirements of the internal logistics system. In fact, this is a customer-supplier relationship. Production is the customer, and logistics must comply with the requirements of production, including supplying the right kind of container.

Advantages of Using Small Containers

The traditional way to supply and locate parts in the border of line is by using the standard pallet-sized container. Using small containers in the border of lines has many advantages in a number of areas. Below I discuss the implications for quality, cost, lead time, and worker motivation.

Quality

The use of pallet-sized or cardboard containers can involve many problems in quality. Some of these problems include the following:

▲ The parts at the bottom of big containers can easily be crushed by the parts at the top or by another container placed on top.
▲ The force needed to close a buckled container can damage the products inside.
▲ The huge number of parts inside a big container means that there is a risk of missing parts or kit components.
▲ Parts can be damaged by the box cutter that opens cardboard containers or by moving against each other.
▲ Similar but different parts, such as cables, can get mixed up when they are in same container.
▲ Large containers are difficult to clean (e.g., to empty of water after rain).

The use of small containers offers an effective countermeasure to most of these problems by reducing the number of parts and by using dunning of parts inside the container. *Dunning* (or *dunnage*) refers to material laid beneath or wedged between parts to prevent damage during transport. Visual control of the quality of the packaging is greatly enhanced.

Cost

Large containers and containers made from cardboard can cause many problems of cost. Some of these problems include the following:

▲ Operators have to make long, nonergonomic movements to pick the parts and sometimes need a lot of time to untangle them.
▲ Fitting individual protection for items transported inside big containers is a waste of material and labor.
▲ The work done in opening and shaping cardboard containers is wasted labor.
▲ Compactors are required to dispose of waste containers and packaging materials.

Small containers are reusable, easy to handle, and encourage better use of space through vertical storage in flow racks.

▲ Costly vibrating bowls are needed to supply parts ready for easy picking.
▲ Big containers require a lot of space (e.g., wide walkways and work surfaces).

Small containers provide the optimal location of the part and easy picking. They are reusable, easy to handle, and encourage better use of space through vertical storage in flow racks.

Time and Ergonomic Factors

Big containers also have serious shortcomings in terms of time and ergonomics. Some of these include the following:

▲ Waiting for forklifts and other picking and moving equipment causes delays in supply.
▲ The large size of the containers means long container replacement times when production runs are changed and a high number of leftovers. This causes long setup times.
▲ The need to bend down to reach the bottom of the container and do other nonergonomic movements means that operators face a greater risk of back injury.
▲ Opening cardboard containers with cutters and handling heavy containers increases the risk of accident and injury.

Easy-to-handle flow containers (e.g., small plastic containers on wheels) minimize time and eliminate most of the ergonomic issues.

Two Types of Border of Line

Let's now analyze the two different methods for supplying parts of any type of material to the border of line. The best layout for a workstation is always the one that allows the operator to pick the part from the same location with the shortest movement. This is a principle of the utmost importance for both manual and automatic picking. In some situations, the picking of parts may be done automatically by robots (usually in situations where the operation is rather difficult, maybe requiring more than one person) but is often just a small and easy movement done by the operator.

There are two possible methods of line supply—continuous (*kanban*) and sequenced (*junjo*). See Table 6.1.

Table 6.1   The Two Methods of Line Supply

Example	aaaaaaa bbbbbbb	aaabbaaabbaaabb
Type of supply	Continuous (or *kanban* supply)	Sequenced (or *junjo* supply)
Frontal supply	Always the same part	Parts change according to product type
Space occupied in BL	One location for each part number (SKU)	One location for all part numbers
Workstation productivity	Variable picking point (depends on product type)	Fixed picking point

Let's consider two products, A and B. Product A is made up of parts x and a, whereas product B is made up of parts x and b. Part x is common to both products A and B and should always be at the workstation (this is called *continuous* or *kanban supply*). The supply of parts a and b, on the other hand, will be more complex because these parts are each specific to one product. There are two types of supplies. Which one would you choose?

Which is the best form of supply in this situation will depend on the size of the part. If the size of the part (and especially the size of the container) allows the part to be within arm's reach of the operator, then we could choose *kanban* supply. If not, we could decide on sequenced supply—especially if it would mean less handling.

I will come back to these two methods when I discuss synchronization (in Chapter 8). The cost implications in terms of logistics are that sequenced supply is more expensive than *kanban* supply because in *kanban* the replenishment signal is quite straightforward (given by an empty container), whereas in sequenced supply the logistics provider must pick according to a fixed sequence of the line schedule. In the end, the decision will be a tradeoff between the savings in worker time (and space) and the logistics cost.

Location of Parts and Containers in the Border of Line

A very important aspect of border-of-line organization is the location of the parts and the containers of parts (Figure 6.1). There are two main types of locations:

▲ Front location
▲ Rear location

Front Location

Front location of parts in small containers is the preferred method. The containers can be presented to the front of the operator's immediate working area. If all parts are located at this value-added area in the workstation, the worker need only make short movements. The shelves on which the containers are presented to the operator should be first-in, first-out (FIFO) dynamic racks, which allow the containers to be supplied from the back so that they flow to the front, facing the operator.

If it is not possible to make the containers flow to the worker's value-added area, identify the best place for the container in relation to this working area. The worker then can move a small box to this location from the container racks as needed.

Rear Location

If the situation is such that it is impossible to use a front location, the rear location of parts or containers of parts will have to be used. In many cases, the size of the product and the parts means that the border of line will have to be behind the worker (e.g., in car assembly).

Border of line is the interface between production and logistics operators. Their work should be completely separated.

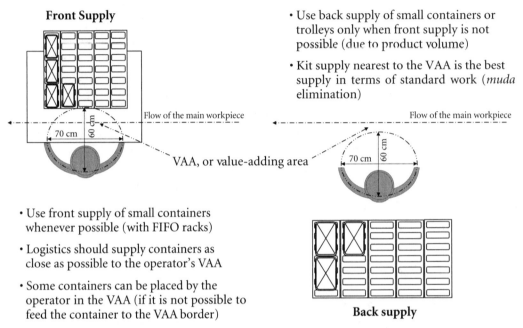

Front Supply

Flow of the main workpiece

70 cm   60 cm

VAA, or value-adding area

• Use front supply of small containers whenever possible (with FIFO racks)

• Logistics should supply containers as close as possible to the operator's VAA

• Some containers can be placed by the operator in the VAA (if it is not possible to feed the container to the VAA border)

• Use back supply of small containers or trolleys only when front supply is not possible (due to product volume)

• Kit supply nearest to the VAA is the best supply in terms of standard work (*muda* elimination)

Flow of the main workpiece

70 cm   60 cm

Back supply

Figure 6.1   Border-of-line organization.

With this location, the worker will have to spin from front to back in a "washing machine motion" to pick the necessary part. One way of avoiding this movement is to prepare in advance one kit of the parts needed for each product in the line. This is called *kitting* (I will discuss this technique in more detail later). Kitting usually implies a *junjo* supply method because the kits have to be in the same sequence as the product schedule of the line.

Summary

The most efficient border of line is the continuous *kanban* supply of small containers on flow racks so that the parts are presented within arm's reach of the operator. If this method is not possible (because of the size and number of different parts), other methods will have to be tried. The possible methods, in order of logistical difficulty, are

▲ *Kanban* front supply
▲ *Kanban* rear supply
▲ *Junjo* front supply
▲ *Junjo* rear supply
▲ *Junjo* kit supply

Flow Containers

Another very important characteristic of the border of lines is that all the parts and containers of parts are able to be moved by hand, without the assistance from a forklift or any other type of mechanical handling equipment. The flow or movement should be as easy as possible. We call this type of containerization *flow containers*.

The type of flow container we use will depend on the size of the part. A *flow container* is defined as a plastic container that with its contents weighs up to 12 kg because a container of this size can be moved by hand without the assistance of any mechanical handling equipment. The same applies to any individual part. A part that weighs more than 12 kg will require some type of mechanical device to move it (as will items that have awkward shapes, such as large floor mats).

> Another very important characteristic of the border of line is that all the parts and containers of parts are able to be moved by hand without the assistance of a forklift or any other type of motorized material-handling equipment.

To be part of a flow, a container weighing more than 12 kg needs to be on wheels. Wheeled bases that have walls function as trolleys and are also flow containers. A standardized classification of the various types of flow containers is given in Figure 6.2.

Containers are classified into three standard sizes: small (600 × 400 mm), medium (600 × 800 mm), and large (800 × 1,200 mm). Anything bigger than this is a bulk container and constitutes a special case (Table 6.2).

Small Container Standard

The standard size of a small container is 600 × 400 mm. To optimize container management, the number of different types of containers used in one operation must be kept to a minimum. Using standard container sizes will maximize the ability of containers to be reused on new product lines. The world transport standard is defined by the available

Table 6.2   Dimensions of Standard Flow Containers

Height of Container (mm)	Standard Container Sizes		
	600 x 400 mm	400 x 300 mm	300 x 200 mm
120	20 liters	10 liters	5 liters
235	45 liters	20 liters	—
320	60 liters	—	—

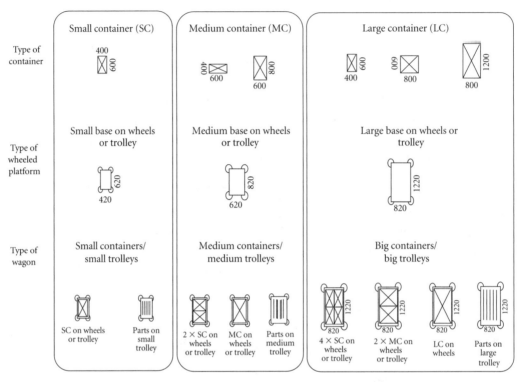

Figure 6.2 Types of containers suitable for the border of line.

truck width of 2,400 mm, which breaks down as 6 units × 400 mm or 4 units × 600 mm. The basic container module dimension is therefore 600 × 400 mm.

A stack of about four to eight small containers (depending on the height of the containers) can be nested for transportation and put on a wheeled base or platform (also called a *roller*). The boxes also can be placed on a trolley with shelves. The border of line can be of the following type:

▲ Individual parts moved to flow racks (or shelves) in the border of line
▲ Small boxes moved to flow racks
▲ A pile of small boxes on a wheeled base
▲ A trolley of boxes or parts

Medium Container Standard

The size of a medium container standard is 600 × 800 mm. This is exactly double the size of the small container, which means that the wheeled bases and trolleys for this size also can be used to move the small containers. The border of line can be of the same type as with the small container.

Large Container Standard

The standard size for a large container is 800 × 1,200 mm (the usual size of a pallet). You can use wheeled bases and trolleys that are a multiple of the small container and use the same type of border of line. The most usual type of border of line will be one big container on a wheeled base or a trolley load of parts—this is also called an *ergo pack* because the parts are located inside the trolley in a way that is very easy to pick. (This method is used for long parts stored vertically inside a trolley.)

For parts that are too long for a standard container, you can use containers that are longer than the standard but still have the standard 400-mm width. This makes it possible to use a standard frontal supply and storage infrastructure. Standard lengths can be 800, 1,000, and 1,200 mm for compatibility with transport dimensions.

Arrangement of Parts and Single Feed

This is a good point to talk about the concepts of the arrangement of parts inside the containers and the single feed of parts. Parts can be arranged in a container to give them adequate protection and ensure precise, efficient picking and put-down. The arrangement of parts in the container is determined naturally by the shape of the part or imposed by dunning. Dunning materials can be of various kinds:

▲   Thermoformed inserts can be adapted to the shape of the part and may form the container itself. However, they require an investment in special tooling.
▲   Dunning in Akylux or any flat, rigid material offers fast, tool-free implementation.
▲   If the dunning material is cardboard, the container can be reused later for other parts.

To optimize workstation productivity, the operator can be supplied with parts one at a time at exactly the same location. This is achieved by using strings of parts, which has the following advantages:

▲   *Quality*—ensures reliable, precise control of picking
▲   *Cost*—optimizes operator motions so that there is minimum variability in part takeup
▲   *Delivery*—increases the number of parts under continuous supply
▲   *Motivation*—avoids difficult and awkward movements

Note: The use of vibrator bowls is often seen as a way of achieving single-part feed, but in fact, it can represent a huge waste of investment and work because of the following disadvantages:

▲   The vibration causes repeated impacts on the parts.
▲   The technology involves a high investment in equipment.

▲ Minor stoppages are difficult to eliminate.

▲ Part change is impossible because the bowl contents are part-specific.

▲ Noise levels are very high.

Defining Small Containers

Standard containers can be defined by creating a database of parts and containers that also will be useful for making a number of decisions in terms of logistics. For each part, the following information will be needed:

▲ *Part identification*—part number, description, picture, or drawing

▲ *Length of the part*

▲ *Weight of the part*

▲ *Consumption rate of the part* (units/min) in the work process

To establish how, when, and where containers will be used in the line (Table 6.3):

1. Go to the workstation and decide the best location for the part by simulating the picking movement.

Table 6.3   Sizes and Uses of the Different Types of Containers in the Border of Line

Type of Grouping	Examples	Type of Container	Notes
Small parts	Electronic components, springs, screws, washers, circlips, etc.	Strings of parts, reels, magazines	Avoid vibrator bowls
Parts smaller than 555 mm	Subassemblies, motors, metal or plastic parts, etc.	Small standard containers	Maximum size: 400 x 600 mm
Parts bigger than 555 mm	Metal parts, wipers, light units, etc.	Small, elongated container	Maximum width: 400 mm Length: 800, 1,000, or 1,200 mm
Parts not possible to accommodate in previous groupings	Wiring harnesses, metal reels, barrels, etc.	Other containers on wheels or trolleys	Maximum width: Preferably no more than 600 mm
Kit of parts	All parts used in one or more workstations	Adapted to the work at each workstation (process and handling times)	Use standard containers as much as possible, with dunning
Raw materials	Fluids, granular materials, etc.	Piping	Container must be specific to process

2. Choose one container, taking note of its type and dimensions (use a picture or drawing).
3. Check the container against the following optimal criteria:
   a. Width less than 400 mm
   b. Number of parts per container in one layer and in the same direction
   c. Weight less than 12 kg when loaded
   d. Autonomy of less than 10 minutes
4. Keep the container if it complies with all criteria.
5. If it doesn't comply, choose another container, taking note of its type and dimension (use a picture or drawing).
6. Check the criteria again.
7. If some of the criteria are not met, consider what the consequences will be. In some cases an allowance will have to be made. Note this allowance for future improvement.

Standard Work

The discipline of work study and time standards was started by Taylor and Gilbreth in the beginning of the nineteen century. Since then, there has been great development in the scientific definition of work methods. One of the most successful ways in which Toyota applied this research has been in the concept of *standard work*, creating a smooth and extremely effective flow of worker movement in the environment of one-piece flow cells and lines.

Creating standard work means achieving a state of fluidity in the worker's movements so that the job will be done in the least amount of time and with perfect quality—in fact, creating value-added work. The worker often appears to be flowing along, glued to the product being worked. This is a powerful way of eliminating both *muda* and *muri*.

The essence of standard work can be summarized as follows: Watch the movements of the worker. From this, make a spaghetti diagram showing the movements around a physical work layout, and measure the time taken to perform each movement. In this way, the *muda* of movement will become visible. To eliminate the different types of *muda*, make improvements and create robust work standards—and you will be creating standard work.

In the Toyota system, standard work is an improvement tool that can be applied to any manual work, whether it's in production,

> *Creating standard work means achieving a state of fluidity in the worker's movements so that the job will be done in the least amount of time and with perfect quality.*

logistics, or the office environment. The principle of watching the worker's movements and improving them is universal.

The Standard Work Improvement Process

Figure 6.3 defines four key words that are related to the concept of standard work. The main elements of a good standard work standard are a clear identification of the worker's movements, the work cycle time, and the standard number of material work in process (WIP).

The five steps of the standard work improvement process are shown in Table 6.4. I will provide a look at each of these steps in greater detail.

1. Define the Target for Improvement

This step means establishing an objective for the improvement team. Standard work is related to the time the worker takes to perform the task, so here the critical *muda* variable is the time of completing a task. You will see that SMED has the same target—to reduce the time it takes to change over from one product to another. So SMED is a special case of standard work.

A quick observation of the worker (sometimes supported by a video of some work cycles) makes it possible to establish a time-reduction target that will serve as the objective for the improvement team. It may or may not be appropriate to transform this target into a key performance indicator (KPI) for efficiency. We calculate efficiency by dividing the standard time by the actual real time. If we reduce the actual real time, efficiency will be increased.

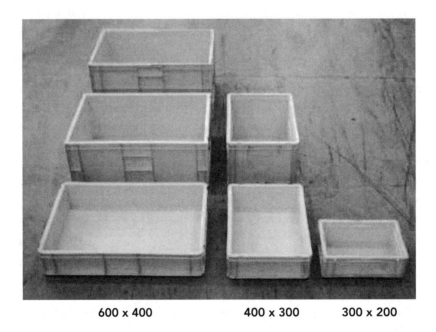

600 x 400   400 x 300   300 x 200

Figure 6.3 Standard work.

Table 6.4   The Standard Work Improvement Process

Steps of the Standard Work Improvement Process	How They Are Achieved
1. Define the target for improvement.	Define the Cycle Time reduction target according to the needed *Takt* Time
2. Observe the work.	Observe carefully the movements of the operator and the time each movement takes. Observe carefully the following *muda*: • Non-value-added operator movements • Materials waiting between operations (WIP—work in process) • Quality defects and rework Observe carefully how abnormalities and difficulties are handled by the operator.
3. Improve the work.	Plan and implement improvement countermeasures to eliminate the various *muda*.
4. Standardize the work.	Standardize: • Operator movements • Cycle time • WIP Present the standard in a visual form: • Charts • Posters • Videos
5. Consolidate the work.	Maintain respect for the new standards by creating strong work habits supported by visual standards.

2. Observe the Work

For this step, you have to collect data on the types of movement that comprise the task or work and the time it takes to perform it. On a line or at a workstation where several people work together on the same product, the movements and times should be measured for each operator individually.

The steps of the observation process are

▲ Calculate the needed cycle time:
   Daily production time/quantity needed per day.

▲ Make a time study of each workstation.

▲ Make a work balancing sheet.
▲ Make a process capacity sheet (for machining operations).
▲ Make a work combination sheet.
▲ Use the most adequate form to capture times and observe muda.

A video recorder can be used, but it is better to use a stopwatch.

The focus of this observation is to identify clearly where the improvements can be made. The aim is not to have a perfect measurement of the current time the operator takes—after all, we wish to improve the work, not to have perfect time standards. Time recording can be something of a trap. It can take so much time and people can get enmeshed in so many discussions that the final goal may be lost.

3. Improve the Work

The goal here is to identify *kaizen* (i.e., change for the better) countermeasures to simplify the work by eliminating any *muda* of movement. When you observe the worker carefully (using a video recorder or just by watching), it will become clear what improvements are needed. Some guidelines for establishing improvements include

▲ Make improvement action sheets.
▲ Ask "Why?" five times.
▲ Concentrate operator movements on the value-added area (VAA).
▲ Where operations involve standing, locate all tools and materials on the operator's working path so that hand movements are always inside the VAA.
▲ Check time-saving rules, and brainstorm possible countermeasures.
▲ Trial suggested solutions.
▲ Implement proven countermeasures as soon as possible.

Figures 6.4 through 6.10 provide examples of various improvements.

4. Standardize the Work

The standard is the end result of the changes for the better (the countermeasures) defined in step 3. The new method is defined and drawn up in a *standard work sheet*, which becomes the basis for training the operators. A special type of standard related to flow cells is the *work combination sheet*. In this sheet, the manual work movements are synchronized with the machine times. This is used in *chaku chaku* lines (low-cost automated lines), where the operator moves material and loads it onto a machine (after loading, the machine will work automatically).

The process of standardization includes the following steps:

▲ Create or update the work balancing sheet.

What Is Standard Work?

Standard	➡	The best, safest, easiest, and most effective way of performing a certain task, achieving the best link between human and machine work.
Work Sequence	➡	The sequence of movements done by each operator is a work cycle.
Cycle Time	➡	Time needed for the operator to complete 1 work cycle (including all movements of 1 part, from start to stop).
WIP	➡	Minimum number of units of work (between operations) needed by the operator to complete the work cycle without interruptions.

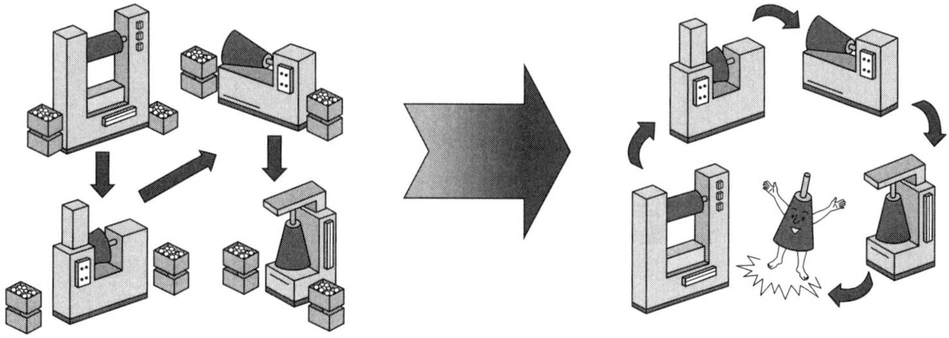

Figure 6.4   Reducing the *muda* of movement—machine layout, 5S, and integrated tools.

▲ Create or update the process capacity sheet.
▲ Create or update the work combination sheet. (These sheets describe the related work components and their sequence.)
▲ Create the standard work sheet.

The reason why a process has variable results can be that an operator does the work in a different way (although operators often will not admit this). Having a standard will reduce the variability of the operation. Standards are the most effective basis for operator training.

5. Consolidate the Work

Consolidating the work means training workers in the new methods and transforming the new methods into an unconscious habit. This is achieved through a good process of job instruction that includes a lot of training and checking. The consolidation of a new method should be done by the worker's supervisor.

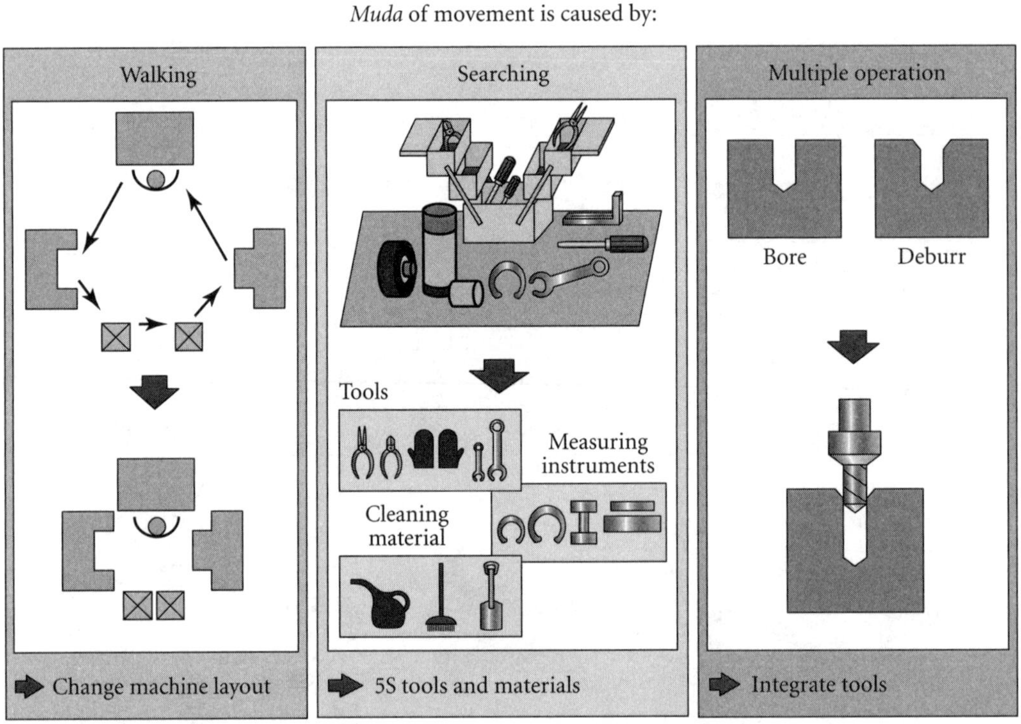

Muda of movement is caused by:

Figure 6.5 Reducing the *muda* of movement—border-of-line design.

The job instruction method used at Toyota is the Job Instruction (JI) module of the Training Within Industry (TWI) program. Figure 6.11 shows how this method works, along with an example of a training card that can be used by the supervisor to follow the procedure. JI says, "If the worker hasn't learned, then the instructor hasn't taught"—an interesting observation and one that puts the responsibility for the success of the training straight into the hands of the supervisor. It takes about 20 days to learn and internalize a new habit. The supervisor needs to be aware of this and be especially observant 20 days after major improvements or changes in work methods have been introduced.

The Role of Containers in the Design of Standard Work

A well-designed border of line that uses small containers located at the point of use is a huge advantage when designing optimal standard work. This is extremely important in all operations that use a lot of assembly workers (e.g., automotive assembly lines and virtually all types of assembly, including consumer goods).

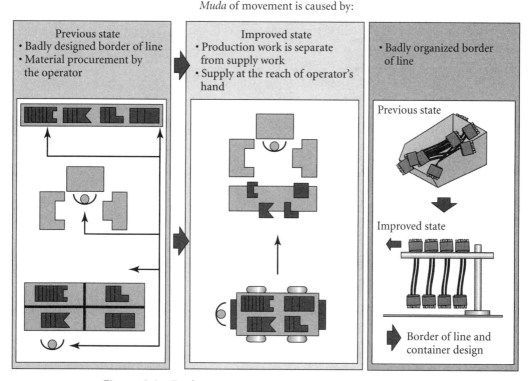

Muda of movement is caused by:

Figure 6.6   Further improvement opportunities—line design.

Toyota developed a special flow system for textiles and shoes called the *Toyota Sewing System* (TSS) that can be applied in any apparel industry. The results of creating flow in this type of traditional industry are amazing and are clear evidence of a huge paradigm change in operations. (One of the changes was to alter the sewing position of the workers from seated to standing, resulting in more productivity and better ergonomics.)

In car assembly lines, Toyota is the leader in terms of using small containers and standard work. In fact, standard work is an obsession with the company. Even now, after 60 years of improvement, Toyota is still refining its standard work. The solutions being applied now are to move from a *kanban*-supplied border of line to a *junjo* supply with kits of parts. The goal is, and will always be, the optimization of standard work. And it is a never-ending story because there will always be some *muda* of movement to eliminate. Winners focus on details.

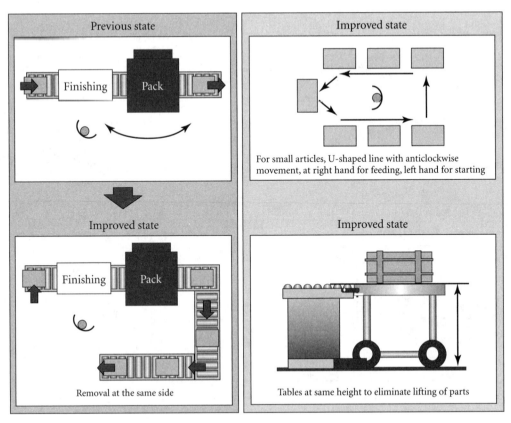

Figure 6.7 Further improvement opportunities—dispensing components.

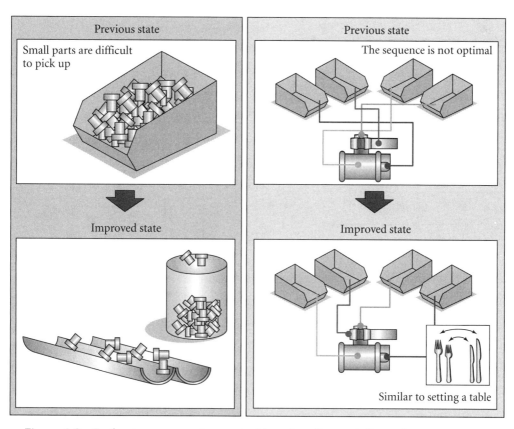

Figure 6.8   Further improvement opportunities—handling and dispensing components.

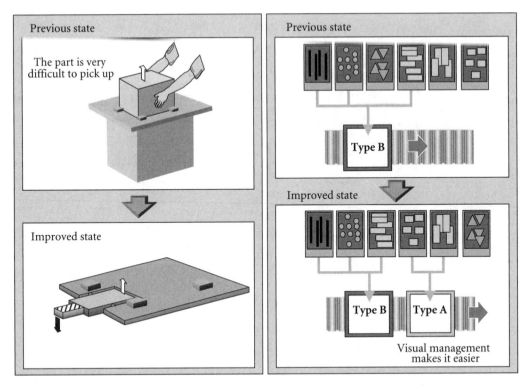

Figure 6.9 Further improvement opportunities—simplification of tasks.

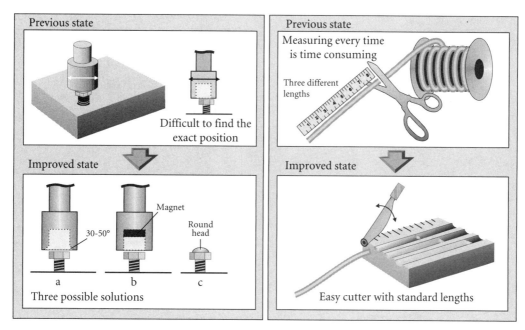

Figure 6.10   Further improvement opportunities—workspace design.

Previous state

Improved state

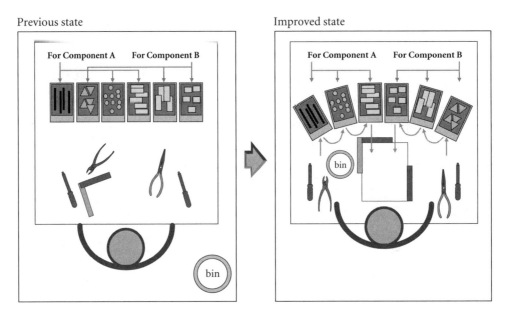

Figure 6.11 Consolidate the work—job instruction.

CHAPTER 7

Production Flow: SMED Flexibility and Low-Cost Automation

SMED

SMED is an acronym standing for *single minute exchange of dies*. It means changing a die to make a different product in a single-digit number of minutes (i.e., <10 minutes). The concept can be applied to any equipment or workstation that loses time or efficiency when changing from one product to another. It is related to increasing the flexibility in product changeover (or service changeover, in the case of an office process).

The person credited with having developed the SMED methodology for improvement is Shigeo Shingo, an industrial engineer and consultant with Toyota. His book, *A Revolution in Manufacturing: The SMED System*, gives detailed information about the SMED system and how it can be applied to many different situations.

Shingo went on to write many books about the Toyota Production System, the most famous of which are the SMED book and *A Study of the Toyota Production System: From an Industrial Engineering Viewpoint*. In 1988, Utah State University honored Dr. Shingo's lifetime of accomplishments in this field by creating the Shingo Prize, an award that recognizes world-class Lean organizations and operational excellence.

Toyota started to apply the SMED method to reduce changeover (CO) time in its metal-stamping presses at the time when Taiichi Ohno was introducing radical changes and creating the Toyota Production System. Taiichi Ohno wanted to implement just-in-time principles and change to smaller, more frequent batches as a way of creating flow and eliminating the material waiting that is the result of big-batch production. At that time, it took four hours to change Toyota's stamping presses from one die to another. The company was aware that a similar die change in a German Volkswagen factory took only two hours. Ohno challenged his team and Shigeo Shingo to find a way of doing the changeover in less than two hours. This was the start of the SMED improvement methodology. Applying it to the stamping presses reduced the changeover time significantly (nowadays, it takes three minutes). Ever since then, SMED has been applied systematically to all Toyota machines.

The Impact of SMED on Capacity, Flexibility, and Flow

The SMED method can increase manufacturing capacity dramatically. In environments where both product variety and changeover time are high, the overall changeover time in a certain period can be the major cause of loss of efficiency. A good example is the printing industry, where changeover time can be the major component of downtime, accounting for about 80 percent of all the efficiency time losses. It is clear that reducing changeover time is one of the major improvement pillars for this type of machine (where in most cases the changeover time takes over two hours). By reducing the changeover time and increasing efficiency, we increase available capacity and reduce the need for capital expenditure (CAPEX) for additional equipment.

Although SMED can be used to increase machine capacity (especially if changeover time is one of the top losses), Toyota started using this improvement method for another reason. Ohno wanted to work with smaller batch sizes to decrease material waiting and so create a flow of materials. In fact, he wanted to improve equipment flexibility in terms of changeover in order to create a flow.

The Wilson model allows us to find an economic order quantity (EOQ, the batch size) by calculating the minimum of a function that is the sum of total inventory costs and ordering costs.

The EOQ model was developed in 1913 by the remarkable F. W. Harris (who, although receiving no formal education beyond high school, made significant contributions as an engineer, inventor, author, and patent attorney). It is also known as the *Wilson model,* after R. H. Wilson, who developed the model further in the 1930s. The EOQ is defined as the order quantity that minimizes the total inventory holding cost and the ordering cost.

The Wilson model allows us to find an EOQ (batch size) by calculating the minimum of a function that is the sum of total inventory costs and ordering costs (Figure 7.1). In a production environment, total inventory costs are the costs of holding work-in-process (WIP) inventory, and ordering costs are the costs of lost equipment efficiency owing to the amount of total changeover time.

Ohno quickly realized that ordering costs (a better name for these is changeover costs) are neither constant nor fixed and can be reduced by reducing the unit changeover time. The result is that the EOQ level drops, and so does the total inventory cost (less *muda* of material waiting). Figure 7.2 shows what can also be called the *SMED effect.*

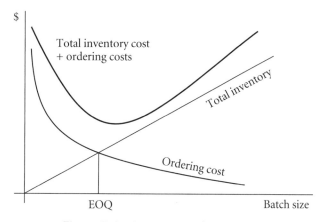

Figure 7.1   Economic order quantity.

Ohno wanted to achieve zero changeover, where the EOQ is equal to one (the material waiting is zero and the flow is perfect—what is known as *one-piece mixed flow*). In this instance, flexibility in terms of the changeover is also perfect, and the mixed product assembly line makes it possible to achieve mixed-variety production. Mixed production also represents a situation in which leveling can be explored to the maximum (this will be explained in Chapters 9 and 10 on internal logistics flow).

The Conflicting Targets of Machine Utilization and Creation of Flow

It can be said that Wilson's formula still applies today. The only problem is when people assume that changeover time (or, generally speaking, ordering cost) is rigid and cannot be

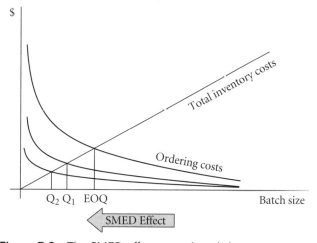

Figure 7.2   The SMED effect on reduced changeover time.

reduced. Many people don't think to do Wilson's calculations because they are still misled by two strong paradigms: *flow at any cost* and *efficiency at any cost.*

The flow-at-any-cost paradigm is currently gaining in popularity. People hear about the wonderful Toyota Production System (TPS) and start to increase flow by reducing batch sizes blindly, without looking at Wilson's formula. What happens is that the CAPEX requirements explode because the small batch sizes together with big changeover times decrease efficiency. The result is that a flow is indeed achieved—but at the expense of CAPEX, not by internally reducing the changeover time and increasing equipment flexibility. You can see this effect in many rich companies that are implementing Lean manufacturing and the TPS.

The efficiency-at-any-cost paradigm was the norm for many years and is the opposite of the flow-at-any-cost paradigm. The problem is that it looks only at the ordering costs and forgets the total inventory costs. The result is a huge amount of inventory, with all the associated losses.

In both cases, people simply forget about Wilson's formula. Ohno's disciples at Toyota still use a simplified version of Wilson's formula today when they calculate *kanban* algorithms for pull logistics loops that include equipment with changeover times (this is explained in Chapter 9, which deals with synchronization).

The key is to keep reducing the changeover time in order to decrease the batch size and create a flow. The batch size needs to be recalculated every time the changeover time is reduced.

The SMED Process

SMED starts by defining changeover time as *the time taken from the finish of the last good-quality part from the previous batch to the first good-quality part of the next batch.* It includes not only the physical die or machine changeover, but also all the preparation work while the machine is stopped or working at reduced speed and all the adjustment and cleaning work at the end while the machine is stopped or working at low speed. It encompasses all the *ordering costs* associated with a change in the production run.

Our experience at the Kaizen Institute shows us that in situations where equipment has never been analyzed through a SMED event, the workers doing the changeover are not really aware of the losses involved, and the opportunities for improvement are huge. In these cases, it is usual to achieve a 50 percent reduction simply by standardizing the work and making some improvements without any investment in additional equipment.

The SMED improvement method consists of five steps (summarized in Figure 7.3):

1. *Study the current situation.* Here we look in detail at the current method, together with the team that usually does the changeover work. The tools used are time analysis, video recordings, and spaghetti charts of the movements necessary to do the work.

2. *Separate internal work from external work.* Using the times and the results of the analysis, we classify each task into internal work—work that can be done only with the machine stopped—or external work—work that can be done while the machine is operating. We take all the external tasks and reorganize them at either the beginning or the end of the process. The internal tasks are organized into a new operative standard. The operators are then trained in this new standard.

3. *Convert internal work to external work.* A detailed analysis of the internal tasks can reveal how, by making some improvements, some of these tasks can be done externally to the changeover. A classic example of such an improvement is a device that preheats the die (preheating will eliminate time wasted in waiting for the die to reach the required temperature before it can be used).

4. *Reduce internal work.* We find countermeasures that allow the remaining internal work to be done in less time—for example, reducing adjustment times by standardizing the geometry of the dies.

5. *Reduce external work.* We find countermeasures that allow the external work to be done in less time—for example, storing the dies close to the equipment.

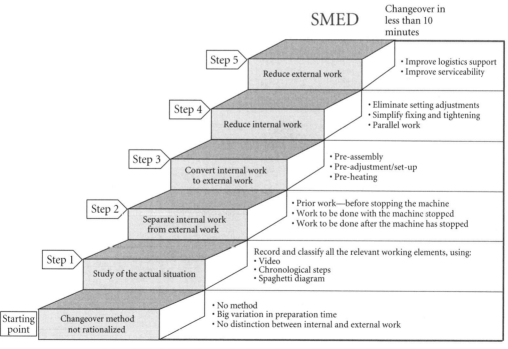

Internal Work: Tasks that can be done only when the machine is not running
External work: Tasks that can take place while the machine is running

Figure 7.3   The five steps of SMED.

By combining some of these steps, Shigeo Shingo achieved quick results in reducing changeover time. After step 1, he would choose the die that took the shortest time to change and challenge the team to organize a perfect changeover. Everything was prepared in advance—the next die was placed close to the machine, all tools were checked, all dimensional adjustments were reduced, and all the people were completely focused on what they were doing. This was a kind of rehearsal. After all this careful preparation, the actual work, of course, yielded very good results. His next step was to discuss countermeasures so that this optimized changeover could be replicated for all the dies and all the different product changeovers. The final result of this process was the actual improved changeover standard.

Changeover work usually involves many departments. First, the changeover operators can be the production operators or can be special mechanics from the maintenance department. These people make up the *focused changeover improvement group* because they are the ones who need to change their daily working habits. Other functions that affect the changeover (I call them *changeover suppliers*) are the die cleaning and preparation shop, the maintenance shop, the quality-control office, and any other supplier of materials or services used in the changeover. It is important that all these functions are involved in the changeover improvement process (Figure 7.4).

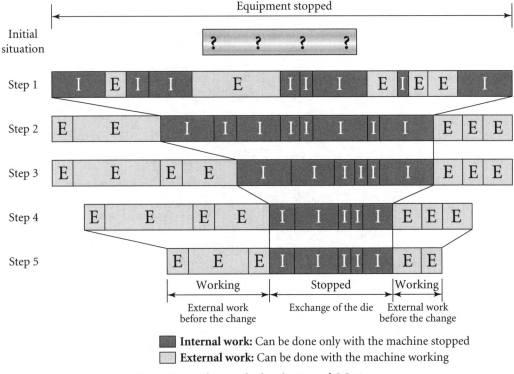

Internal work: Can be done only with the machine stopped
External work: Can be done with the machine working

Figure 7.4 The gradual reduction of CO time.

By systematically applying the SMED method, a permanent reduction of changeover time can be achieved, leading eventually to zero changeover. This optimal situation usually requires some investment in die changeover automation, the cost of which can be justified by the benefits it will bring. Today many equipment manufacturers offer zero changeover options to enhance basic equipment functions.

Developing standard work standards and training workers in them are key elements of the SMED method. An effective standard and a well-trained team can make fast and frequent changeovers in an easy and natural way, simultaneously achieving both good material flow and good machine efficiency.

Low-Cost Automation

Low-cost automation (LCA) deals with the cost-efficient mechanization of manual tasks performed by operators. It is a further step in the concept of standard work, aiming to increase productivity by reducing the manual work content. A difference between LCA and full automation is that in LCA we are interested primarily in taking simple, linear movements that are part of the work cycle and automating them at low cost by mechanical devices that use levers, cams, chutes, guides, and gravity.

Table 7.1 shows the main differences between LCA and conventional automation. LCA strictly follows the production-flow concepts we have explored so far, such as one-piece flow, border-of-line effectiveness, standard work, and SMED capability (flexibility).

Table 7.1   Comparison Between Low-Cost Automation and Conventional Automation

	Low-Cost Automation	Criteria
Cost	Very low cost	High cost
Size	Small and flexible	Big and heavy
Development time	Short	Long
Maintenance/reconfiguration	Easy	Difficult
Design and fabrication	Internal	Usually subcontracted
Information feedback to operators	Good	Weak
Simultaneous engineering level	Good	Weak
Design know-how	Maintained inside company	Belongs to subcontractors
Type of energy employed	Operation depends on natural physical forces (*karakuri*); low energy consumption	Automation of *muda*; high energy consumption
Construction	Simple	Complex

Another word used to describe LCA devices is *karakuri*—the mechanized puppets or automata that were a feature in eighteenth- and nineteenth-century Japan. The most common example of a *karakuri* mechanism today is a tea-serving robot, which starts moving forward when a cup of tea is placed on the plate in its hand. It moves in a straight line for a set distance (moving its feet as if walking) and then bows its head, signaling that the tea is ready for drinking. The robot stops when the cup is removed from the plate. When the cup is replaced, the robot raises its head, turns around, and returns to where it came from. These robots use mechanical energy and usually are powered by a clockwork spring made of whalebone. The actions are controlled by a set of cams and levers.

LCA uses many kinds of *karakuri* to present parts to the operator at hand's reach or as time-saving devices generally.

Automation Levels

The process of deciding what movements to automate in this way can be helped by using an automation checklist that is applied to all operations in a given process (Figure 7.5). The current situation can be quickly evaluated by looking at the full cycle time of each operation. The time components of an operations cycle are usually loading, machining, unloading, and transportation. A good one-piece flow line with improved standard work will offer a good starting point for LCA, and we can now start looking for opportunities to mechanize. Time-saving devices such as jigs or fixtures can help to free operators and reduce the time needed for many operations.

After simplifying the manual work of operators, we can next automate machine time. This is a key element in the process of creating the *chaku chaku* ("load-load") cells (these were explained in Chapter 4). If machine time is automated, the operator will move along the process doing mostly loading and transfer of parts from operation to operation.

Poka yoke is a Japanese term that means "to make fail safe or mistakeproof." *Poka yoke* devices detect and avoid errors and should be located in key operations in the process in order to guarantee zero defects. *Poka yoke* devices also can be LCA in form.

The final work element to be classified as LCA is *unloading time*. Unloading a part after finishing the machining value-added work is a quite straightforward movement and can be done by LCA.

Full automation (and significant investment) starts by mechanizing machine loading movements and movements that transfer parts from one machine to the other. The complex, precise loading and transfer movements this entails usually require the use of robots or complex transfer machines.

One example of full automation is a fully automated assembly line with a very fast cycle time (<15 seconds) and a very small amount of manual work. In general, this type of

Type of automation	Levels of automation	Process operations								
		1	2	3	4	5	6	7	...	n
Manual work	1. Manual work	▓							▓	▓
	2. Time-saving devices (attachments and fixtures)			▓						
Low-cost automation	3. Automation of machine time (MT)		▓							
	4. Automation of MT with *poka yoke*					▓				
	5. Automation of unloading time				▓					
Full automation	6. Automation of loading time (robots)						▓			
	7. Automation of transport time (transfers)							▓		

1. Integrate process operations into one-piece *shojinka* flow lines

2. Check the automation level of each operation using the automation checklist

3. Set automation targets

4. Make implementation plans

Figure 7.5 Automation checklist and steps.

line presents some flexibility problems in terms of very long CO times or limitations in the number of different products it can handle.

The decision to automate also can be driven by the need to eliminate *muri* (difficult operations) where the ergonomics or the environment of the operation is too demanding for a human operator. The best strategy is to start by designing the machines or lines according to flow principles and only then checking what levels of automation are feasible, based on calculating the return on investment. In many cases this will avoid very expensive, fully automated solutions. What is seen in practice is a jump from a no-flow design to full automation, in which case it is impossible to judge whether a more gradual strategy of flow design and LCA would not have yielded a much better result.

Examples of LCA Devices

Time-saving devices minimize many movements and are helpful in developing standard work. Table 7.2 lists some of the types of devices that can be used for reducing the times of certain tasks.

Automation of machine time depends on the flexibility and adaptability of the technology being used. Most equipment manufacturers today offer this feature. For instance, the introduction of flexible computer numerical control (CNC) machines radically changed

Table 7.2 Types of Time-Saving Devices

Type of Device	Function
Weight elevation	Part elevators
	Load platforms
Transport aids	Belts
	Boxes
	Racks on wheels
	Homemade automation-guided vehicles
Presentation of components	Chutes
	Dunning
	Strings of parts
	Point-of-use supply of unit (*seiretsu-sochi*)
	Kitting
Mobile platforms for assembly	Seating platforms
	Moving trolleys
Jigs and fixtures	To facilitate the operations

the manufacturing industry. Curves are now as easy to cut as straight lines, complex three-dimensional (3D) structures are relatively straightforward to produce, and the number of machining steps that require human action has been reduced dramatically.

The increased automation of manufacturing processes brought about by the introduction of CNC machining has meant considerable improvements in consistency and quality without strain on operators. CNC automation has reduced the frequency of errors and given CNC operators time to perform additional tasks. CNC automation also allows for more flexibility in the way parts are held in the manufacturing process and the time required for changing over a machine to produce different components. Error-detection features now give CNC machines the ability to call the operator's mobile phone if they detect that a tool has broken. While the machine is awaiting replacement of the tool, it will run other parts that are already loaded up to that tool and wait for the operator.

It is easy to design low-cost solutions to the automation of machine time using pneumatic and hydraulic circuitry to replace the manual power of the operator (Figure 7.6). One example of a simple *poka yoke* might be that the jig for holding pieces for processing allows pieces to be held in only one orientation. Alternatively, the jig may have switches to detect whether or not a hole has already been cut, or it may count the number of spot welds to ensure that (for instance) four have been executed by the operator.

Shigeo Shingo in *A Study of the Toyota Production System: From an Industrial Engineering Viewpoint* (Productivity Press, 1989, p. 22), recognized three types of *poka yoke*:

▲   The *contact method* identifies defects by whether or not contact is established between the device and the product. Color detection and other product-property techniques are considered extensions of this.

Automatic application of sealant in five locations

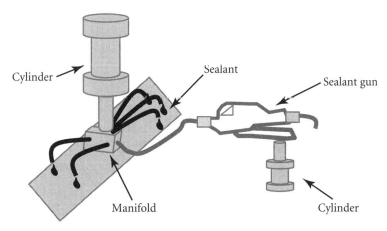

Figure 7.6   Automation of machine time.

▲ The *fixed-value method* determines whether a given number of movements have been made.

▲ The *motion-step method* determines whether the prescribed steps or motions of the process have been followed.

Poka yoke either gives warnings or can prevent (or control) the wrong action. I suggest that the choice between these two should be based on what happens in the process. Warnings may be sufficient for occasional errors, whereas errors that are frequent or are impossible to correct may warrant a control *poka yoke* (Figure 7.7).

Unloading time can be automated by means of mechanical devices (*karakuri* solutions) or by using pneumatic and hydraulic solutions to eject parts after finishing the machine time cycle. The Japanese word for this type of mechanism is *hanedashi*. The machine switches are located on the operator's path of natural motion after picking the ejected part, allowing the operator to switch on the machine *while walking away to the next process*. These are called *nagara* switches from the Japanese word meaning "while doing" something. This refers to a lever-type switch that requires only a small natural "flick" motion by the operator

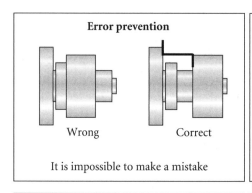

Error prevention

Wrong   Correct

It is impossible to make a mistake

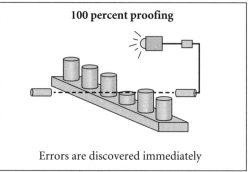

100 percent proofing

Errors are discovered immediately

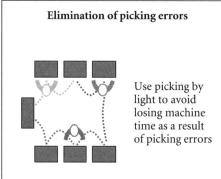

Elimination of picking errors

Use picking by light to avoid losing machine time as a result of picking errors

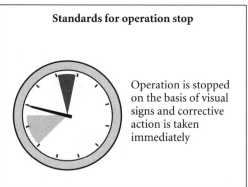

Standards for operation stop

Operation is stopped on the basis of visual signs and corrective action is taken immediately

Figure 7.7 Automating machine time with *poka yoke*.

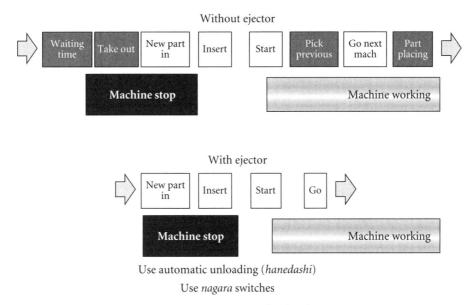

Figure 7.8   Automation of unloading time.

while walking past, instead of stopping to push a button, requiring a deliberate extra movement (Figure 7.8).

LCA Design Guidelines

Although LCA design and solutions depend on the particular technological field in which they are to be used, here are some general guidelines:

▲ Use
  ▼ Simple mechanisms using natural laws (*karakuri*)
  ▼ Gravity (chutes, rollers, mechanisms)
  ▼ Natural balancing forces (counterweights)
  ▼ Flow solutions (simple AGVs [automatic guided vehicle], rollers, tables on wheels)
  ▼ Small sizes (the target is to reduce cost and eliminate the *muda* of motion)
  ▼ Miniaturization (reduce size and weight of tools, work areas, etc.)
  ▼ Reduce distance (reduce distance between work areas to minimize walking)
  ▼ Automatic testing machines
  ▼ Automatic unloading
  ▼ Low-cost materials and components
  ▼ General-purpose materials (sensors, tubes, motors)

▼ Machine construction based on *gemba* and user needs simultaneous engineering
▼ Easily modifiable construction
▲ Recycle old components (use of old equipment).
▲ Modify old machines.
▲ Incorporate SMED principles.

It is advisable to create an LCA *kaizen* experts team inside the production department to facilitate the design and fabrication of tools and equipment. The usual procedures for tool and equipment modification are too rigid and bureaucratic to answer the needs of the *gemba*. The LCA *kaizen* team will be responsible for making the LCA devices.

The mission of this team can be to design and fabricate LCA devices based on *gemba* needs and proposals. The members of this team can be experienced operators or supervisors reporting to the head of the production department.

The general steps involved in creating LCA solutions include

1. Provide *gemba kaizen* training (based on *gemba* observation).
2. Create an LCA *kaizen* experts team dedicated to LCA fabrication.
3. Apply the automation checklist to each process, and decide where LCA is needed (see Figure 7.5).
4. Decide the base concept for each LCA.
5. Make a prototype, and assemble the LCA in the *gemba*.
6. Test the LCA, involving the operators.

Low-cost automation will allow a constant increase in productivity at a very low level of investment. One of the major goals of applying *kaizen* to logistics and supply chains is to reduce CAPEX costs. Low-cost automation makes a major contribution to the achievement of this goal.

CHAPTER 8

Internal Logistics Flow: Introduction and Supermarkets

Introduction

The third pillar of the Total Flow Management (TFM) model is *internal logistics flow* (Figure 8.1). The challenge of internal logistics flow is to create *one-small-container flow*. We have already seen in the border-of-line domain how to choose the best containers to ensure the flexibility and productivity of the lines. Now we need to organize internal logistics in order to supply all the needed parts according to the line cycle time (which should be working close to the customer *takt* time).

Another target of internal logistics flow is to create information flow, starting with the customer's actual order or replenishment orders. The orders (or customer requirements) need to be transformed into production orders as quickly as possible and sent to production for picking and delivery of parts to the production lines.

Internal logistics flow integrates production and logistics so that the system works according to the customer *takt* time in a synchronized way to provide the products "just in time."

The internal logistics flow pillar combines with the previous pillar, production flow, to organize all the improvements needed to create Pull Logistics Loop 2 (finished-goods production) and Pull Logistics Loop 3 (production parts picking). The domains of the TFM model that are involved are shown in Figure 8.2. The domains of the third pillar can be explained as

- ▲ *Supermarkets.* How to organize easy picking areas for flow containers of all the materials and parts needed.
- ▲ *Mizusumashi (literally "water spider" for logistics transport workers).* How to transport the flow containers quickly to the border of lines.

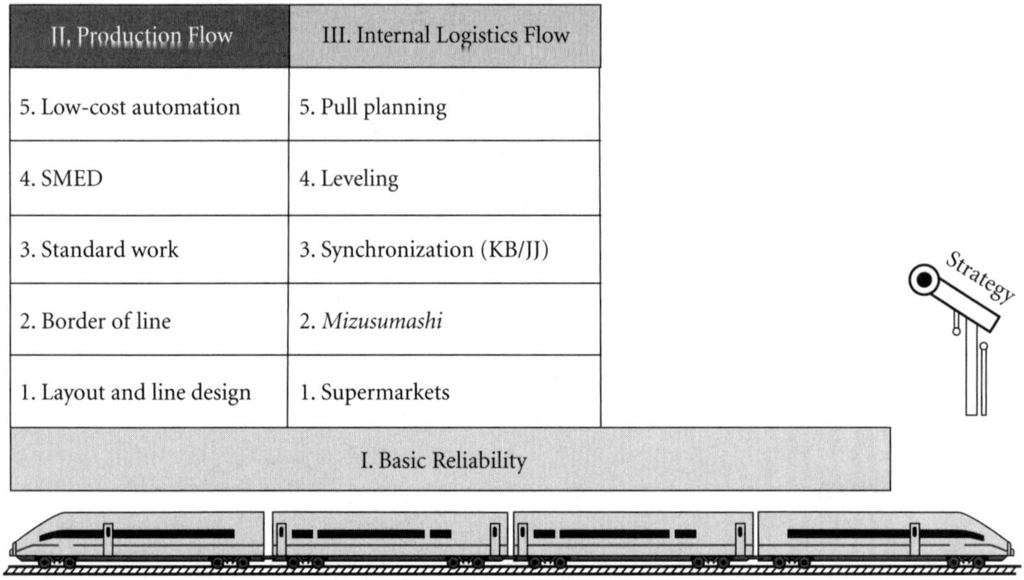

II. Production Flow	III. Internal Logistics Flow
5. Low-cost automation	5. Pull planning
4. SMED	4. Leveling
3. Standard work	3. Synchronization (KB/JJ)
2. Border of line	2. *Mizusumashi*
1. Layout and line design	1. Supermarkets
I. Basic Reliability	

Figure 8.1   Pillars I, II, and III of the TFM model.

▲ *Synchronization.* How to start the production, picking, and delivery of the needed materials and parts in a synchronized way.

▲ *Leveling.* How to schedule the production orders in the pacemaker processes (the point in the overall process that is scheduled).

▲ *Production pull planning.* How to set up the production capacity and calculate the customer needs.

The goal is to work according to customer demand at the highest quality and lowest cost. To achieve this, we need to integrate logistics with production and create one-small-container flow and one-piece flow inside the plant. We will see how this can be done in the following chapters.

Traditional Supply versus Flow Supply

The traditional way to organize internal logistics is based on optimizing logistics for its own sake without worrying too much about the needs of production in terms of efficiency. Usually, the production department tends to make its own improvements (which are limited by the existing logistics processes and tools) without ever exploring the concepts of production flow to the maximum. The result is that many types of *muda* coexist in both production and logistics.

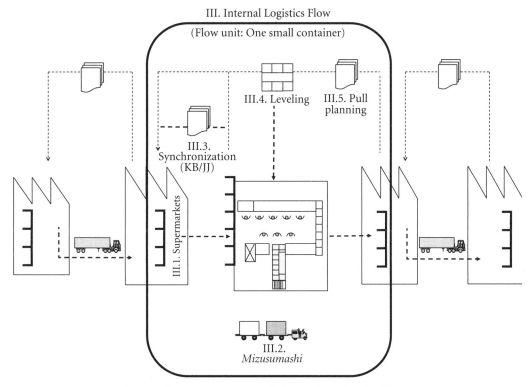

Figure 8.2   Integrated logistics and production flow.

The traditional way to organize logistics is based on the following principles:

▲ Minimizing internal transportation, which results in supplying the lines with large quantities in each transport (usually once per shift)

▲ Minimizing the area needed for the storage of incoming materials and parts, as well as work in process (WIP), which implies storage at height

▲ Using forklifts to handle pallet-sized containers

▲ Minimizing repacking or unpacking work and pushing it to the production lines (e.g., picking parts into the border of lines and opening carton boxes)

▲ Planning large production orders to minimize changeover (CO) time and increase efficiency

The flow way of organizing logistics is based on different principles. These are

▲ Supplying the right-sized containers needed to maximize efficiency and flexibility in the production lines

▲ Organizing picking areas to supply the right-sized containers frequently and with efficiency

▲ Using the appropriate transport equipment to deliver in standardized routes with a fixed cycle time (e.g., a small train that carries a load just large enough to supply the stations along its one-hour route)

▲ Working with suppliers and customers to use the same right-sized containers (or doing all the necessary repacking and unpacking) in order to supply production with the right material, at the right location, in the right quantity, and with the right presentation

▲ Planning the customer orders and creating conditions to smooth the orders to suppliers through leveling

The flow way is a breakthrough in terms of organizing logistical effectiveness and efficiency. It creates a whole new way of integrating logistics with production, allowing the complete optimization of the internal logistics loops.

The traditional way of organizing logistics can be described as a *push-flow system*. Push flow works according to the general model shown in Figure 8.3. Fixed customer orders are sent to the finished-goods warehouse for picking. If the right inventory is available, the orders may be fulfilled immediately; if inventory is unavailable, orders may wait until inventory becomes available. The amount of inventory in the finished-goods store is usually high (values from 10 to 30 days are common in many industries), but at the same time, the service level is low (values from 80 to 90 percent for on-time delivery are common). The situation is the classic problem of *dysfunctional inventory*—too much of what we don't need now and too little of what we do need. It's a synchronization problem.

The system for synchronizing finished-goods production with the fixed customer orders (also called *call-off* orders in the automotive industry) is based on a central planning department that runs an *enterprise resource planning* (ERP) software system. The modules of the ERP system that make the most of the synchronization work are based on the logic of *materials requirements planning* (MRP). Because the system wants to plan and synchronize all the quantities and start times of all production orders, the starting point is usually a forecast of demand for a certain period of time depending on the lead times for production and sourcing (this can be from one to several weeks). The system also has information on the standard times for each production line, the standard defect rates, and the inventories of WIP. The MRP algorithm takes all this information and extrapolates the final forecasted demand into synchronized production and supplier orders. If everything goes according to plan, what you now have is a functional inventory that serves the customers "just in time."

Where things can go wrong is that most of the information used to synchronize the orders changes quickly and is subject to errors. Call-off orders differ from forecast orders (a forecast without forecast error is not a forecast), real production times differ from

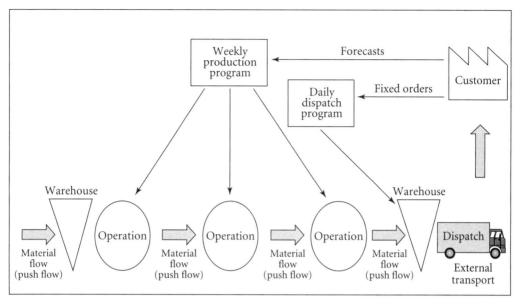

Standard MRP execution model
Programs based on grouping (batching) and forecast
Manufacturing and purchase orders issued by central planning
Big batches, long lead time, slow (no) flow

Figure 8.3 The push-flow model.

standard production times (as do defect rates), and the information on WIP changes so quickly that most of the systems don't have time to maintain reliable information (a match between what the system tells us we have and what we actually do have). Reality is a complex system that involves the four *M*s (i.e., manpower, machines, materials, and methods) and is constantly changing and adapting. A centralized system cannot maintain a perfectly synchronized system.

The performance of a push system will vary according to the environment, but the performance of a pull system will always be better. We will see why.

A pull-flow system doesn't attempt to plan in a centralized way. Figure 8.4 shows how a pull-flow system starts with the fixed customer orders and schedules these orders either for production or for picking depending on the customer service policy defined. Some components may be defined as *make to order* and others as *pick to order* (made to stock). These fixed orders are sent to only one point in the supply chain. Consumption of materials and parts starts at this point, and the consumption generates replenishment orders.

These replenishment orders then generate further replenishment orders, and the process is repeated upstream of the supply chain. The process is as simple as this—the system reacts to real consumption, not to planned orders. It is a self-adjustable system. If

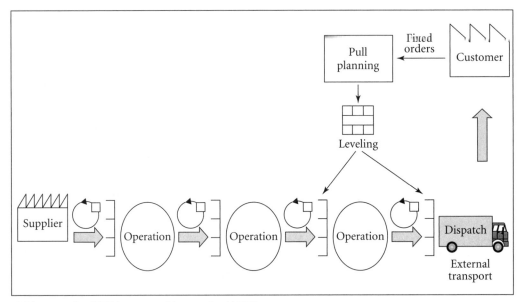

Picking to order (PTO), or assembly to order (ATO)
Build to replenish (BTR)
Pull material from supplier
A good production and logistics flow

Figure 8.4 The pull-flow model.

problems delay the flow, the orders also will be delayed and will be issued only when consumption restarts. People then can concentrate on fixing the problems that caused the delay in the flow, and the synchronization will work automatically.

A pull-flow system is the new supply-chain paradigm. Let's see how we can implement it.

The Logistics Domains

Supermarkets

The first domain of improvement in internal logistics flow is *supermarkets*. The term is somewhat vague, but the basic concept is to have the same ease in picking goods as we have when we go to a supermarket to shop. The customers pick what they need without looking into a computer system or ordering the goods, as in a traditional warehouse. The goods are so neatly and handily displayed that the only thing you have to do is pick what you need and go on to the next shelf. It is said that Taiichi Ohno saw this in the United States and thought it was a very good improvement to apply in the *gemba* because it saved time.

For flow to be achieved, the *gemba* needs this type of easy storage system. Imagine a logistics worker coming to a store to pick a pallet of material. The pallet he needs is on the fifth level of a traditional warehouse. The worker has to find a forklift that allows him to pick a pallet at such a height. Then he has to drive it to the pallet location and pick it, being very careful not to damage other pallets—or drop the one he needs—in the process. The worker must bring the pallet down, then find another forklift, and load the pallet onto it. Then he probably will have to inform the computer system that he took a pallet out of the store. He will also have to drive carefully close to the point of use and put the pallet on the ground. He may need to move an empty pallet away, which means several movements with the forklift. Finally, he may have to open the package by cutting the carton. This is a lot of work. It's mainly non-value-adding work that includes a lot of waiting and doing things very slowly in a nonlinear way.

Now imagine that the same logistics worker comes to a supermarket to pick the same pallet, but now the pallet is a flow container and is stored in a supermarket. In this case, the pallet will be mounted on a wheeled base (a roller base) and will be stored at ground level. The location of the product will be clearly visible (visual management). The worker comes with a small train, stops close to the pallet, moves the pallet to the train, goes to the border of line, moves the pallet close to the production worker (maybe removing an empty pallet, also on wheels)—and that's it. A fraction of the time is used. This is made possible by using flow containers stored in supermarkets and handled by logistics workers called *mizusumashi*.

The Mizusumashi ("Water Spider") System

The second domain of improvement in internal logistics flow is *mizusumashi*. This Japanese word means "water beetle," and this internal logistics worker is often called a "water spider" in English. This term probably was chosen for this concept because of the water beetle's agility as it swims across the water. Here a *mizusumashi* is a logistics worker who does the internal transportation of goods, using a standard fixed cycle route. I will use the terms *water spider* and *mizusumashi* interchangeably.

The *mizusumashi* is a key element in the creation of internal logistics flow. This worker moves all the information related to production orders (*kanban*), as well as all the flow of containers. The water spider moves the flow containers between supermarkets and border of lines by repeating the same movements in a fixed cycle (usually 20 or 60 minutes). During this cycle, the water spider will stop in a certain number of stations along the route and check whether they need materials. The water spider uses a small train that has a suitable load capacity to serve all the stations on its fixed route, delivering information to several points along the way.

The *mizusumashi* fixed cycle time is also called the *pitch time*. This pitch time is a multiple of the *takt* time. If the *mizusumashi* is moving one piece at a time, the pitch time would equal the cycle time. Because the *mizusumashi* is moving small containers, the pitch time is designed to move several small containers to many points of use in the border of several lines.

The customers are the production operators on the lines. They have a reliable logistics provider who comes every 20 or 60 minutes, looks to see if more material is needed, and removes the empty containers and any garbage generated during the process (reverse logistics). Production is assured of a reliable and frequent supply.

Synchronization

The third domain of improvement in internal logistics flow is *synchronization*. Synchronization is related to the information system used to signal the start of production, or the start of the picking and delivery of materials. In a Lean environment, synchronization is done on the *gemba* with physical devices that can be seen (visual management). The worker using the synchronization information is the water spider, who sees when a container needs to be moved to a certain point of use and who orders a line to start production of a certain item.

Synchronization can be achieved successfully with physical devices. The system can always be automated later by means of an information system. It is important to have an efficient and effective physical (visual) information system that the users understand and are able to react to quickly.

There are two main ways of achieving synchronization: the *kanban* logistics loop and the *junjo* logistics loop. These were discussed in Chapter 9 within the section on border of line improvements, but now I will explain how these loops work in the *mizusumashi* context.

In a *kanban* loop, the water spider arrives at the border of line and checks to see if there are any empty boxes available. Each box has a *kanban* card that identifies the part number, the quantity, the customer location (in the border of line), and the supplier location (in the supermarket). The water spider picks the empty box with the card attached and goes back to the supermarket and picks another identical box to deliver in the next loop. This is the most basic *kanban* delivery loop. (If there is any production in the middle of the logistics loop, the *kanban* will be more complex.)

In a *junjo* loop, the *mizusumashi* receives a picking list that has the parts listed in the sequence needed by the operator (who is the internal customer of the water spider). Let's assume that the operator will need parts 1, 2, and 3 in the next *mizusumashi* cycle. The *mizusumashi* picks these parts and delivers them in a box in the border of line in the required sequence (i.e., 1, 2, and 3). The operator will have what is needed for the next cycle (and will receive the next sequence in time for the cycle after that). *Junjo* means "sequenced delivery" and has the advantage of reducing the size of *kanban* supermarkets (in this example the border of line will not have to maintain a location for the three different parts but only one location in which to put the sequence).

Leveling

The fourth domain of improvement in internal logistics flow is *leveling*, also called *heijunka* in Japanese. Leveling includes all the activities necessary to sequence the pacemaker lines with the production orders. The process starts with the production orders (either replenishment orders or fixed orders). These orders are then broken down into smaller batch sizes in *kanban* containers. The right day to start production and the daily sequence of production are decided, and this sequence is sent to the pacemaker lines.

The term *leveling* also includes the concept of sequencing the quantity batches of different products in a *leveled* (or equal) way within a planning period. This is also called the *EPEI concept*. EPEI stands for "every product every interval." For example, to achieve an EPEI of one day, you have to sequence all the part numbers that will be needed during that day. If the EPEI is one half day, you would need to sequence all references during that half day and repeat the sequence again the next half day. The smaller the EPEI, the better the leveling will be. In other words, an ideal EPEI will allow a single reference sequence, also called *mixed production* (as in many car assembly lines, where you can see a sequence of different models flowing on the lines with no batches of similar models).

What is the advantage of mixed production? Basically, in this model, the consumption of different parts is smoothed or leveled, which eliminates spikes in consumption and gives the suppliers a smoothed *takt*. Mixed production also makes it possible to use a fixed crew size on the lines independent of the work content of the various products being assembled. This will be explained in more detail in Chapter 10. For the moment, just remember that leveling deals with the sequencing of small or unit batches to create a better flow. It also includes all the necessary synchronization mechanisms to facilitate the sequencing.

Production Pull Planning

The fifth domain of improvement in internal logistics flow is *production pull planning*. This domain includes important planning decisions that determine the success of all the other domains.

First, you need to decide the planning strategy for the finished goods. There are two basic strategies here: *make to order* and *make to stock*. For each part number in the *bill of materials* (a graph showing the structure of the materials that are necessary to make one finished product), you have to decide the strategy, starting from the finished-goods inventory. Some of the finished-goods inventory you will supply from stock, which means that you can promise immediate delivery. For others, you will only make it to order. There are also some variants in between, which I will discuss later.

Second, you look at your medium- and long-term capacity and make the necessary adjustments. You check how many operators you will need on each line next month or how many shifts you will have working. You also may want to check that the size of your supermarkets or storage facilities is large enough or even the number of external transport routes that will be needed. This kind of planning is usually done monthly but can be done every two weeks. The main information needed is forecasts of demand. In this model, you use forecasts to prepare capacity in advance, not to start executing orders in the forecasted quantities.

Third, you must decide on a short-term basis (usually daily) the execution orders to be started. The main input for this will be either customer orders or consumption replenishment orders. Orders will have to be calculated and sent to the right place in the supply chain every day or even on a continuous basis.

How the Supermarket Concept Works

Let's now look a little more deeply at the supermarket domain. A supermarket is a storage area that is set up according to the following rules:

▲   It has a fixed location for every part number.
▲   It provides easy picking access (ground-level storage).
▲   It allows visual management.
▲   It keeps to the first in, first out (FIFO) principle.
▲   It is designed to enable flow and easy handling of
   ▼   Small containers
   ▼   Containers on wheels (rollers)
   ▼   Trolleys

(The starting point of good supermarket design is the set of standard internal transport units, containers, that were created in the border-of-line process discussed in Chapter 6.)

Having created flow in *production*, you now must create more *logistical* flow:

▲   From incoming goods storage to the production cells and lines
▲   From incoming goods storage between production cells and lines
▲   From incoming goods storage to the final product storage areas

Supermarkets are the internal storage infrastructures that allow a good internal logistics flow to operate. A supermarket allows very easy picking of parts. This is a major element in achieving productivity in internal logistics. Traditional in-plant storage uses conventional shelves to stack pallet-sized containers. Because it holds a large number of containers, minimizing the storage area is always a concern. Figure 8.5 compares traditional storage areas with flow supermarkets.

You can see that flow supermarkets allow very easy picking of flow containers. The type of storage is either shelves with flow racks (no higher than 2 m, just as in a supermarket) or ground-level storage of containers on wheels or trolleys. Space constraints can be a problem. If the flow is high, the quantities to be stored (storage is, by definition, waiting time) will be small, and the plant can operate with supermarket-sized storage areas only. However, this can take some time to achieve. In the meantime, you may need some reserve storage areas that use traditional storage methods.

Internal logistics flow can be defined as a sequence that starts in supermarkets of materials or parts, includes all the WIP storage, and finishes with the finished-goods supermarkets. This means that your internal logistics flow pillar involves the organization of all supermarket storage areas and all the associated logistic movements. It is a supermarket-to-supermarket flow network.

Traditional Storage	**Flow Supermarkets**
• Poor protection of parts	• Good protection of parts
• Difficult to apply first in, first out (FIFO)	• Good FIFO
• Difficult access to parts	• Easy access to parts
• Multiple storage locations for the same item (difficult to create picking habits)	• Single dedicated locations for the same item (easy to create picking habits)
• Risk of parts falling	• No risk of parts falling
• Batch production paradigm	• Flow production paradigm

Figure 8.5   Traditional storage compared with a flow supermarket.

Types of Flow Supermarkets

There are five different types of supermarket storage:

▲ Flow rack (Figure 8.6)
▲ Ground storage on wheels (Figure 8.7)
▲ The logistic cell
▲ Border of line (Figure 8.8)
▲ The kitting supermarket (Figure 8.9)

Flow Racks and Ground Storage on Wheels

The flow-rack supermarket is used to store small plastic containers that can be moved by hand. The definition of *small container* is a plastic case, one less than 12 kg in weight when loaded, that can be moved by hand. Because it can be easily moved by hand, it is classified

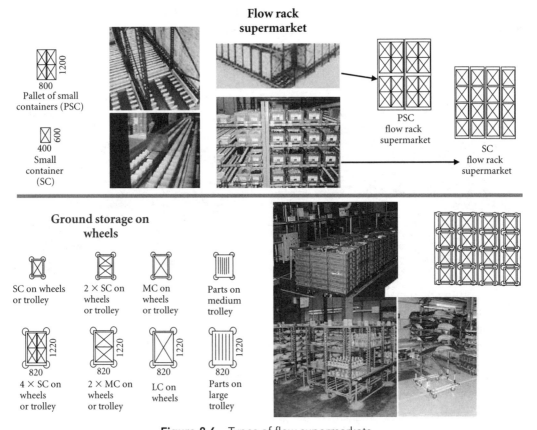

Figure 8.6 Types of flow supermarkets.

as a flow container. This type of supermarket also can store pallets of small containers, using flow racks that present the pallet so that the *mizusumashi* can pick containers.

The ground-storage supermarket stores medium to big containers on wheels, as well as trolleys of parts. In fact, the difference between containers on wheels and trolleys is that while both are on a wheeled base, the trolley also has walls and shelves (or some other types of fixtures). This supermarket has a very simple format. When the wheeled containers are aligned along guiding lines, it is also known as a first in, first out (FIFO) lane.

Figure 8.6 shows some examples of flow-rack supermarkets. You can see that their design is rather simple—the racks flow to a picking alley (outbound or customer alley) from inbound alleys on the outer perimeter. Wheeled ground storage supermarkets have the same design, but on wheels (Figure 8.7).

The Logistics Cell

It sometimes may be necessary to include some reserve capacity in a supermarket. This is usually done by designing some traditional storage shelves above the supermarket areas

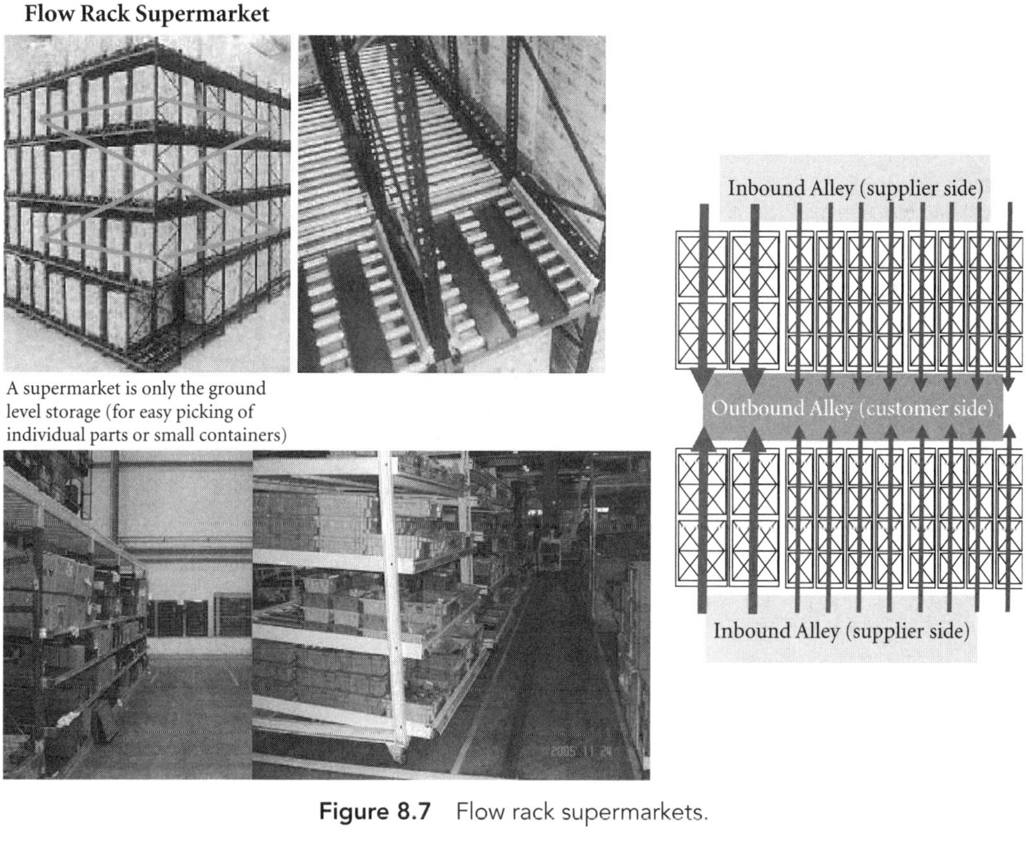

Flow Rack Supermarket

A supermarket is only the ground level storage (for easy picking of individual parts or small containers)

Inbound Alley (supplier side)

Outbound Alley (customer side)

Inbound Alley (supplier side)

Figure 8.7   Flow rack supermarkets.

on which pallet-sized containers can be stored. Similarly, a traditional shelved storage area can be transformed into a supermarket at ground level, with the shelves above being used for reserve storage. A special form of this supermarket plus reserve is the *logistics cell*.

The concept can be used to store the materials and parts needed in a production cell, as well as the finished goods of the same cell. There is a picking alley with flow racks on both sides, and at the far end of the cell there is space for containers of finished goods. This space can be used to build pallet-sized containers of small plastic containers or to repack from the containers used in production to the containers used for customer delivery. Above the flow racks there are some shelves ready to store reserve stock. The outside of the cell is used to load all the incoming parts and to remove the outbound finished goods. In this way, the logistics cell functions as an interface between external logistics (done in pallet-sized containers) and internal logistics (done in small container sizes).

Border-of-Line Supermarket

Another type of supermarket is the *border-of-line supermarket*. This term applies to the storage infrastructure designed around the workstations in the production cells, lines, or machines. You have seen that the border of line can be of two types: *kanban* or *junjo*. Figure 8.8 shows the characteristics of *kanban* and *junjo* supermarkets.

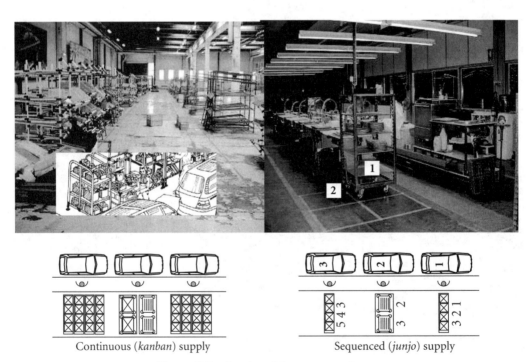

Continuous (*kanban*) supply   Sequenced (*junjo*) supply

Figure 8.8   Border-of-line supermarkets.

You can see that a *kanban* type of border-of-line supermarket can be organized using any kind and any size of container. Of course, flow racks of small containers are the preferred method, but *kanban* supermarkets can equally well be organized for big parts using ground storage on wheels. In this case, the minimum number of containers will have to be two, and the supermarket should allow easy handling of these containers on wheels by means of a turntable or by creating lanes for full containers and lanes for empty containers. All the movement of the containers to and from the storage area is done by pushing the wheeled containers by hand.

Kitting Supermarkets

Kitting supermarkets are yet another type of supermarket. Here the principle is easy. A *kit* is a special container organized to store the different parts used to make one product. If all the parts needed for the product are inside the kit, then one single unit of finished product can be produced by picking from the kit. A kitting supermarket is very similar to a border-of-line supermarket in the sense that several parts must be picked to produce a kit of parts. This kit of parts then can be sent to a particular point in the production line, from where it will follow the product through all the workstations.

Figure 8.9 shows two examples of a kitting supermarket and a schematic of the basic design. Kits are used to concentrate picking movements for an individual operator and

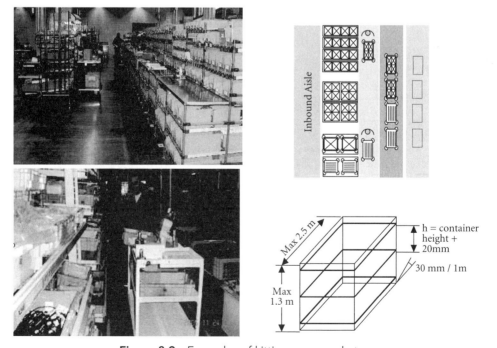

Figure 8.9   Examples of kitting supermarkets.

simplify the final picking necessary for making the product. In situations where there are many different parts and a large number of options, kitting supermarkets organized with *kanban* logic can be the answer.

Deciding Supermarket Size

Now I come to the more difficult task of deciding the size of the supermarket. By definition, a supermarket will always be the waiting point at the end of a logistics loop, so its size depends mainly on the characteristics of the lead time of this logistics loop.

Figure 8.10 shows that the size of a supermarket will depend on the type of logistics loop it is supplying. In the case of a *junjo* logistics loop, the size of the supermarket is the area necessary to accommodate a batch of sequenced parts equivalent to the period of the *mizusumashi* cycle, after which the sequence is frozen (once you freeze the sequence, you can send it to the line).

A more complex situation is the *kanban* supermarket at the end of a *kanban* loop. Such a supermarket will have to be designed to accommodate the maximum number of parts to be stored. This, in turn, depends on two main parameters:

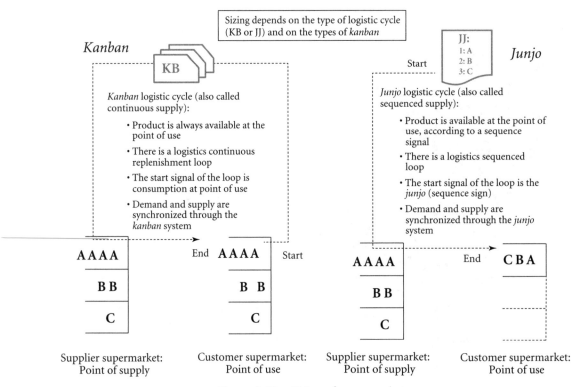

Figure 8.10 Sizing of supermarkets.

⚐ The production or transport batch size

⚐ The replenishment lead time

The replenishment lead time is used to define the trigger point for ordering a replenishment of parts to the supermarket. Therefore, the quantity of parts stored needs to be large enough to serve the customer while the information that replenishment is needed and the material needed move through the logistics loop.

Let's suppose that you have reached the trigger point in one supermarket, and you issue a replenishment order, and after the replenishment, no further consumption took place. In this case, the remaining quantity in the supermarket is equal to the forecasted consumption during the replenishment time. However, the machine that you use to make the product may require a minimum batch-size quantity, or there may be a minimum transport load required on the truck. In both cases you will receive a certain batch, and you will have to store it anyway.

The maximum storage space needed in the supermarket, therefore, is the quantity required to supply the customer during the replenishment process *plus* the minimum batch size requested. This is why a quick changeover between different products and a frequent supply are so important to keep the supermarket size down and create flow.

Chapter 9 will explain the different types of *kanban* loops and how to make the necessary calculations.

There is, however, a third parameter used in calculating the size of a supermarket. It is related to the customer's frequency of picking. If the frequency is low (e.g., once a week), then the supermarket probably will have to be bigger because it can reach its maximum storage point during the week. If the picking frequency is high, the maximum storage point will not be reached so often. If you can keep the customer's picking frequency at a constant high level, then the size of the supermarket can be reduced (I will discuss this again when I address logistics pull planning in Chapter 11).

There is an interesting scenario called the *supermarket size simulation* that demonstrates the combined effect of batch size and customer picking frequency. The conclusions of this simulation are summarized in Figure 8.11.

To be able to interpret the results shown in the figure, you need to understand the logistics loop in the scenario:

⚐ The simulation considers the results of one day of work.

⚐ There is a production cell that makes three different products.

⚐ There is a supermarket at the end of this cell to store the three products.

⚐ Customers come to this supermarket one, two, or four times a day to pick their needs.

⚐ The production cell can be sequenced to make 3, 6, or 12 changeovers—3 changeovers a day means an EPEI of one day (making all three products every day), 6 changeovers

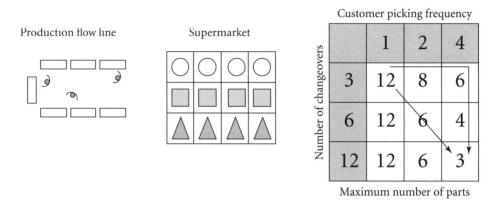

Figure 8.11 Supermarket sizing simulation.

a day means an EPEI of half a day (making all three products in half a day), and 12 changeovers a day means an EPEI of a quarter of a day.

You can draw some conclusions from the results of this scenario:

▲ Both frequent setups (small batch sizes) and high transport frequencies have an effect on inventory.
▲ Best results are achieved when batch sizes (EPEIs) match transport frequencies and both are minimized (i.e., one-piece production and transport batches).
▲ When transport frequencies are low, moves to reduce batch sizes have no effect at all.

Internal Logistics Flow: *Mizusumashi* and Synchronization

Mizusumashi

Mizusumashi is the name of the second improvement tool set of the internal logistics flow pillar. As we saw in Chapter 8, the *mizusumashi* (the "water spider") is a logistics operator who is responsible for moving materials and information inside a plant.

The *mizusumashi* system is one of the most important means of creating flow in internal logistics. The water spider operates like a shuttle service at an airport. The shuttle service has a fixed route (e.g., Arrivals 1, Arrivals 2, Hotel 1, Hotel 2, and Hotel 3) that it keeps on following cycle after cycle. The cycle timing can be calculated—if we allow 4 minutes for each shuttle stop and 20 minutes for the driving time between stops, we have a cycle of 40 minutes. There will be a time schedule at every shuttle stop that shows the

> The mizusumashi *operates like a shuttle service at an airport.*

estimated time of arrival. The users know that every 40 minutes the shuttle will arrive. Once they are onboard, they know what time they will arrive at their destination.

The *mizusumashi* system operates the same way. It has the following characteristics:

▲ The *mizusumashi* "shuttle" stops are at supermarkets (i.e., picking supermarkets, border-of-line supermarkets, kitting supermarkets, or finished-goods delivery supermarkets).

▲ The cycle is calculated in the same way, by measuring the work to be done at the several stops and adding the travel time.

▲ At this level of organization, the containers to be moved onboard the shuttle service are the equivalent of customers or passengers.

The water spider's *standard work* means that there is a fixed route (i.e., a plan that shows the travel route and the stopping points) and a constant cycle time determined by the sum of the times involved. Because we are using supermarkets and flow containers, we can in fact improve the productivity of the *mizusumashi* by improving the operator's standard work, just as we improved standard work to achieve production flow.

As well as moving materials and empty containers and doing other driving tasks, the *mizusumashi* also moves the information associated with replenishment and other synchronization needs. I will discuss the flow of information in more detail in Chapter 10. For the moment, let's just remember that the *mizusumashi* moves *kanban* cards between supermarkets and production cells or lines.

Traditional Forklift Supply *versus* Mizusumashi *Supply*

Traditional line or machine supply is done by using a forklift to move a pallet-sized container close to the point of use. The same transport method is also used to deliver the finished goods to the finished-goods warehouse. In many cases, the supply of the border of the line starts with the line workers or the supervisor, who decides that it is time to order another load. The order can be issued on a computer system. The order is received in the parts warehouse, where a load is picked and prepared. Then a forklift will deliver it and also move the finished-goods pallets into the warehouse.

This process is not standardized at all because there is no fixed route and no fixed cycle. The forklift driver operates according to orders as they are received, and there is no capacity control. By this I mean that during some periods of the day the forklift can be overloaded with orders and during others not loaded at all. Because there are no supermarkets storing flow containers, the logistic tasks involved are nonlinear, which makes them very time-consuming. The load capacity of the forklift is also limited in terms of the number of parts it can carry at any given time. Usually it can carry only one pallet at a time, which is the equivalent of one carriage in a *mizusumashi* train. This means that the forklift has to make many empty trips back and forth. Sometimes the forklift can be stacked two or three pallets high. The forklift is very rapid in terms of travel time, but in many cases safety or traffic considerations mean that the speed must be reduced. The *mizusumashi*, on the other hand, can carry up to eight carriages at one time or even more (depending on the size of the carriages).

The traditional forklift form of supply works like a taxi, in the sense that you call it by ordering a supply through the computer or by calling the driver or through the driver's own decision made by looking at the border of line and checking what needs to be moved. A simple calculation will illustrate the point. Let's say that a company has 10 forklifts, which are busy 90 percent of the time. The probability that they are all busy at the same time is calculated as 90 percent ^ 10, which is 35 percent. This means that one-third of the time the customer will have to wait because the capacity of the system is overloaded. This is why everybody in a plant or warehouse always thinks that there are not enough forklifts. They are aware of the waiting time, and they ask for more forklifts. The logistic manager, however, thinks that there are enough forklifts because the number fits the overall number of cases needing to be moved. It's the problem of eating the average chicken—in an average meal, everybody can eat, but some eat the whole chicken, and others eat nothing.

The water spider, on the other hand, operates by standard work, which means that there is a fixed route and a fixed cycle time. The most common cycle times are 20 and 60 minutes. During this time, the *mizusumashi* will make many logistic movements at stopping points and also will drive between the stops. The equipment for this is a small electric train.

This is a shuttle-line mode of operation, as we have already seen. This type of organization ensures a constant service between supermarkets and points of use. It is also less costly and easier to operate than the forklift system. The train is made up of an electric locomotive and wagons. The number of wagons can vary but will be determined by the nature of the load and the design of the carriages (Figure 9.1).

Why Forklift Trucks Are Not Adequate

Forklift truck

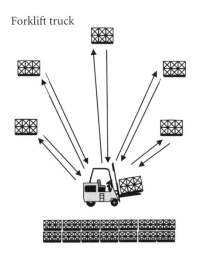

Mizusumashi

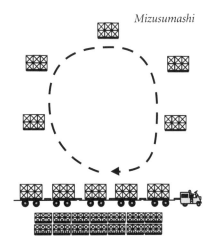

- Operates in a "radio taxi" mode (you have to call it)
- If the company has 10 forklifts and they are occupied 90% of the time, the probability of all being occupied simultaneously is 90% ^ 10 = 35% = >1/3 of the time the customer will have to wait
- High equipment costs and difficult to operate
- Low productivity
- Operation prone to accident

- Operates in a "metro line" (bus route) mode
- Arrives at each station exactly on the scheduled time (every 20 min is the most common cycle)
- Less costly and easy to operate
- High productivity and standard work
- The *mizusumashi* will also move information on the shop floor (*kanban* and *junjo*)

Figure 9.1   The advantages of using *mizusumashi* over forklifts.

For the sake of simplification and standardization, we divided the trains into three standard types: small, medium, and large. We also can have special trains that are custom made to fit the characteristics of the unit case loads to be moved.

Figures 9.2 and 9.3 show these three types of train in more detail, along with the types of containers and parts they can carry. The most important aspect here is the wheeled base of the wagon (see "Type of wagon platform" in Figure 9.3). The simplest train is just a locomotive pulling some platforms on wheels, on which you can pile standard containers or even full pallets.

The simple wheeled platform then can be designed to carry different types of loads. It is possible to dedicate one wagon to one part number, designing some fixtures to hold the parts in the most ergonomic way (this is also called an *ergo pack*) or to accommodate a kit of different parts. We can even build shelves on top of the platform to ease the loading and unloading.

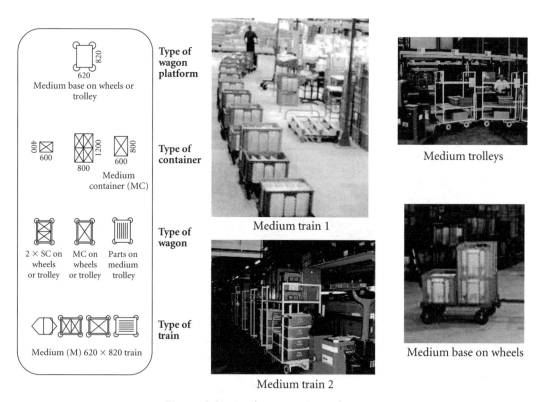

Figure 9.2 Medium *mizusumashi* train.

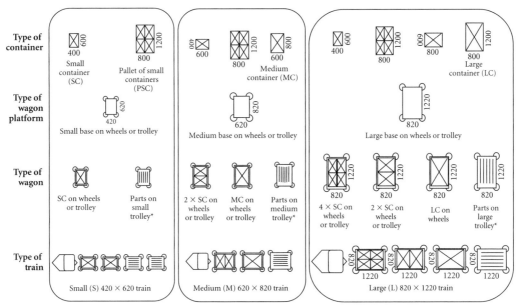

Figure 9.3   Train standards.

Assembly-Line Supply (Kanban *and* Junjo *Flows)*

A *mizusumashi* service will make use of the supermarkets (designed in Chapter 8) that are storing the appropriate flow containers (designed in the border-of-line domain) to optimize the work in the production cells. The supermarkets are also designed to optimize handling. The operator of the *mizusumashi* line is the one who will do all the manual work necessary to operate the line. A *mizusumashi* line is, in fact, a kind of advanced logistics service that connects all the production cells inside the plant. It is an indispensable element of a pull-flow system. Without the *mizusumashi* line, the one-piece flow lines are isolated in a sea of inventory and will not work to their full potential because—despite being surrounded by inventory—they do not have an adequate supply of materials and parts.

Figure 9.4 shows how a *mizusumashi* service can be configured around a certain number of production cells and a logistics cell (the concept of the logistics cell was explained in Chapter 8). In the figure we can see a standard *mizusumashi* route that uses the logistics cell and serves three production lines by means of a small train. Here all production value-added tasks are concentrated in the line workers, and all logistics tasks are concentrated in the logistics worker (i.e., picking, supplying, handling empties and cartons, and moving information using *kanbans*).

What Is a Water Spider?

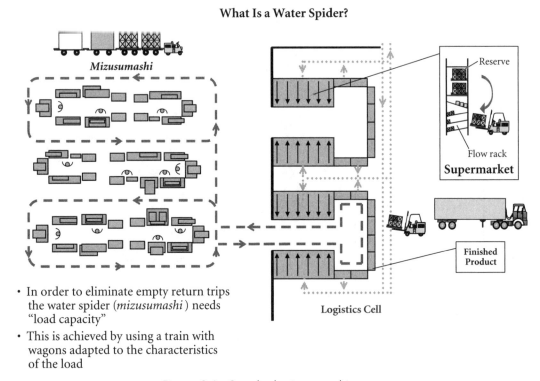

- In order to eliminate empty return trips the water spider (*mizusumashi*) needs "load capacity"
- This is achieved by using a train with wagons adapted to the characteristics of the load

Figure 9.4 Standard *mizusumashi* route.

The border of line is organized according to the *kanban* supply principle, so in the border-of-line supermarket the *mizusumashi* has all the necessary parts, and the replenishment signal is the empty boxes. At the end of the route, the *mizusumashi* will send finished-goods orders to the line. These orders are in the form of finished-goods *kanbans* and will be picked by the *mizusumashi* (at the beginning of the cycle) in a device called a *leveling box* (this will be explained in Chapter 10). The finished-goods containers are removed from the production line on the first in, first out (FIFO) principle—when one case is finished, it will be moved to the finished-goods area in the logistics cells.

Figure 9.5 shows a *kanban mizusumashi* route to supply a car assembly line. This type of line is usually used to handle small plastic containers that can be moved by hand and are located with *kanbans* in the border of the assembly line.

Figure 9.6 shows a water spider's route that provides *junjo* supply to a car assembly line. This line can handle and deliver kits of parts according to a *specific junjo* ("sequence"). It is interesting to note that the border of line is quite free of parts (which makes a better

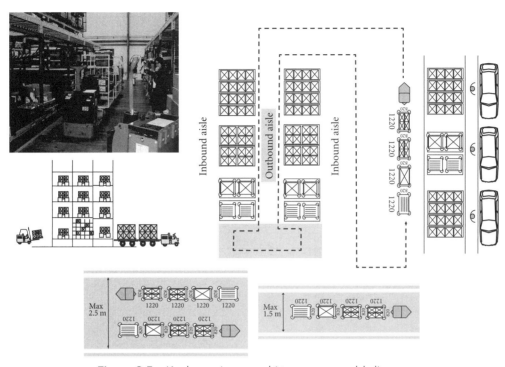

Figure 9.5   *Kanban mizusumashi* to a car assembly line.

working environment) compared with the *kanban* type of border of line. You also can see that the kitting consists of pushing back the *kanban* supermarket in the border of line, starting the picking to a kit or case, and then delivering the line sequence using the *mizusumashi*. In some simple lines, the *mizusumashi* function can be automated by using an automated guided vehicle (AGV).

The Water Spider's Standard Work

For each *mizusumashi* line, a visual standard describing the standard work features of the line will have to be prepared (Figure 9.7). The main elements of this standard are

- ▲ Drawing of the route in the layout
- ▲ The route cycle time
- ▲ The tasks along the way (marked in the layout)
- ▲ The times for each task

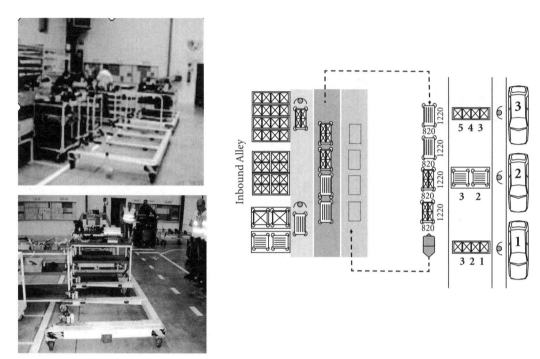

Figure 9.6 *Junjo mizusumashi* to a car assembly line.

Designing a *Mizusumashi* Line

The main steps involved in designing a *mizusumashi* line are

1. Make a list of all the tasks that will be assigned to the *mizusumashi*. (The start of the cycle is the leveling box or *kanban* box where the *mizusumashi* picks the information on the products to pick or make.)
2. Make an initial estimate of how much time each task will take (if necessary, go to the *gemba* and conduct trials).
3. Draw a circular route in the layout (a round trip that starts and finishes in the same place).
4. Identify the stopping points (stations).
5. Build an appropriate prototype train. Three types can be built (ideally, different wagon sizes should not be mixed in the same train):
   a. Small train: 10 to 12 small wagons
   b. Medium train: 8 to 10 medium wagons
   c. Large train: 6 to 8 large wagons
6. Do a trial run with the train empty. Make sure that it goes in a straight line. Any turns should be 90 degrees, without cutting corners. (Beware of getting the *snake effect*! This

Water Spider Standard Work

The standard work cycle of the water spider (*mizusumashi*)
is a multiple of the line *takt* time.

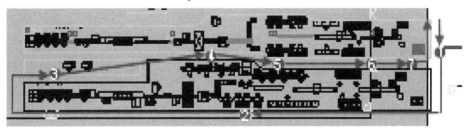

Mizusumashi Standard Work Sheet							
Area: Assembly L23				Name: J. Carvalho		Date: 03/07/99	
Product: Compressor D				Mizu cycle: 20 minutes			
Nº	Operations	Time					
		Operatn	Transp	5	10	20	
1	Pick orders from leveling box	5	5				
2	Pick components	15	10				
3	Pick FP and put order on the sequencer	10	5				
4	Replace boxes	20	10				
5	Repack FP	10	15				
6	Remove orders used	10	5				
7	Bring empty containers	20	5				

Figure 9.7   Example of a *mizusumashi* standard.

means that the train will move like a snake. This is easily solved by changing the geometry of the axes and wheels.)

7. Make sure that the supplier and customer supermarkets are ready.
8. Choose the *best* operator to be the *mizusumashi*. This is important because the flow of the entire loop depends on the good performance of this worker.
9. Run the train for four or five days, measuring times and eliminating *muda*.
10. Draw up the final *standard work sheet*.
11. Train the *mizusumashi* worker for at least 20 days so that following the standard becomes an unconscious habit. Make sure that the worker can go through the process automatically (remember when you learned how to drive, and the effort you had to

make in the beginning, until you got to the point where your attention was on the traffic and not on the mechanics of driving).

The design and operation of *mizusumashi* lines is as important for the creation of flow as the design and operation of one-piece flow lines.

Synchronization

So far I have talked about using

▲ Flow containers that you can move easily by hand
▲ Storing those flow containers in supermarkets, where you can identify, pick, and deliver quickly
▲ *Mizusumashi* services that will complete all the logistical tasks in a reliable and routine way

I have defined the necessary physical infrastructure that will allow you to operate a flow system. This, together with flexible one-piece flow lines, completes the physical flow structure that represents a breakthrough in productivity and the reduction of lead time. You have completed the internal design of the plant and organized the material flow of the existing logistics loops. So what still needs to be done?

What is missing is the information flow. You have already prepared many of the devices you will need to handle the information flow. For example, I said that a container should have a *kanban* card that tells you what part should be inside it, how many pieces there should be, and who are the suppliers and customers of the part. You also saw that in a *kanban* supermarket an empty container is the replenishment signal to move it back to the supplier (what the supplier will do with it is another matter) and that the *mizusumashi* operator will handle all the containers and associated information.

The *mizusumashi* operator also handles other information about the execution orders that need to be started at several different points of the flow. The *synchronization domain* explains the several types of *kanban* information loops and the mechanism of the *junjo* loop. I will now develop the details inside these loops. *Kanban* loops will be discussed in detail because they are more common in a pull-flow system (they represent the consumption-replenishment model). The *junjo* system is also being used more and more and can be a valid solution for reducing material waiting and improving productivity (Figure 9.8).

What Is a Kanban *Replenishment Logistics Loop?*

At this time, it is useful to recall what a *kanban* card is and what type of information can be found on it. Figure 9.9 explains the meaning of a *kanban* card. The *kanban* card can be fixed to a container or separate from the container.

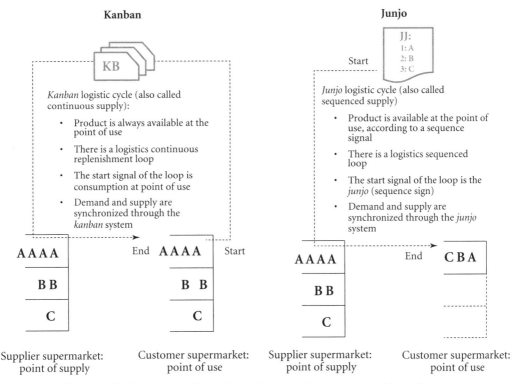

Figure 9.8   Two types of supply basic loops, the *kanban* and *junjo* loops.

A *kanban* replenishment loop will always operate according to the following principles (see Figure 9.10):

▲ The *kanban* is part of a *kanban* loop (or system).
▲ The loop starts at a customer inventory location.
▲ The part is available for immediate customer delivery.
▲ The part must be replenished when the stock reaches the reorder level.
▲ Reorder level = demand during replenishment lead time + safety stock.
▲ Safety stock = demand variation + lead-time variation.
▲ The *kanban* (or set of *kanbans*) is usually a replenishment order.

The total replenishment lead time depends on the time it takes to perform the following groups of tasks:

▲ Order-processing lead time
▲ Order-picking lead time
▲ Transport or production lead time
▲ Inbound lead time

What Is a *Kanban*?

- The word *kanban* means "sign board"
- The *kanban* is often a card (or a document) that represents an order of material from one customer to one supplier
- The basic information printed on the *kanban* is
    - Material identification (and code)
    - Customer identification
    - Supplier identification
    - Quantity to be supplied

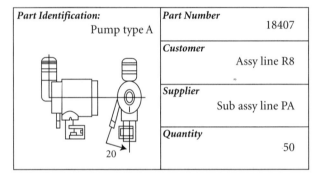

Figure 9.9   Example of a *kanban* card.

You will see that the order-processing lead time can be greatly reduced by using planning boxes (logistics and leveling boxes will be explained in Chapter 10) with *kanban* cards. The lead time for picking the order can be greatly reduced by using supermarkets with flow containers. The internal-transport lead time can be greatly reduced by using *mizusumashi* shuttle lines. The inbound lead time also can be greatly reduced by using supermarkets with flow containers. But what about the production lead time?

The presence of production is the first factor to consider in establishing *kanban* logistics loops. Some loops will not include production but will consist only of transport. When you use a *mizusumashi* service for this, this lead time becomes extremely short and reliable.

The loops with production in the middle are a bit trickier to consider. The lead time will depend mainly on the waiting time in front of the machine. The waiting time depends on the degree of leveling (the flexibility to make quick changeovers and work with small batches). The ideal situation is to have a *one-container quick changeover capability* (or even a one-piece changeover capability) so that whenever you receive a *kanban*, you can make it immediately and not wait to build a batch. Unfortunately, in many situations you have to build a batch based on the Wilson formula, and this increases the lead time as well as the maximum size of the supermarket.

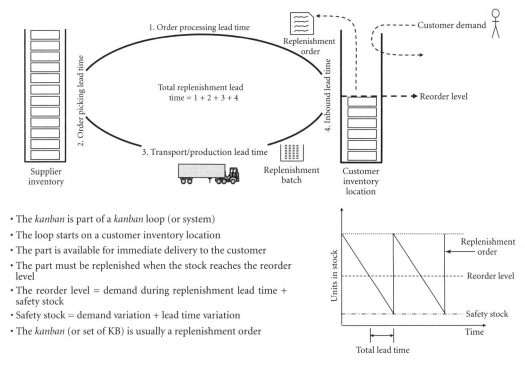

Figure 9.10   *Kanban* replenishment loop.

The Six Types of Kanban *Loops*

If you look at a typical plant-based supply chain (in which the production and internal logistics operations inside the plant are at the midpoint of the chain), which will also need the source side and the delivery side of the chain, you can find at least six types of possible *kanban* logistics loops (as shown in Figure 9.11). These six types can be divided into two groups: those without production in the middle and those with production in the middle. The first group consists of transport *kanban* loops and the second of production *kanban* loops.

The three transport *kanban* loops are

▲ Transport-delivery *kanban* (received from a customer and delivered to another customer from a finished-goods supermarket)

▲ Transport-internal *kanban* (internal consumption/replenishment loops)

▲ Transport-source *kanban* (sent to a supplier and received in an incoming supermarket)

The three production *kanban* loops are

▲ Production-flow *kanban* (going through a zero-changeover line or machine)

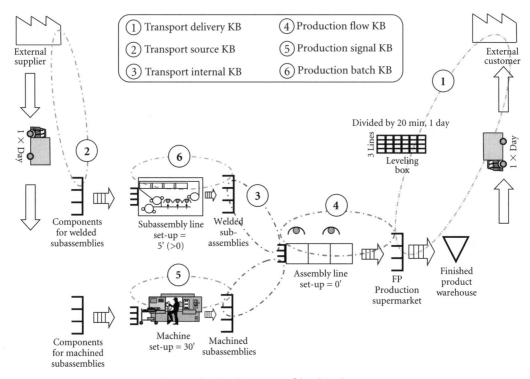

Figure 9.11 Six types of *kanban* loops.

▲ Production-signal *kanban* (going through a higher-than-zero-changeover line or machine and not using *kanban* cards associated with containers)

▲ Production-batch *kanban* (going through a higher-than-zero-changeover line or machine and using cards associated with containers)

Appendix A explains the complete process for designing transport *kanban* loops, including all the necessary calculations. Appendix B explains the complete process for designing production *kanban* loops, including all necessary calculations. The calculations also will give the size of the supermarkets to be considered at the end of each *kanban* loop.

The main variables to be used in the calculations are

▲ The immediate customer demand
▲ The size of the lead-time components of the loop
▲ The batch-size calculations for the production *kanban* loops
▲ An estimate of the variation in demand and lead time

This is a good point to explain the impact of demand and lead-time variation in the logistics loops. The basic mechanisms are explained in Figure 9.12.

- If demand during lead time is greater than average, inventory can go into the safety stock (red line)
- The longer the lead time, the greater the demand variation will be
- If demand increases above safety stock, there is a stock out situation
- Demand variation can be reduced by the following improvements:
  - Reducing the average lead time
  - Leveling final customer demand
  - Using an ABC (PQ) analysis, product A will vary less than products B and C

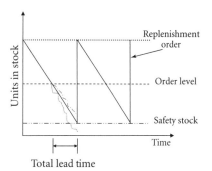

- If lead time is longer than average, inventory can go into the safety stock (dotted line)
- Above-average demand plus above-average lead time is the worst scenario
- Lead time variation can be reduced by the following improvements:
  - Reducing the average lead time (creating flow in the process)
  - Standardizing the work, especially through the *mizusumashi* and milk run concepts
  - Improving production reliability (TPM)

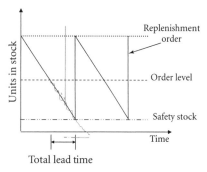

Figure 9.12   The basic mechanisms of demand and lead-time variation.

It is very important to have a stable demand and a stable lead time (lead-time stability is ensured by *mizusumashi* shuttle lines). The same principle can be applied to external logistics (called *milk runs* in my external logistics model). Following a fixed cycle time reduces the variation in transport lead time to a minimum.

Demand stability is more difficult to achieve but also depends on the size of the lead time. In many cases, demand varies less in a short lead time than in a long one, but the main way to reduce demand variation is leveling. I will discuss this in detail in Chapter 10, but for the moment, think of it like this: If I have to make 100 units in 10 days, I can order the 100 parts in one day and only order again in 10 days' time, or I can order 10 units every day. The constant daily batch of 10 units (some days it may vary between 12 and 8) is much more stable than having to make 100 in one day, 0 for the next 9 days, and then maybe 50 or 150 in the next 10-day period. Leveling stabilizes or smoothes the demand, which is very beneficial to your *kanban* loops in terms of stock levels and supermarket sizes.

What Is a Junjo *Logistics Loop?*

Junjo is the Japanese word for "sequence." By assigning a sequence number to a part, you can arrange to have it delivered just in time, when the product using the part needs it. Both the part and the product will need to have the same number. *Junjo* delivery is also called *just-in-sequence delivery*. It has the big advantage of reducing the size of the border of lines and considerably shortening the movements of the line worker who uses that part to make the product.

But this form of delivery requires a sequencing process or loop—the *junjo loop*. In terms of complexity, the *kanban* loop is really simple—it has no sequencing needs because the consumption is the sequencing signal (also called the *replenishment signal*).

Both methods can be extremely good in terms of *synchronization effectiveness* (meaning that the user will always have the needed part when it is needed). *Junjo* offers the additional feature of saving both space and worker movement. When the parts are large or there is a big variety in parts, this is the only viable supply method. The loop works according to the principles shown in Figure 9.13.

The *junjo* method can be used to supply individual parts according to a sequence list, or it can be made more sophisticated, supplying kits of parts according to a sequence list. The difference is in the picking. In the case of individual parts, a trolley is usually arranged with a sequenced batch of parts (e.g., a wheeled base is designed to hold 15 bumpers fixed vertically, with the final assembly sequence number on each bumper). For a kit, a picking list is generated for each kit container, and each container is assigned a number.

Figures 9.14 and 9.15 explain the principles of both these operations. In these figures, a physical device called a *sequencer* is introduced in our Total Flow Manufacturing (TFM)

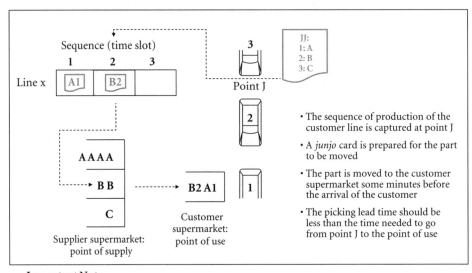

Important Note

Junjo loops will only work well if:
- The sequence is frozen during lead time (point J to point of use)
- The lead time (point J to point of use) variation is minimal

Figure 9.13 The *junjo* loop.

- The sequence of products to produce is sent to a sequencer
- The sequencer can be of two types:
  - With time scale
  - Without time scale
- Components necessary for location 03-01 will be delivered in the *junjo* sequence of the product
- The same *junjo* number will be given both to the product and to the component
- It is also possible to use a "changeover" *junjo* on a sequencer with time scale
- This *junjo* will inform the water spider to pick another component reference

Sequencer without time scale

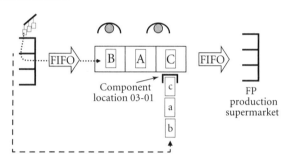

Figure 9.14 Unit *junjo*.

			Hourly			Scheduling	Post
1	2	3	1	2			3
8-9	4-6	12-1	▱	▱			
9-10	5-6	1-2	▱	▱			
10-11	6-7	2-3	▱	▱			
11-12	7-8	3-4	▱	▱			
12-1	8-9	4-5	▱	▱			
1-2	9-10	5-6	▱	▱			
2-3	10-11	6-7	▱	Change over card			
3-4	11-12	7-8	▱	Next product to reach signal			

Sequencer with time scale

- In the kit *junjo* situation the water spider is preparing a kit of several components to be put together with the main product
- The kit will have all the sequenced components needed by the operators in each line workstation
- The kit will receive a *junjo* number exactly according to the main product sequence
- This will minimize the wasted of picking by the operator

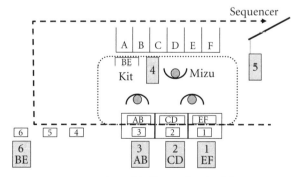

Assembly line, unit mixed flow

Figure 9.15 Kit *junjo*.

model. This device is part of the leveling domain and serves to hold the sequence of orders to be completed in a production cell or line. Its purpose is to hold *kanbans* in the sequence in which they are to be made. Chapter 10 will discuss the sequencer, together with other physical leveling and scheduling devices used to regulate and synchronize the flows.

Some Examples of Supermarkets, *Mizusumashi,* and Synchronization

Example 1

Let's now look at an actual example of how an internal logistics supply operation can be greatly improved by using the border-of-line, supermarket, *mizusumashi,* and synchronization solutions. This example is a typical situation in any electronics industry.

The issues are

▲   How to supply several assembly lines with thousands of parts
▲   How to achieve zero stock-out and zero production stops because of missing components
▲   How to greatly reduce the work in process (WIP) at the same time

Step 1: Standardize Containers

In this case, all the parts are small. The first step is to standardize containers in the border of line by using small and very small containers. (The standard small container size is 600 × 400 mm, and even this can be too big for small electronics and plastic parts.)

Step 2: Locate the Containers in the Border-of-Line Supermarkets

The location of these containers at the point of use is a key decision. It is the second step. The traditional situation was that the size and location of the containers in the border of line were not optimized and not being managed by a physical *kanban* system. Here the most efficient solution is a border-of-line supermarket that will operate a two-bin (or full and empty) *kanban* supply system.

To estimate the size of the supermarket, you need to calculate the *mizusumashi* cycle that would be needed. Three cycles of the *mizusumashi* pitch time (you can check the calculations for this case in Appendix A) give us a rough estimate of the size of supermarket that will be needed. The former solution in this plant was to pile the boxes close to the line and have the line's logistics provider send a replenishment order to the area warehouse by checking boxes and using nonstandard or inconsistent ways of counting. You can imagine how much work was involved and how many opportunities there were for errors.

Step 3: Design the Area Supermarket for Easy Picking

At the same time, the area supermarket is prepared for easy picking of the same containers used at the border of line. Flow racks provide the most effective storage of the flow containers. The former situation was a warehouse with shelves piled up with boxes and containers of several types, including cardboard boxes. The time it took to find the right part and pick it was enormous, and the logistics providers needed to spend a lot of time in the warehouse.

Step 4: Organize *Mizusumashi* Shuttle Lines

When the border of line and the area supermarkets are ready, you can organize the *mizusumashi* service. The cycles have already been established at 20 minutes. A number of tasks are given to each water spider based on the sum of the total task time matched with the cycle time. A train with an electric locomotive is used, with wagons that have shelves to handle plastic boxes. These are designed and tested.

Step 5: Test, Prepare Standards

The *mizusumashi* standards are written, tried out, and fine-tuned.

Step 6: Implement

Finally, the lines start operating one by one. In the old system, a single logistics provider with a small trolley moved back and forth between the lines and the supermarket, counting parts, picking, and delivering. The worker's everyday experience was many back-and-forth, nonlinear movements (which produced nice spaghetti charts).

The results obtained by this kind of flow project typically include the following:

- ▲ Productivity improvement in logistics: 32.4 percent
- ▲ Line stops owing to missing parts: decreased from 10 to 0 percent
- ▲ Productivity improvement in production: 25 percent
- ▲ 5S level (housekeeping): changed from 50 to 90 percent in the internal audit checklist

It is worth mentioning that this project included a logistics loop for replenishing the area supermarket from the incoming-goods warehouse. This warehouse can be considered the reserve stock because of the high lead time and the lack of flow from exterior suppliers.

Another operation in this supermarket replenishment loop is to repack some of the parts from the supplier's container to the right-sized standard containers used in-house. This signaled another project—to coordinate the container sizes with the suppliers and so eliminate the biggest part of the repacking task. The dimensions of the logistics loop between the supermarket and the reserve stock were calculated according to the transport-internal *kanban* rules explained in this chapter.

I will explain the mechanism of leveling and show how it can be used to design more sophisticated systems in situations where the *junjo* form of supply is essential in Chapter 10.

Example 2

Another interesting example of applying the TFM model involved organizing flow in the supply of a car assembly line. Car assembly lines involve thousands of components. The size and variety of parts they handle make them far more complex than the preceding electronics example. In a car assembly line, there are very small parts, such as screws, together with big parts, such as bumpers. The variety is created by the potential options in the models and colors of the cars. Just to supply the bumpers is paradigmatic, in the sense that their color must match the body color, and the number of options is so varied that the only possible method for line supply is *junjo* ("sequence").

In these lines, you can have all the various types of borders of line, namely:

▲ *Kanban* front supply (in subassemblies)
▲ *Kanban* rear supply
▲ *Junjo* front supply (in subassemblies)
▲ *Junjo* rear supply
▲ *Junjo* kit supply

In terms of *mizusumashi* lines, the usual ones for this situation include

▲ A train of wagons with shelves supplying small and medium plastic containers with 60-minute-cycle inside *kanban* loops
▲ A train of wagons with pallets on wheels supplying big containers with 20-minute-cycle inside *kanban* loops
▲ A train of wagons with wheeled bases with special fixtures supplying parts with variable-cycle inside *junjo* loops
▲ AGVs to transport kit containers from picking supermarkets

The types of supermarkets seen in car assembly flow plants include

▲ Flow racks (also called *kanban* racks) for small and medium-sized plastic containers and pallets of plastic containers
▲ Big containers on wheeled bases at ground level
▲ Special trolleys with *junjo* parts

Originally, Toyota flow assembly lines were organized mostly using the *kanban* type of border of line and all the necessary supply logistics. Since the early 1990s, the company has evolved to the *junjo* type, with kitting border of lines. As the range of options and models increases, the size of the *kanban* borders of line has to increase with it. This begins to hurt productivity, so the *junjo* form of supply becomes an attractive solution.

A Toyota press release issued in 2006 said:

> Toyota Motor Corporation has introduced a new material-handling system based on kitting to reduce complexity and improve quality in assembly areas. A spokesman for Toyota Motor North America said the kitting system was being introduced on "more and more lines" at the Georgetown facility and elsewhere in North America. He said it was "not a complete sea change" in parts presentation and wasn't applicable to all production areas.
>
> At Georgetown, the correct parts for a particular Camry or Avalon are selected into a tray that is placed inside the car as it heads down the line. Because part selection is done upstream, assemblers can "focus on the quality of installation," according to the Toyota spokesman. Variety and the resulting complexity have proliferated as more and more features are offered to customers. For instance, before the new system was introduced for the current generation Camry and Avalon, team members had to choose between 24 varieties of sun visors.

The switch also eliminates reaching, stretching, and searching for parts by assembly operators. The new arrangement also makes training operators and material handlers easier because the job responsibilities are narrower.

CHAPTER 10

Internal Logistics Flow: Leveling and Production Pull Planning

Leveling

Leveling, also known as *heijunka*, is the fourth domain in the pillar for internal logistics flow. It represents the concept of scheduling production in small batches—specifically, making a constant amount (or level) of the same product on a regular frequency (e.g., every day). Maintaining a constant production of all product varieties on a daily basis (or even in a smaller period of time, such as half a day) implies making small batches. The original idea was that making a constant demand for parts from suppliers would facilitate the adoption of an inventory-replenishment model based in physical *kanban*. This type of model can be very sensitive to variations in demand.

The Process of Leveling

The process of leveling consists of several planning operations that convert orders into programmable batches and launch an optimized sequence of production, one that respects capacity and smoothes the quantities to be produced. The process starts with the results of the production pull planning process (the fifth domain of internal logistics flow) and transforms the quantities to be made into scheduled orders. These orders are then picked by the *mizusumashi* to start picking or production in the *gemba*.

> *The process of leveling consists of several planning operations that convert orders into programmable batches and launch an optimized sequence of production.*

The operations of the process can be summed up as follows:

▲ Transforming production orders into *kanban* order cards (smaller batches)

▲ Shuffling the *kanban* order cards according to the production start days (this levels the monthly load)

▲ Scheduling the *mizusumashi* picking cycle and leveling the daily load (respecting daily capacity)

▲ Sequencing the production lines

Designing the Format

The main tools used in the leveling process are physical device holders that show the planning in a visual format. The goal is to build a perfectly synchronized visual planning system that reacts to real-time events in the *gemba*. This section introduces the concept and basic elements of leveling.

The main decisions and actions taken in leveling are as follows:

▲ Deciding which line or machine will receive the order *kanbans* (i.e., the pacemaker line)

▲ Leveling the variability in the demand of the outside customer (i.e., sending to production a fixed amount of daily products—the agreed-on daily production capacity)

▲ Leveling the mix of different part numbers to
  ▼ Allow production to use a fixed constant operator's crew
  ▼ Reduce the bullwhip effect on the demand of supplied components

▲ Defining the picking cycle and the *mizusumashi* cycle time (pitch time)

▲ Defining the production batch size (according to the every product every interval [EPEI] parameter)

▲ Defining the sequence to be sent to the production line

Before I discuss the leveling process in detail, let's take a look at the classic Toyota definition of leveling. Toyota is one of the world's best examples of the application of leveling within its production system. Although this chapter began by giving a brief explanation of the concept of leveling, it is worth beginning my detailed discussion with the Toyota definition.

The Toyota Definition of Leveling

In the Toyota system, *leveling* means repeating a product in a constant cycle of time (also called the *every product every interval* [EPEI]). The EPEI is a number that tells you the cycle time needed to repeat all the product references. It can be very easily calculated by dividing the number of product references by the number of changeovers in a given machine for a given period of time. It is also equal to a fixed batch size calculated in days of demand.

Let's assume, for example, that in one month three product references can be made in a machine with three changeovers. In this case, the EPEI is 3 divided by 3, which equals 1, giving us an EPEI of 1 month. Every month, we repeat the three product references. This EPEI is not very flexible because the customers of each reference made during the month will have to wait until the beginning of the next month to receive their supply of the product. The suppliers of the parts needed to make the product references will get big monthly orders that can vary significantly from month to month depending on demand.

> *Leveling means repeating a product in a constant cycle of time (also called the every product every interval [EPEI]).*

The logic behind leveling is shown in Figures 10.1 and 10.2. The five levels (or degrees) of leveling recognized in the Toyota system are shown in Table 10.1.

It is worth noting that level 5 is the most demanding EPEI. It can be seen in car assembly lines that use mixed-model production. Here it is possible to repeat a sequence of different models so that the sequence in effect acts as one product (see Figure 10.2).

The progress in leveling is linked to the number of changeovers—the greater the number of changeovers done, the higher is the level of leveling. This is why single-minute exchange of dies (SMED) is so important. When changeover is zero, batches can be eliminated completely, resulting in one-piece scheduling. It is possible to have one-piece flow and big batches, but, as you'll see next, the ideal is to have one-piece flow and one-piece scheduling. So why have small batch sizes? What is the advantage?

The Bullwhip Effect

The advantage of having small batch sizes is that it reduces the so-called bullwhip effect in the supply chain and enables the production lines to work with a fixed number of operators

Table 10.1   The Five Degrees of Leveling in the Toyota System

Level	Description	EPEI
1	Big batch, monthly production	Equal to 1 month
2	Smaller batch, more than one batch per month	Equal to 10 days (1 month has 20 days of work—see Figure 10.2)
3	Daily production, different quantity	Equal to 8 hours (1 day has one shift of 8 hours of work)
4	Several batches per day, constant batch	Equal to 4 hours (see Figure 10.2)
5	Unit batch, mixed production	Equal to 0.8 hour (see Figure 10.2)

• Production leveling means to repeat a product in a constant cycle of time (also called EPEI—every product every interval)
• According to Toyota, there are five levels of leveling

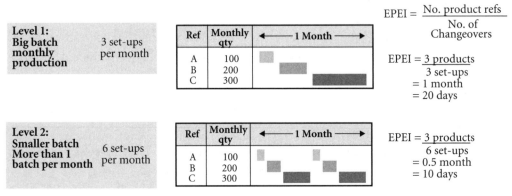

Figure 10.1   Toyota's definition of leveling (a).

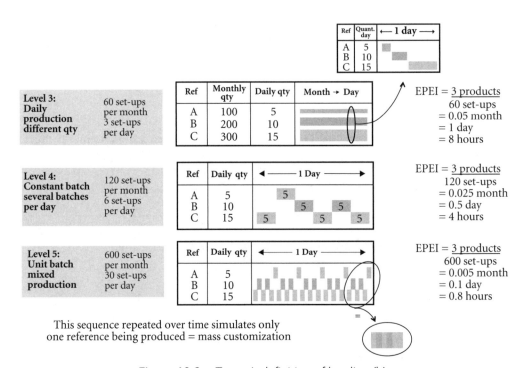

This sequence repeated over time simulates only one reference being produced = mass customization

Figure 10.2   Toyota's definition of leveling (b).

(independent of the work content of the different products). The bullwhip (or whiplash) effect can be seen in forecast-driven supply chains. The concept has its roots in J. Forrester's 1961 work on industrial dynamics and thus is also known as the *Forrester effect.* As a result of this dynamic, an increasingly oscillating demand upstream of a supply chain is rather like a cracking whip—it became famous as the *bullwhip effect.* This sequence of events is well simulated by the Beer Distribution Game developed by the MIT Sloan School of Management in the 1960s. Figure 10.3 shows how the bullwhip effect works: Small changes in the final customer demand generate demand increases at every step of the supply chain.

Many factors can give rise to the bullwhip effect. One of its main causes is the use of forecasts. Because forecasting errors are inevitable, companies often carry an inventory buffer, called the *safety stock.* As you move up the supply chain from the end consumer to the raw materials supplier, each participant in the chain experiences a greater variation in demand and so has a greater need for safety stock. In periods of rising demand, downstream participants will increase their orders. In periods of falling demand, orders will fall or stop in order to reduce inventory. This creates the oscillation pattern shown in Figure 10.3.

You will see in the next Total Flow Management (TFM) model domain how pull planning greatly diminishes the effect of forecast errors. In this domain, leveling, we deal with another cause of the bullwhip effect—batch size.

• Small changes in the final customer demand will generate demand increases in every step of the supply chain

• This phenomenon is the main direct cause of the *muda* of stock and *muda* of excess production

• Causes:

  • Order grouping to increase lot size (low leveling)

  • Using data from the immediate customer, instead of data from the final customer

  • Excessive reaction to small changes in demand (non-standardized building of safety stock)

  • Anticipated buying of seasonal products

  • Lack or excess capacity to respond to real demand

• Most of the ERP systems are modeled with rules that increase this effect

• Only pull planning and leveling can strongly reduce this effect

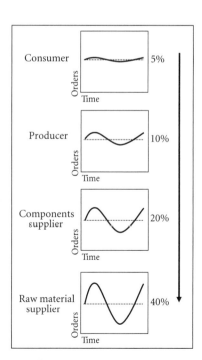

Figure 10.3   The bullwhip effect.

Reducing batch levels from Toyota's level 1 (monthly) to level 3 (daily) in the pacemaker process can make a big difference in customer service. By eliminating spikes and giving the suppliers a constant demand that is close to the final consumer demand, it also helps to smooth the consumption of materials. You are not amplifying the demand.

Going from level 3 to level 5 probably will not affect customer service, but it will allow you to smooth even more the consumption of parts by internal parts suppliers. You have very quick internal transportation processes (i.e., *mizusumashi* cycles with hourly frequencies). Therefore, the actual demand can be quickly conveyed to internal suppliers. This is essentially a one-piece-flow supply chain working at the final customer *takt* time.

Leveling also will smooth the work-content load, allowing lines to work with a fixed crew regardless of the different products being produced. Let's that you we have one product reference that requires 100 minutes of work and 10 workers. Another reference may have 80 minutes of work and require only 8 workers. Depending on the batch to be made, you will need to change from 10 to 8 workers. With level 5 leveling, you can work with a crew of 9 workers who alternate between work cycles of 10 and 8 minutes. By using the *mura* line-balancing technique explained in Chapter 5, you can concentrate the variation in a few workers and assign a constant workload to the rest. In this way you can work with a constant crew of 9 operators instead of having to change from 10 to 8 with every change of batch type.

The Steps of Kaizen for Leveling

It is necessary to use visual management to implement leveling. The leveling process consists of the following operations:

1. Deciding the pacemaker line (the line that will receive the production orders)
2. Converting orders into *kanban* cards—two types of orders can be transformed into *kanbans*:
   a. Customer orders
   b. Replenishment orders
   c. The *kanban* is a subset of the order. (The use of *kanbans* is covered in Chapter 9.)
3. Creating a logistics box:
   a. Shuffling the order of *kanbans* according to the production start day and leveling the monthly load
   b. Respecting the daily production capacity agreed to in the production-logistics contract (*capacity leveling*)
4. Creating a leveling box:
   a. Scheduling the *mizusumashi* picking cycle and leveling the daily load
   b. Respecting the production capacity available in the picking cycle

Line Sequencing: Sequencing the Production Lines

Step 1: Deciding the Pacemaker Line

In most cases, this is a straightforward operation. The *pacemaker line* is the line that is used to define the capacity of the plant (or area of the plant). It is usually the main assembly line or the machine that gives the product differentiation. If there is a high degree of process integration into one-piece-flow cells or lines, the pacemaker will be the integrated assembly or production line (that does most of the operations). Some subassemblies or production of components may have been left out of the main line, but in most cases the pacemaker is quite easy to spot. It will be the machine, cell, or line doing the most important value-added work, the one that defines the capacity of the whole logistics loop in which it is integrated. Figure 10.4 summarizes the process.

Step 2: Converting Orders into *Kanban* Cards

In the next leveling operation, the execution orders are recorded on *kanban* cards that can be used for the visual management of the planning and synchronization process. There are two tasks in this operation:

▲ Deciding the size of the *kanban*
▲ Making the *kanbans*

• Assembly operations: It will be the final assembly line that uses most of the manpower and that needs to aggregate a usually large number of components

• Generally it will be:

  • The machine or line that is used to establish the plant capacity

  • The machine or line that usually starts the production orders

  • The machine or line that makes the product differentiation

  • The machine or line that is most difficult to program because of set-up time or components supply

• Examples:

  • Car assembly lines

  • Main components assembly lines

  • Injection machines

  • Welding assembly lines

THE PACEMAKER

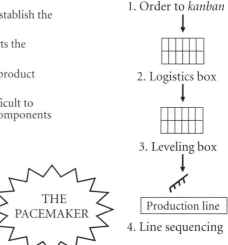

1. Order to *kanban*

2. Logistics box

3. Leveling box

Production line

4. Line sequencing

Figure 10.4 The pacemaker.

Deciding the Size of the *Kanban* The *kanban* container will have to be equal to or smaller than the production output during the *mizusumashi* picking cycle (also called the *pitch time*). The two most common pitch times are 20 and 60 minutes.

Calculate the production time of one finished-product container. If this time is less than the *mizusumashi* cycle, then the container size is fine. If the production time is greater than the *mizusumashi* cycle, consider changing to a smaller container.

A *kanban* size that is a multiple of 20 or 60 minutes of production is a good choice. Another useful way is to consider 20 or 60 minutes divided by the product work content.

Making the *Kanbans* The tasks here are to

▲ Transform each order into *kanbans*
▲ Keep track of the delivery due date

The key driver for the size of a *kanban* order card is the size of the finished-goods container used in the pacemaker line. For example, if you ship in pallet-sized containers of 16 units, then the size of the *kanban* can be 16 units. If the product is larger than this, the *kanban* size can be one unit.

Step 3: Creating a Logistics Box

When the *kanban* cards have been decided and created, it is time to use the first physical planning tool—the logistics box. This box is a set of pigeonholes like the one for holding room keys that you can see behind the reception desk of many hotels. For our purposes, each column represents one day, and each line can represent one product reference, one product family, or even one production line.

The *kanban* cards are put in this box according to the date of the planned production start day. You may work backwards from the delivery day to decide a certain day as the final deadline for the start day and assign this start day to the logistics box to signal when to begin production.

Each column of the box has a limited capacity. The capacity is decided on a monthly basis during the capacity-planning process (this is called the *production-logistics contract* and is explained in the discussion of the production pull planning domain in the second half of this chapter). This capacity limits the number of cards that can be placed in each column.

During this planning exercise, it is possible to do some leveling by trying to achieve an EPEI of one day (for the most common products, at least) so that you can plan small batches of all the references that can be done on a daily basis (or at least do it for the high runners). Figures 10.5 and 10.6 show some examples of these physical logistics boxes and explain how they are used.

- It is a physical device (a box) in which each column corresponds to 1 day

- It is maintained and used by logistics (or production control)

- Holds the *kanbans* (multiple of orders) in order of the production start day

- Gives a visual image of the order nook

- Arranges the quantity leveling according to the contract

- Is a buffer of orders before the leveling (*heijunka*) box

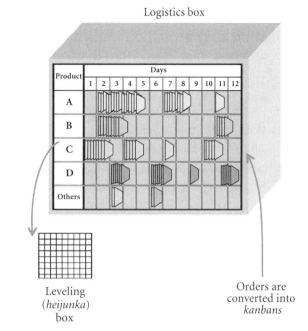

Logistics box

Leveling (*heijunka*) box

Orders are converted into *kanbans*

Figure 10.5   The logistics box.

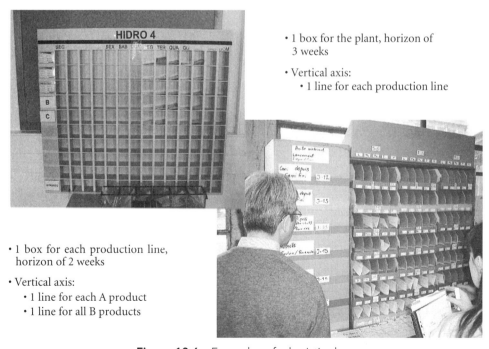

- 1 box for the plant, horizon of 3 weeks

- Vertical axis:
  - 1 line for each production line

- 1 box for each production line, horizon of 2 weeks

- Vertical axis:
  - 1 line for each A product
  - 1 line for all B products

Figure 10.6   Examples of a logistics box.

Step 4: Creating a Leveling (*Heijunka*) Box

Once the start day of the *kanban* cards has been decided, it is necessary to schedule the details of each day. This is done with a leveling box.

This is also a physical box and is similar to the logistics box. However, the time scale is not one day but is equal to the *mizusumashi* pitch cycle (usually 20 or 60 minutes). The leveling box is the starting point of the *mizusumashi* cycle. From it, the *mizusumashi* picks the *kanban* cards containing information about the product to be made at the pacemaker line. The *mizusumashi* also may be able to pick some associated information such as picking lists.

Figures 10.7 and 10.8 show some examples of these leveling boxes and explain how they are used. The scheduling in the leveling box can be used to sequence the *kanban* cards with the level 3 to level 5 logic explained earlier in the discussion of the Toyota leveling model. The scheduling will depend on the flexibility of the pacemaker line—the more changeovers the pacemaker line is capable of, the smaller are the batches that can be scheduled at shorter intervals. The leveling box holds the targets for what has to be completed in each *mizusumashi* cycle. Everybody knows that each time the *mizusumashi* comes to a line, a certain number of *kanbans* will have to be ready. This system gives good visual control of the production performance.

- Located in the picking or dispatch area (the starting point of the water spider cycle)

- Respects the line capacity (each column has a 20- or 60-minute interval, and the right number of *kanbans*)

- The time in each column is equal to a full water spider standard cycle (also called the *pitch time*)

- Sets the line *takt*

- The leveling inside the day is physically done here:

    - A products: < EPE of 1 day

    - B products: = EPE of 1 day

    - C products: "reserved slot," EPE > 1 day

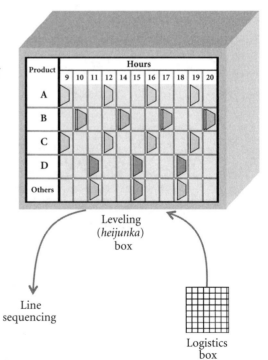

Leveling
(*heijunka*)
box

Line
sequencing

Logistics
box

Figure 10.7 The leveling box.

Figure 10.8   Examples of leveling boxes.

Step 5: Line Sequencing

The final step of leveling is line sequencing. For this step you may have to use two devices—the lot-making box and the line sequencer.

The lot-making box is a holding box in which a certain number of cards can accumulate before they are sent to the line for production. The number of the cards equals the defined batch size for the line. This also can be planned in the leveling box, but it may be more efficient to have this *poka yoke* close to the production line.

If the production line has zero-changeover capability, you can send the *kanban* cards directly from the leveling box to the *line sequencer*. This is a device that holds the cards in the order in which they arrive at the line (brought by the *mizusumashi*). It is a visual management tool that makes it possible to see the load to be made on the line immediately. Too many cards (too much load) may mean that the line is late, and too few may mean that the line is advanced or has less work. Figures 10.9 and 10.10 show how lot-making boxes and line sequencers are used.

The Standard Leveling Model

The leveling process using visual management and visual planning can be summarized in what I call a *standard leveling model*. This is shown in Figure 10.11. Here you can see that the orders to be executed (the result of the pull-planning process) are translated into smaller orders called *kanbans* (usually the size of the containers used in production) and that the start day for production is decided using a logistics box based on the fixed daily capacity.

At the start of the day, the cards are transferred to the leveling box, which gives the detailed daily sequence to follow. This is the interface point between planning and execution

- Two situations are possible:

  - Production line with a set up time greater than zero

  - Production line with a set-up time equal to zero

- In the first case it is necessary to receive the *kanbans* from the leveling (*heijunka*) box until a lot is built (for the sequencer)

- The number of slots is equal to the batch size −1

- Note: The final target will be to eliminate the need for this device, after set-up time is reduced and flexibility is achieved

- The batch size can be calculated using the production batch *kanban* algorithm

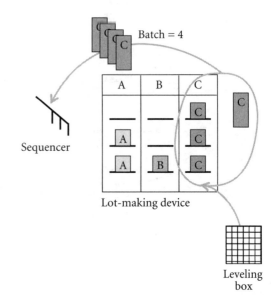

Figure 10.9 Line sequencing (a).

- Next it is necessary to place the *kanbans* at the start of the production line

- The water spider will do this task (included in the standard worksheet)

- The sequencer assures the FIFO order of the *kanban*

- It shows an image of the line advance or delay

- It helps in deciding whether to reinforce capacity (extra time, more workers, etc.)

- When set-up time is zero, there will be no lot-making box

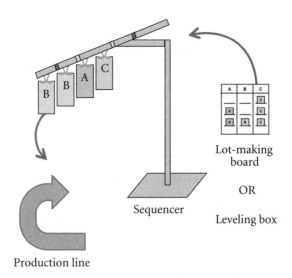

Figure 10.10 Line sequencing (b).

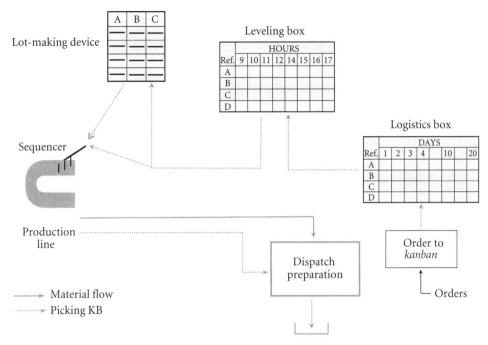

Figure 10.11   The standard leveling model.

because this box is the point from which the *mizusumashi* logistics worker gets the information to go and start the picking and production work for that particular product cycle.

At every pitch cycle, the *mizusumashi* will send the *kanbans* to either a line sequencer or a batch-building box. This is the point from which the production cell receives its instructions. This is a standard process that can be adapted to any plant or value stream inside a plant.

In Figure 10.11, the orders are being sent directly to the production cell. This is a situation in which a product (or assembly) is being made to order. Alternatively, the orders could be sent first to a finished-goods inventory, and then the final customer orders would be picked from the finished-goods stock. The standard model can be adapted—the purpose of this chapter is to show what tools are available. How you combine these tools for each logistics loop will give you the solution for each particular situation.

Often the logistics box or the batch-building box is not necessary. However, the leveling box and the line sequencer are essential tools in most pull-flow logistics loops.

Production Pull Planning

The last domain of the internal logistics flow pillar is production pull planning. In this domain we decide the

- ▲ Planning strategy of the final product varieties and also all parts varieties (either make to stock or make to order)
- ▲ Required capacity in terms of logistics and production
- ▲ Execution plan—what orders to start on the production pull system

The output of production pull planning is the input to the leveling process.

At this point you have to decide *what* and *how much* to launch in production. By working according to pull principles instead of push principles, you will see that it is possible to greatly reduce the use of production forecasts.

Steps in the Production Pull Planning Process

The production pull planning process consists of three steps:

1. Deciding the planning strategy for
    a. The finished goods
    b. The parts needed to make the finished goods
2. Capacity planning
3. Execution planning

Deciding the Planning Strategy

The first step in production pull planning is to decide the planning strategy of the finished goods and then the parts needed to make the finished goods (the bill of materials needed to make the product).

Finished Goods Strategy   Here you have two basic planning strategies to choose from:

1. *Make to order (MTO)*—meaning that you will not have the product ready for picking in the finished goods inventory, and the customer will have to wait for the order to be completed
2. *Make to stock (MTS)*—meaning that the product will be ready for customer delivery when the order arrives, and you will have to make more product to replenish the consumption

In most cases, you will have a mix of fixed customer orders and replenishment orders. Fixed customer orders can be transformed immediately into *kanban* cards (the beginning of leveling), but for MTS products you will need an algorithm to calculate the replenishment orders. You also will need a process for the advance checking of capacity so that everything is ready when the orders arrive. Figure 10.12 shows a method of deciding the planning strategy for different kinds of products.

According to product quantity analysis, the *high runners* are the best candidates for the MTS strategy. These are the repeat items that customers order frequently, which means that the risk involved in maintaining a finished goods inventory of these items is small. The *low runners*, on the other hand, are required in lower quantities and therefore are ordered less frequently. They are good candidates for the MTO strategy.

The decision on which finished goods strategy to use also depends on the company's commercial strategy because for some customers it may be advisable to plan all products as MTS, even the low runners. The planning strategy is related to management of the finished goods portfolio and should be reviewed frequently (at least every year) because the ranking in the product quantity analysis list may change (especially as new products are introduced).

In the automotive industry, the planning strategy for making cars is almost exclusively MTO at the final product level. Two types of orders can be received in the plant—orders from dealers to replenish a small stock and final customer orders. Dealer orders are not the same as final customer orders—the product may sit in the dealership until a final consumer decides to buy it. So the models in the dealer orders are very carefully chosen (the colors

A product quantity (*pareto*) analysis will usually show the following pattern:

- A products, responsible for 80% of the sales quantities (10 to 20% of all product references)

- B products, responsible for 15% of sales (20 to 30% of all product references)

- C products, responsible for 5% of sales (50 to 70% of all product references)

Based on the product portfolio, the company will have to decide a planning strategy for the execution of each product reference, namely:

- MTS—Make to stock: available for immediate delivery; PTO (picked to order); and build to replenish (BTR)

- MTO—Make to order: the customer will have to wait the order lead time

Planning strategy:
- MTO (make to order)
- MTS (make to stock)

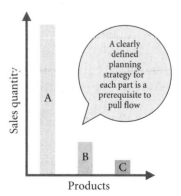

Figure 10.12   Deciding the planning strategy.

are high runners, and the options are those considered to be safe guesses of the likely final consumer choice). The dealer orders may be considered MTS orders and the final consumer orders MTO orders. Both types of orders are then leveled to be made in the assembly line (you may call it an *assemble-to-order strategy*).

Parts-Supply Strategy

Another decision to be made is the planning strategy for the parts at the assembly-line level in the bill of materials. Some parts can be MTS and others MTO. This is related to the choice of *kanban* or *junjo* supply of the parts to the assembly line. *Kanban*-supplied parts are MTS parts and ideally are located in the border of line within hand's reach of the line worker. Some parts in the assembly line will have *junjo* supply. Here you can have two situations—either the parts will be transported just in *sequence to the line*, or they will be *made just in sequence* on the line. The latter is an MTO strategy. In both cases, the order (the sequence) will have to be delivered from the final assembly schedule.

> Another decision to be made is the planning strategy for the parts at the assembly-line level in the bill of materials. Some parts can be MTS and others MTO.

Generally speaking, defining the planning strategy of the parts (the level below the final product in the bill of materials) is quite straightforward and evident once the final product strategy is defined. It depends a lot on having *commonality of parts* (the same part used in many final products). Parts that go into high runners can be easily classified as MTS, and less common parts that go into low runners usually can be classified as MTO.

The MTO classification also depends on the delivery time. The acceptable delivery time is determined by the market, and this acceptable delivery time is also called the *decoupling point* in the planning strategy (this is the point in the process at which the parts belonging to an MTO product need to be available when the MTO order is received). The lead time from this point in the supply chain to the end of the supply chain should match the acceptable delivery time. The decoupling point is the last point in the chain at which you can find an MTS part. Parts will be picked at this point according to customer order (or linked to the customer order).

Capacity Planning

The second step in the production pull planning domain is capacity planning. The result of this process is also called the *establishment of a production-logistics contract*. This contract sets the capacity that will have to be ready to fill short-term customer orders.

The capacity-planning process is defined the following way:

1. Capacity planning is needed to anticipate variation in market demand (including seasonality).
2. The usual capacity planning horizons are
   a. Annual (coinciding with the annual budget exercise)
   b. Quarterly or monthly (a three-month rolling plan can be used)
3. Customer *takt* time must be calculated, and capacity decisions must be made to cope with the expected *takt* time.
4. The decisions here will be related to
   a. Assembly-line capacity
   b. Specific machine capacity
   c. Supermarket size
   d. Transport capacity
5. The production-logistics contract is the way to standardize the forecasted monthly capacity required.

Demand forecasts provide the information input for capacity planning. In many cases, the forecast can be done by product family.

In the automotive industry, it is usual to provide the supplier with two types of information regarding product quantities—the forecast and the call-off. The *forecast* can cover a certain period of time and be updated frequently (e.g., a six-week horizon with an update every week, also called a *rolling forecast*). The *call-off* is the real fixed customer order, used to plan production (in the MTO strategy) or to pick the goods for dispatch (in the MTS strategy).

> *Demand forecasts provide the information input for capacity planning. In many cases, the forecast can be done by product family.*

The forecasts can be used to calculate the capacity plan. The necessary resources for the next planning period (usually one month) then can be prepared in advance. Figure 10.13 shows the production-logistics contract. It is worth noting that the contract may specify some acceptable variations in the product mix and that logistics will then comply with this mix even if the real customer demand is different. In this case, logistics will have to plan for extra safety stock in the more volatile references.

Execution Planning

The third step is execution planning. To be done effectively, this needs to come after the planning strategy and capacity planning. Execution planning decides what and how much

• Capacity planning is needed to anticipate market demand variation (including seasonality)

• The usual capacity planning horizons are

  • Annual (coinciding with the annual budget exercise)

  • Quarterly or monthly (a 3-month rolling plan can be used)

• Customer *takt* time must be calculated. Capacity decisions must be made to cope with the expected *takt* time

• The usual decisions will be related to

  • Assembly line capacity

  • Specific machine capacity

  • Supermarket size

  • Transport capacity

• The logistics–production contract is the way to standardize the monthly forecasted needed capacity

Capacity planning:
• Lines/machines
• Logistics

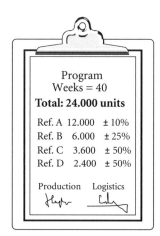

Figure 10.13 Capacity planning.

to manufacture and deliver to customers. The result of the process will be a production order list containing three types of production orders:

1. Final customer orders for MTO products
2. Replenishment orders for MTS products
3. Special final customer orders for MTS products where the size of the order is big and hence the delivery date is longer than usual

When the production order list is complete, the leveling process can be started. This should be done on a daily basis.

Final customer orders for MTO products are easier to process in terms of execution planning. You just take them and add them to the list of production orders to be scheduled.

Execution planning decides what and how much to manufacture and deliver to customers.

Special final customer orders for MTS products are big MTS orders for which the selling department agreed on a delivery time longer than the usual immediate delivery. The delivery time for each MTS product is determined by establishing a quantity limit. Delivery time will depend on the quantity—larger quantities mean that the plant will require more time to work. Execution planning will define a maximum batch size for the immediate delivery of MTS products. This type of order will be planned in the same way as MTO orders, with immediate transfer to the production order list.

Replenishment orders for MTS products are calculated using a pull planning model that will establish a reorder level and a batch size. The model is similar to the *kanban* replenishment loop explained in Chapter 9. There are many algorithms that can be used to implement this model. An example is given in Appendix C—this is a pull planning algorithm that can accommodate both MTO

> *Delivery time will depend on the quantity—larger quantities mean that the plant will require more time to work.*

and MTS orders in the same run. This algorithm will generate replenishment orders that will be transferred to the production orders list.

Dealing with Demand Seasonality

An important question is how to handle demand seasonality within the production pull planning process. Figure 10.14 summarizes the process.

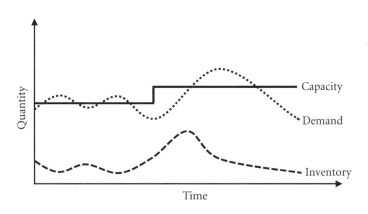

There are two ways of coping with seasonality.

1. Adjust capacity (done monthly in the logistics–production contract)
2. Use inventory to offset demand spikes:
    - Can be done by adjusting the leveling stock (checking supermarket capacity)
    - Can be done by leveling orders on the logistics box (adjusting the delivery dates of big orders is done on the logistics box)
  - The best way is the first, but in some cases, both or only the second will be needed

Figure 10.14   How to cope with demand seasonality.

There are two basic ways to deal with demand seasonality:

▲ Capacity adjustment
▲ Using inventory to offset demand spikes

Capacity Adjustment

Capacity adjustment means adjusting the level of manufacturing capacity to handle the expected fluctuations in demand. The capacity-planning process uses forecasts to decide the next month's capacity. In this way, capacity can be increased or decreased by adjusting the number of people, the machine speed, or other capacity factors. The solutions are industry-specific, but in each case the company must be prepared to have a capacity-adjustment solution.

Using Inventory to Offset Demand Spikes

Using inventory to offset demand spikes is another way of dealing with seasonality. Two situations can occur here:

▲ When the real demand (the production order list) is smaller than the agreed capacity, it is possible to anticipate some orders. If there are no orders to anticipate, a decision can be made to increase the stock levels of the MTS products, starting with the high runners (this is always a risk that must be thoroughly considered).
▲ When the real demand is bigger than the agreed capacity, the inventory levels can be used to serve the customer. If you find that this is happening every day over a long period of time, then you will have a stock-out situation. This can be minimized if the reorder levels are adjusted in line with the seasonality. For example, if you know that for three months the demand will be less than capacity, you can increase the reorder levels for high runners. During the peak months, you can reduce the reorder levels and use the stock to deliver.

Every situation is different and will require a specific strategy for handling seasonality, established by using capacity and inventory. The best strategy is one that allows great flexibility in adjusting capacity. This is the type of situation in which you can adjust the capacity to make only what the customer needs on a daily basis. If you have extra machine capacity, you may be able to pull workers from other departments to work in the peak periods. On the other hand, the low periods can be used to work on *kaizen* activities.

> *Every situation is different and will require a specific strategy for handling seasonality, established by using capacity and inventory.*

Two Models of Pull Flow

To round off this chapter, I present two scenarios for using production pull planning together with leveling and synchronization:

▲ A standard 100 percent MTS pull-flow model
▲ A standard 100 percent MTO pull-flow model

Scenario A

Figure 10.15 shows a 100 percent MTS pull-flow model. In this model, the customer orders are converted to a *kanban* format and are sent to a picking leveling box and then to a finished goods supermarket. From there the product is picked and dispatched to the customer.

   The next step is to replenish the supermarket. You can run a pull-planning algorithm (based on a *kanban* replenishment loop) and generate replenishment orders in the format of *kanban* cards that are sent to a batch-building box close to the final process. Then, when the batch is built, the *kanban* set is sent to the machine sequencer to start production. The parts replenishment process works in the same way. Here you have four pull-flow logistics loops—a solution designed specifically for this situation by the architect of the supply chain.

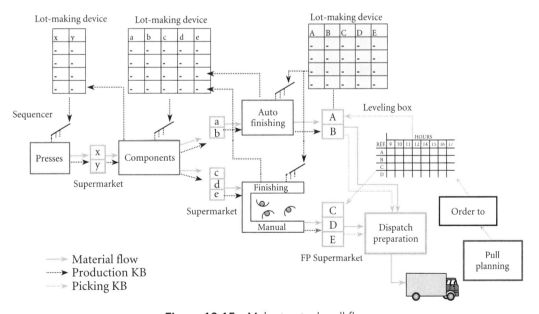

Figure 10.15   Make-to-stock pull flow.

Scenario B

Figure 10.16 shows a 100 percent MTO pull-flow model. Here the customer orders are received, are transformed in smaller *kanban* batches, and are sent directly to a logistics box process. This determines the starting date of production and also provides an initial leveling in terms of daily capacity and how batches are split over the days. The planning horizon may be 10 or 20 days depending on the delivery time agreed with the customer and the decoupling points of the MTO strategy.

Each day the *kanban* cards are transferred to a leveling box and sent to the beginning of the process (operation 1) by the *mizusumashi*. Before the initial machine sequencer, it may be necessary to use a batch-building box. At the first machine, you will have a sequencer. Let's say that after operation 1 you have two possible product routes, operation 2.1 and operation 2.2. In front of operation 1 you will place a FIFO supermarket that has the two next operations as destinations.

When you finish the batches, you will send the *kanban* cards to the sequencer of the next operation. The *mizusumashi* will the pick the batches in the supermarkets according to the sequencer information and will deliver them to the next machine. After the first operation, you have a synchronization system based on *junjo* and FIFO that will keep the lead time to a minimum. When the product is ready, the dispatch to the customer can start.

Many different supply-chain models can be designed using the processes and tools of production pull planning, leveling, synchronization, *mizusumashi*, and supermarkets. Each solution will be a breakthrough from the traditional push systems to state-of-the-art pull-flow systems that follow the *kaizen* way.

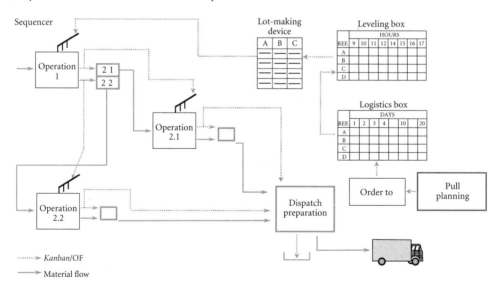

Figure 10.16 Make-to-order pull flow.

CHAPTER 11

External Logistics Flow: Introduction and Storage/Warehouse Design

Introduction

The fourth pillar of the Total Flow Management model is external logistics flow. The challenge of external logistics flow is to create one-pallet container flow, which is the basic unit for external transport, usually by intermodal container or truck. As the container moves in and out of storage points, many separate packing, repacking, and storage operations may be necessary. The goal is to eliminate all types of *muda* from all the external logistics flows and provide a value-added service to the various customers along the supply chain.

You have seen in the internal logistics flow pillar (Chapter 8) how to create a one-container flow by using supermarkets, *mizusumashi*, synchronization, leveling, and production pull planning. You saw that the starting point of internal logistics is the supermarket, which stores flow containers that are moved in cycles of 20 or 60 minutes across all the internal layouts. You also saw how one-piece flow in the production line virtually eliminates material waiting time and that the finished goods are quickly put into the final supermarkets by the *mizusumashi* shuttle networks, ready to be moved to a distribution warehouse or to be picked to supply an external customer.

> *"How do we deliver the required products with the shortest possible delay, at a level of 100 percent customer service, at the same time minimizing the overall stock of the complete logistics chain?"*

II. Production Flow	III. Internal Logistics Flow	IV. External Logistics Flow
5. Low-cost automation	5. Production pull planning	5. Logistics pull planning
4. SMED	4. Leveling	4. Delivery flows
3. Standard work	3. Synchronization (KB/JJ)	3. Source flows
2. Border of line	2. *Mizusumashi*	2. Milk run
1. Line and layout design	1. Supermarkets	1. Storage and warehouse design
I. Basic Reliability		

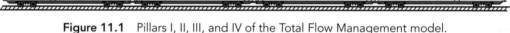

Figure 11.1 Pillars I, II, III, and IV of the Total Flow Management model.

Many companies saw the supply-chain tools of the 1990s as a solution to the question, "How do we deliver the required products with the shortest possible delay, at a level of 100 percent customer service, at the same time minimizing the overall stock of the complete logistic chain?" This is still the goal of applying *kaizen* in logistics and supply chains through the creation of a pull-flow system. How, then, does the *kaizen* model differ from traditional supply-chain tools?

The traditional approach (which is still the current paradigm in many supply chains) is based on integrating information systems (to eliminate the bullwhip effect) and also in many cases on push-based ordering algorithms. So the traditional approach puts emphasis on

▲ Materials requirement planning (centralized push order planning based on pushing inventory and so creating *muda*)
▲ Order forecasts (80 percent) and real orders (20 percent)
▲ A high level of safety inventory
▲ Data reliability—information systems planning is based on forecasts and estimates (of consumption, lead times, defectives, and inventory)

Applying *kaizen* in logistics and supply chains, on the other hand, complements the traditional information systems integration approach by minimizing the data reliability issues through standard operations and short lead times at the *gemba* level. This is done by creating a physical flow of materials and information and reacting to real customer orders and real customer consumption. The *kaizen* approach model puts emphasis on

- ▲ Physical supermarkets
- ▲ Real orders and real consumption
- ▲ Optimization of flow
- ▲ Reliable standard work

Besides the big advantage of working with customer pull signals, the TFM model also strives to eliminate all *muda* related to productivity, both in production and in logistics operations. In the following chapters you will see how to achieve these targets.

Summary

The targets of external logistics flow are to

1. Minimize inventory (material waiting time)
2. Achieve greater than 98 percent delivery in full, on time, and in specification (DIFOTIS)
3. Eliminate the *muda* of logistics operators' movements (by defining standard work)
4. Minimize the total logistics cost

Source and Delivery: The Two Parts of External Logistics Flow

In any manufacturing company we can divide the external logistics flow in two divisions—*source* and *delivery* (Figure 11.2). Source means all the logistics processes that take place

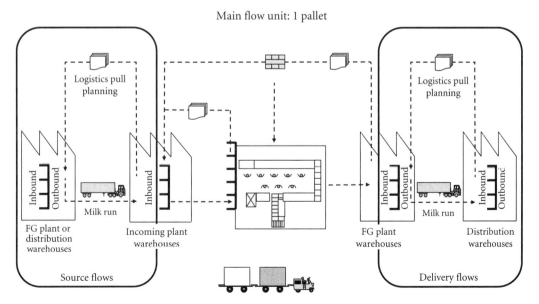

Figure 11.2   External logistics flow.

before the delivery of the materials and the arrangement of the internal materials and parts supermarkets, including any reserve stock and all the plant warehouse inbound work (as well as the transportation and outbound operations at the suppliers). Delivery covers all logistics operations that take place from the point of the finished-goods supermarket, including the distribution inventory, the outbound work, transportation to customers, and the inbound supplies to the customer's storage points.

Any distribution company (a company that buys, sells, and maintains an inventory) will subdivide its operations in the same way into the source flows of incoming goods and the delivery flows of outbound goods. A manufacturing company can be viewed as a distribution company that has many value-adding operations between the inflow of goods (materials) and the outflow of goods (finished goods). I have already discussed how to create a flow in production and internal logistics inside a manufacturing company. Now you have to create a pull-flow system in the external logistics flow in both source and delivery.

Elements of External Logistics Flow

The external logistics pillar consists of the following domains:

▲ Storage and warehouse design
▲ Milk run
▲ Source flows
▲ Delivery flows
▲ Logistics pull planning

Storage and Warehouse Design

The first domain in external logistics flow deals with the layout of the warehouse and the type of storage for the pallets, cases, or items to be stored. Traditional warehouse layouts focus mainly on optimizing the use of space, with the concept of "one size fits all." This requires a lot of personnel for the picking and shipping, and the complexity of these operations results in many errors and mistakes.

The storage and warehouse design domain approaches storage and layout by defining cells or lines grouped in value streams (making it similar in many ways to the line and layout design domain in the production-flow pillar). The criteria for the grouping can be the volume of parts (i.e., small, medium, or large), groups of customers, or types of orders. Storage zones are grouped and organized to meet the criterion of flow. This means organizing the layout according to which items are high runners, medium runners, and low runners as defined by PQ (Parts Quantities, or Pareto) analysis. In warehouse design, the quantity element of the PQ analysis will be the quantity of the logistics units being moved and stored (i.e., full pallet, full case, or item).

In production, one talks about *unit output* or *item output*; in logistics, one talks about *logistics unit output*. This can be measured and analyzed in terms of full pallets, full cases, or even items (order lines moved).

As you have already seen when I discussed internal logistics, the logistics cell is a set of products that have similar characteristics in terms of internal customers. The same applies inside the warehouse, creating several logistics cells that then can be managed to achieve lower inventory numbers and maximum flow and productivity.

Milk Run

The milk-run domain of external logistics flow deals with the organization of transport between the various elements of the supply chain. The name *milk run* is used to emphasize the need for the same *mizusumashi* principles that were used in internal logistics.

As you have seen, the *mizusumashi* system is a shuttle line that operates with a predetermined route and frequency. The users of the line, both the shipper and the receiver, know that the materials will arrive at a fixed time. This means that they can plan operations to load or unload just in time. The material planners also have access to regular transport with a quick response time that allows for the frequent replenishment of inventories.

The difference between this system and the *mizusumashi* of internal logistics is that milk runs go to external suppliers and so may have to cover large distances (potentially across the globe). The concept of milk run has to include using continental and inter-continental modes of transport to create reliable and fast shipment routes.

The detailed discussion of milk runs later in this chapter will cover how to use intermodal transport (e.g., by sea, train, and truck) of freight containers and especially long-, medium-, and short-distance truck haulage to create a milk-run type of delivery.

Source Flows

The source-flows domain deals with the physical operations in the source logistics loops, especially within the inbound process at a customer storage facility. The goal is to create a flow in all the operations (this will be a pull flow because the orders are calculated with pull algorithms) and increase productivity at the same time. It is the old paradox of how to reduce inventory, improve customer service, and reduce logistics costs all at the same time.

My example of the new paradigm for this will be the flow supply logistics in a car assembly plant. The transport and inbound operations in this example can be really complex because car assembly logistics must deal with thousands of incoming materials and hundreds of vendors. The materials also vary—they can range from small screws to big and complex parts such as axles and other major automotive parts.

The loop begins and ends in the supermarket of materials available to the *mizusumashi* drivers inside the customer plant. The challenge is to streamline these complex logistics operations.

For many years, Toyota has been working with *kanban* milk runs (adaptation of the *mizusumashi* principle to external transport) and supermarkets, with no reserve stock inside the plant. The shortest milk-run pitch times are two hours (for the vendors located nearby), which makes it possible to establish supermarkets that have a maximum inventory equal to six hours of consumption. There are also just-in-time deliveries (by *junjo*, or the delivery of made-to-order [MTO] sequenced parts) with short pitch times from outside suppliers located nearby. The further away the suppliers are, the bigger is the size of the supermarkets. (Above a certain amount of inventory, the supermarket turns into reserve stock.) For distant suppliers, the reserve stock is kept in a nearby warehouse (belonging to the vendor and managed by either the vendor or a third-party logistics operator).

The supply-chain design of a source-flow strategy is an essential part of *kaizen* in logistics and supply chains. This strategy also should involve vendors and suppliers because they are part of the pull logistics loops to be modeled and improved. In the sections on internal logistics flow (Chapters 8 and 9) I explained that you start the design of a flow system by building supplier and border-of-line supermarkets and then organizing a *mizusumashi* shuttle line between them using a *kanban* information system.

Some source flows require a similar solution. This means discussing with the vendor or supplier their participation in the tasks involved in the loop. At a minimum level of involvement, the vendor's or supplier's goods will have to be organized in a supermarket from which the milk-run driver can pick (remember the definition of supermarket: storage for easy and quick picking). At a maximum, the vendor or supplier will need to accept responsibility for running a complete vendor-managed inventory (VMI) loop. The degree of participation will depend on the size of the logistics flow and other economic considerations, but the vendor/supplier will have to be involved in the supply design phase of the source-flow strategy.

Delivery Flows

This domain deals with all the physical operations in the delivery logistics loops, especially the inbound and outbound operations of the product distribution facilities. It is interesting to see that the elements of these logistics loops are quite similar to those in the source-flow domain because they share the same pull planning, outbound, milk-run, and inbound operations. The goal is also the same—to create a flow in all these operations and increase productivity at the same time.

The new paradigm for streamlining delivery flows is the flow distribution warehouse. A distribution warehouse receives thousands of goods from hundreds of vendors and distributes hundreds of consignments to hundreds of customers. One big difference from the logistics of car assembly supply (or any manufacturing supply logistics operation) is that the outbound warehouse process is not based on a *mizusumashi* shuttle picking directly from supermarkets. Here the outbound operations are more complex than the inbound operations, and the customers are external customers located many kilometers away. So the delivery-flows domain will focus on how to streamline the outbound operations dispatch and transport to customers. The inbound operations of a distribution center also will need to be improved because of their importance to lead time and productivity.

The supply-chain design of a source-flow strategy is an essential part of kaizen *in logistics and supply chains.*

Here you are concentrating on the dispatch of outbound goods and transportation. When you are designing a source system, you deal with the incoming transport and inbound materials. In both cases you need the full logistics loop concept, with the awareness that at least two parties are involved (if you are outsourcing transportation and storage, this will involve three or four parties) who may not belong to the same company.

A good example of a delivery-flow strategy is Toyota's logistics for spare parts. The first loop in the logistics chain is the final customer needing his or her car repaired. The customer would like to be served in less than one day, so the dealer will need to provide the service quickly and efficiently and will need to maintain a small inventory of spare parts. The second loop is the replenishment of this inventory. The supplier is a local warehouse. This local warehouse will have to supply requested parts several times a day and have them available. The third loop is a regional warehouse that supplies the local one in the same way. (In Europe, Toyota has one local warehouse in almost every country and a regional warehouse in Belgium.) The fourth loop connects with other elements of the chain spread all over the world (a central warehouse in Japan, which manufacturing plants supply directly as consolidated orders). This complex delivery supply chain is extremely effective in terms of quality, cost, and customer service. You will see how pull flow is the model that makes it possible.

Logistics Pull Planning

The logistics pull planning domain deals with how to

▲ Decide the planning strategy of each product reference (starting with the basic made-to-order and made-to-stock strategy)
▲ Use forecasts to plan capacity in the logistics loop
▲ Plan the real orders (either the final customer orders or replenishment orders)

The difference between this and production pull planning is that in this type of external logistics loop, we don't have manufacturing operations in the middle of the loop. We have transport operations that can have very long lead times (increasing globalization means that transport operations will have to be considered on a worldwide scale). You will see how it is possible to order on a daily basis, even with big lead times (such as when ordering from Europe or America to Japan).

Another interesting question in logistics pull planning is who in a logistics loop should be responsible for it. Should it be the customer or the supplier? I am talking about made-to-stock (MTS) goods (also called *stock-keeping units* [SKUs]) that are maintained in a finished-goods inventory and that need to be replenished in line with consumption. One model that is often used today is *vendor-managed inventory* (VMI). As its name suggests, in this model the vendor (or supplier) in the loop is responsible for managing the loop, including all the steps of the replenishment process, such as pull planning, outbound, transport, and inbound. Customers will have immediate access to the parts they need and will pick only from the supermarket zone of the inventory. It is at this point that the materials or goods become the property of the customers. I will discuss VMI and consignment stock in more detail in the next chapters.

Storage and Warehouse Design

Storage and warehouse design deals with the organization of spaces necessary to perform the warehouse functions for the different types of warehouses. These spaces need to be designed to allow a flow of materials. This domain parallels the first domain of the production-flow pillar, line and layout design. Here, however, you are interested in defining the main lines or groups of logistic operations and how to lay out operations and storage points to fit those groups.

Organization and Availability

A warehouse is a place that houses materials in a storage point, to wait there for some time until they are required to be delivered to a customer. The main function of a warehouse is to make the products available to final customers at a reasonable delivery time. What is a "reasonable" delivery time will depend mainly on the type of product, but often there is also a drive to reduce the delivery time in order to be more competitive. Customers increasingly choose suppliers that have the right product available at a faster delivery time. When a customer needs a product, it should be available and delivered quickly because this is the essence of a pull system—driven by customer demand. The main function of the warehouse is to synchronize the offer of available product with demand from customers.

The challenge for storage and warehouse design, then, is how to have the least amount of materials while offering the highest level of customer service. This means that the flow warehouse will have to

▲ Quickly receive the incoming goods and put them away to storage (binning)
▲ Quickly pick and dispatch outgoing goods to customers in the required packaging (see below)
▲ Synchronize all material movements with customer need in order to reduce the amount of goods waiting in storage inventory

The competitive warehouse will have to do all these things at the lowest possible cost of investment and personnel.

Customer Packaging Requirements

This is another important concept affecting warehouse and storage design. Each warehouse in the supply chain will have to consider the right form of presentation for its immediate customers. Let's look at the five main types of warehouses found in a supply chain:

1. Plant raw materials and components warehouses
2. Plant finished-goods warehouses
3. Main distribution centers
4. Regional distribution centers
5. Local distribution centers

The customers of warehouse type 1 are the manufacturing workers who have to load the machines. The right materials presentation for them will be the one that best simplifies their loading movements. You have seen how the small container is the optimal size of package in the border-of-line domain of the production-flow pillar because it minimizes the picking and workstation-loading movements of the operators. So warehouse type 1 will need to be ready to supply the small standard containers efficiently. This means receiving, putting away in storage, picking, and dispatching this type of packaging.

> Each warehouse in the supply chain will have to consider the right form of presentation for its immediate customers.

The same reasoning applies to warehouse type 2, except that here the right customer presentation will be different. The customer is warehouse type 3, which needs to receive pallets of full cases. While the task of each type of warehouse remains the same, the right form of presentation will depend on the requirements of each set of customers.

The five types of warehouses are shown in Figure 11.3. You can see that the challenge for plant warehouses is how to change from pallet loads to handling small standard boxes (cases) and finally go back to pallet loads. The challenge for distribution warehouses, on the

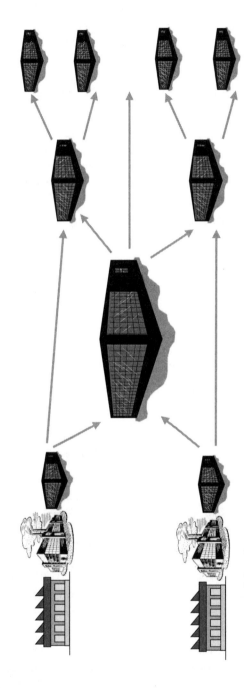

Raw material and components warehouses

Purpose: To hold materials at, or near, the point of introduction into the manufacturing or assembly process

Usual flows: Pallets in, pallets or cases out

Finished goods warehouses

Purpose: To hold inventory used to buffer variation between production and demand

Usual flows: Pallets or cases in, pallets or cases out

Main distribution centers

Purpose: To accumulate and consolidate from manufacturing; located centrally in relation to manufacturing or customer bases

Usual flows: Pallets or cases in, pallets or cases or single items out

Regional distribution centers

Purpose: To receive, pick, and ship small orders for local warehouses and individual customers

Usual flows: Pallets, cases or single items in, cases or single items out

Local distribution centers

Purpose: Close to customers for quick response; shipment one or several times a day

Usual flows: Cases or single items in, single items out

Figure 11.3 Types of warehouses.

other hand, is how to progressively change from pallet loads to single items (this is also called *broken-case handling*).

To simplify and summarize, you can say that the flow warehouse will have to deliver

▲ The right material
▲ At the right location
▲ In the right quantity
▲ With the right presentation
▲ With efficiency

Achieving these targets will require minimizing the following types of *muda* ("waste"):

▲ People waiting
▲ People movement (too much motion)
▲ Material movement (too much transportation)
▲ Material waiting (too much inventory)
▲ Overdelivery (too great a quantity)
▲ Overprocessing
▲ Errors and defects

Warehouse Paradigms

The traditional paradigm for storage and warehouse design is characterized by delivery to customers from inventory on hand and a focus on "one size fits all" storage locations and space utilization. This means that the warehouse will have the following characteristics:

▲ There is too much inventory that is not ordered by customers and too little inventory that is needed.
▲ Storage locations are randomly allocated.
▲ Lead time and operator productivity are not an issue.
▲ There is a high rate of errors and abnormalities.
▲ The warehouse output capacity is too rigid to respond easily to changes in demand.

Traditional warehouses are designed on the basis of push-type planning and big-batch orders to handle a large amount of inventory that has to be moved in, stored, and moved out. Space is a big issue, which is one of the reasons why the focus is more on the use of space and less on flow. Another factor is the lack of leveling—the less the orders are leveled

> *Traditional warehouses are designed on the basis of push-type planning and big-batch orders to handle a large amount of inventory that has to be moved in, stored, and moved out.*

(so that they are big and infrequent), the more space and personnel the warehouse needs—and wastes.

The flow warehouse, which is based on logistics pull planning, aims to have a flow of incoming materials on a daily basis (leveled, small, and frequent orders) so that it needs less space for each SKU. The focus is on a customer-responsive flow system that will work according to

▲ Synchronized-flow inventory (the size of the inventory is geared to pull flow)
▲ Fixed storage locations
▲ Short lead times
▲ Efficient use of personnel (standard work)
▲ Visual management
▲ Flexible capacity

Thus the new paradigm of the flow warehouse will show a breakthrough in performance by having less inventory, better customer service, and lower costs. Figure 11.4 shows how the traditional warehouse compares with the flow warehouse with all flow principles applied.

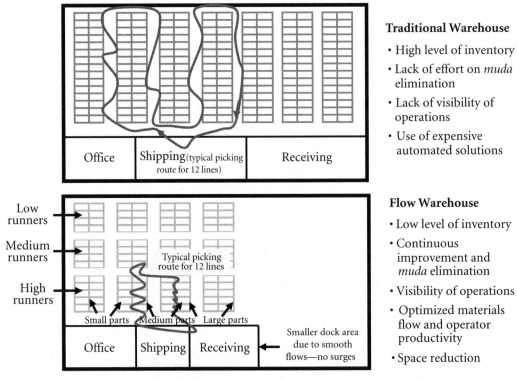

Figure 11.4 The traditional warehouse compared with the flow warehouse.

Warehouse Flow Principles

The storage and layout principles of the flow warehouse include the following:

▲   Product is stored by type and turnover in storage cells.
▲   There is one product-specific storage location for each part by part number.
▲   The storage of delivery packages is accommodated.
▲   Layout is flexible.
▲   The system uses visual management.
▲   Fewer abnormalities are seen.

Product Is Stored by Type and Turnover

The flow layout can be organized by turnover and by the size of parts. To optimize storage and handling solutions, products of the same type should be stored in the same area. Products may be stored by weight, dimensions, shape, or packaging.

For example, storage facilities could be grouped within the same zone according to the following criteria:

▲   Different products of the same type (e.g., different models of exhaust system or different types of alcohol)
▲   Different products that are usually sold together (e.g., paint and paint brushes, seeds and gardening tools)
▲   Items that are similar; products that have similar weight, dimensions, and shape

The layout will be made up of several cells that have similar characteristics in terms of available space and ease of binning and picking. The aim is also to help create work habits that improve the productivity of the workers who do the binning and picking. Figure 11.5 shows a possible flow storage layout.

In some cases, it is also possible to organize logistics cells by customer (I mentioned this in the section on internal logistics in Chapter 9). The aim here is to create zones for different customer value streams (Figure 11.6) with the following characteristics:

▲   Each individual value stream within the warehouse will have its own dedicated space and equipment.
▲   Each value stream will have a dedicated flow.
▲   Each value stream will be designed to eliminate long journeys and empty returns.

The result will be better customer service, faster response, and less material waiting (i.e., inventory) or shorter waiting time before delivery.

The storage zones inside each group (or cell) must be organized according to the output volumes of the products stored, as shown by the PQ analysis. The quantity or size of the

Products of the same type should be stored in the same area to optimize storage and handling solutions

Products may be stored by:

- Weight
- Dimension
- Shape
- Type of packing

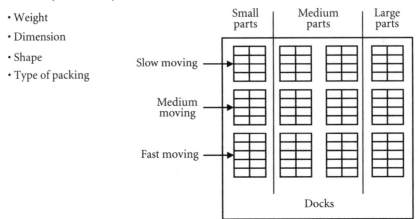

Figure 11.5 Flow storage layout.

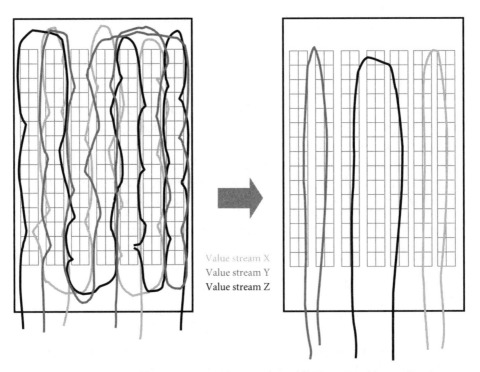

Figure 11.6 Product stored by turnover and type using different zones for each value stream.

flow will be measured in terms of the number of logistics units being moved in a certain period of time (i.e., full pallets, cases, or lines of items). Products with a high turnover must be stored near the docks. Products with a low turnover will be stored in more remote zones. This principle may lead to the organization of high-turnover storage zones that are close to the docks and hold a small number of very high-turnover products (this is also known as the *golden*, or *fast*, *zone*).

One Product-Specific Storage Location for Each Part by Part Number

In many traditional warehouses, there is more than one location for the same SKU. If the warehouse has a random, nonfixed location system, the warehouse management system will manage the locations, which will vary based on the free space available. Other warehouses may have one location for picking and several others for reserve inventory. For the sake of clarity, I will define the picking location as the *primary location* and any other location as the *secondary locations* used for holding reserve inventory.

The principle of "one product-specific storage location for each part by part number" means that

▲ Each product (part number or SKU) must be stored in one primary location only (there are no different locations for the same part).
▲ The size of the location will depend on the quantity to be stored.
▲ The location should be fixed in order to create habits of use in workers, although it must be reviewed periodically to reflect turnover.
▲ If the quantities to be stored are such that more than one location is necessary, a visual system can be used to manage these reserve locations.
▲ The storage location must be configured to the product's shape, size, weight, or handling solution.
▲ The quantity to be stored and the appropriate form of packaging obviously must be taken into account when deciding location.

This principle of product-specific storage for standard pallets or cases (containers), where all articles will fit in, contradicts the traditional paradigm of randomly allocated storage locations. For the system to work well, it is necessary to have a very good location management system that periodically reviews the size and suitability of the locations. This should be done quickly and efficiently, and it should be easy to create and delete locations as required.

> It is necessary to have a very good location management system that periodically reviews the size and suitability of the locations.

Storage of Delivery Packages Is Accommodated

This principle means that the products should be stored in the primary location already packaged according to their unit of final use (i.e., the standard sales or delivery package). Supplying the products for storage in their final unit packaging also means that the operator does not have to open bulk or case packaging to repackage individual items.

Layout Is Flexible

Flexible layout can be achieved by following these rules:

▲ Plan for spare capacity (keep 80 percent of locations free).
▲ Locations need to be easy to reconfigure for different sizes and should be labeled.
▲ Operators should be trained in standard work.
▲ Personnel needs to be flexible so as to be deployed within inbound and outbound processes.
▲ Equipment used for handling reserve stock (if used) should have sufficient free capacity.
▲ There should be physical separation between pedestrian and machine aisles (they also can be separated by the use of different timetables).

The System Uses Visual Management

This and the final principle (controlling abnormalities) are closely related to the basic principles of *kaizen* in logistics and supply chains and are very important for management of the flow warehouse. Visual management consists of facilitating all the inbound and outbound tasks by the correct and widespread use of visual aids such as colors and signs to identify storage zones, storage locations, aisles, gangways, and products. The aim is to improve work habits among the operators; improve the productivity of binning, replenishing, and picking; and reduce the opportunities for errors and mistakes. Visual identification complements the use of technologies such as bar-code scanning.

Fewer Abnormalities Are Seen

This is achieved by identifying, measuring, and continuously reducing all problems related to

▲ Missing products
▲ Wrong quantities
▲ Wrong locations
▲ Wrong packaging and wrong identification

Application of this principle starts by the use of mistake-proofing devices (*poka yoke*) that prevent the occurrence of abnormalities. The system must highlight any abnormality and ensure that corrective action is taken immediately.

A good example of such a system is a warehouse management system that manages SKU locations in a dynamic way. This type of system uses the concepts of *movable location* (ML) or *fixed location* (FL). An ML is a location that moves (it can be a container or a trolley). An FL is a primary or secondary fixed storage location. Bar-code scanners can be used to monitor the location of all SKUs inside the warehouse. As the SKUs move in and out of storage, the status of their location changes from ML to FL and back to ML. *Poka yoke* software checks also can be built to ensure that no mistakes are made.

Toyota's Journey to Lean Distribution

Toyota's journey to Lean distribution is an almost perfect example of changing a warehouse from the traditional no-flow paradigm to the flow paradigm. In the 1980s, Toyota started applying flow concepts to its parts-distribution supply chain. The main steps of Toyota's journey to Lean distribution are shown in Table 11.1.

Chapter 13 will provide a detailed look at the delivery-flows domain, including warehouse flows and the solutions used to create flow in the inbound and outbound operations of a distribution warehouse. By applying flow principles for storage and warehouse design, you will be able to reduce the work content in all warehouse operations and provide an excellent functional inventory in terms of reduced size and improved customer service.

Table 11.1 Steps in Toyota's Evolution of Lean Distribution

Year	Step
1989	Relocate parts according to frequency of demand and size
1989	Reduce sizes of storage bins
1989	Most frequently used parts located near the start of picking process
1990	Introduce standard work for pickers by dividing workday into 15-minute cycles and using visual management to control processes
1992	*Kaizen* activities to modify construction of picking carts and create other improvements
1992	Use of leveling to smooth runs among operators
1995	Transition from weekly to daily deliveries to dealers
1996	Creation of pull systems between PDC (parts delivery center) and its suppliers to strongly reduce the need to hold reserve inventory

CHAPTER 12

External Logistics Flow: Milk Runs and Source Flows

Milk Runs

The *milk run* is the second domain of the external logistics flow pillar. The term refers to a repetitive transport system (operating one or several times each day) that follows a standard route and carries a mixed load of different goods. The name comes from the milk deliveries of the past in the United States, a daily and standard route that came every morning and exchanged full bottles of milk for empty bottles (returnable containers). It was a reliable and frequent service, bringing fresh milk on a daily basis. Today people use nonreturnable containers, which are probably more cost-effective but are certainly less environmentally friendly, and buy milk every week at the supermarket because the supermarket milk, being pasteurized, doesn't spoil—but is less natural.

For transport between stations in the supply chain, either for source or delivery, these features of the old milk run are key elements in the creation of flow. Such an approach also allows work to be leveled on a daily basis (or even more often), which, in turn, helps to prevent the whiplash effect (with its amplification of demand) and stabilizes personnel in warehouse facilities and all across supply chains. Figure 12.1 shows how the milk-run system reduces material waiting time.

Another advantage of the milk-run type of transport is that it improves the productivity of the unloading and loading tasks performed by the driver and other people at drop points because consolidated deliveries will always take place at the same times and will be done by the same people. It is possible to further reduce unloading and loading times by good truck design (side loading) and streamlining the driver's movements through standard work.

Frequent, reliable transport allows more frequent ordering (or replenishment), which greatly reduces waiting time.

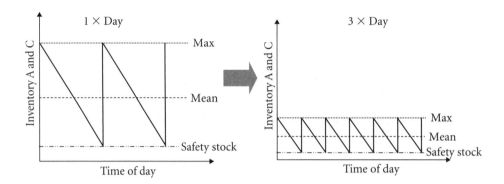

• Reduction of inventory

• Reliable replenishment lead times

• Better visibility of inventory

• Improved supplier comunication

Figure 12.1   Advantages of a milk-run system.

Depending on the distance of the route, it is possible to operate milk runs with a pitch time of two hours. This is done in the car industry with suppliers that are located close to the assembly plant. The paradigmatic case is Toyota City, where suppliers drive small vans every two hours to replenish the many *kanban* supermarkets surrounding the assembly lines.

Later in this chapter you will see that the milk-run concept also can work over long distances (the pitch times, of course, increase to one day or even longer) and can be used with *line-haul transport* (full truck loads) and *intermodal containers* (containers that can be transferred from one mode of transport, such as rail, road, or sea, to another).

Customer-Service Policies

To use the milk-run concept effectively, it is necessary to define customer-service policies for the frequency and times of delivery. The supplier of any type of good needs to set up a service policy consisting of a table that defines the type and frequency of deliveries. As an example, let's look at a local warehouse containing spare parts for cars and serving a region of 100,000 km² (a small country in Europe).

The service policy establishes three types of service provided to customers:

1. *Same-day service, self pickup* (customers can come to the warehouse at a certain time each day).

2. *Same-day service for orders received until 10 a.m.* Delivery will be made until 3 p.m. for customers located in certain places (the two main cities).

3. *Next-day service.* For orders received before 4 p.m., delivery will be made by 8 a.m. the next day for all customers in the region (the most distant customer is 900 km away).

This type of policy allows customers to plan their inventories along flow lines and order their supplies as needed on a daily basis. To be able to serve every customer according to the service policy, the supplier will have to organize shipment schedules and standardized routes for delivery.

The same-day service can be done with a local milk run and a dedicated daily truck. Several routes can be defined with standard start/stop times. The next-day service can be done with a line-haul truck that transports an aggregated daily load to a *cross-dock* or *transport hub* during the night. Small trucks then can deliver from the cross-dock or hub point to small groups of customers according to the established schedule.

If every supplier in the supply chain draws up such a customer-service contract (one even may call them *flow service contracts*), then the entire supply chain will receive the benefits of Total Flow Management and pull-flow systems.

In this way, every customer will be served according to a milk-run service contract. This means a frequent and reliable transport service that creates a good flow of materials.

The example I have provided shows the delivery side of the supply chain, but the same concept will work for the source side as well. A milk-run source service contract is also needed. But who should define and enforce the contract—the supplier or the customer? The answer will depend on the relative strength of each business. When a small supplier is dealing with a big customer, it may be the customer who specifies the service levels, although it is always possible for the supplier to take the initiative.

In the automotive industry, it is usually the customer (the car assembly line) that establishes this type of standard. In this chapter, I will use examples of milk runs for both the source and delivery sides of the supply chain, with the assumption that in delivery, the starting point of the milk run is the supplier, and in sourcing, the starting point is the customer (Figure 12.2).

You can see that there are some advantages to reducing the distances driven on the routes, but the main advantage is the acceleration of flow. By using frequent transport cycles, it is possible to supply on demand directly to internal supermarkets (storage areas) that in their turn are serviced by *mizusumashi* (the milk-run concept applied to internal logistics within a plant). This means that there is a frequent and reliable supply of many

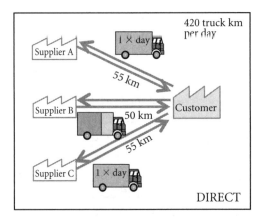
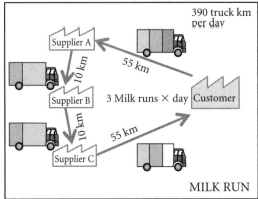
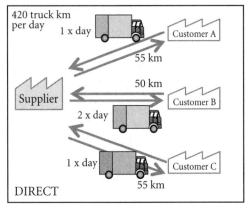
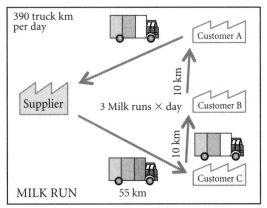

Figure 12.2 The concept of the milk run.

different materials to the production areas. It also means a frequent and reliable supply to final customers through the delivery side of the supply chain.

The unit load is usually a pallet or pallet-sized container. To use the car industry example once again, on the source side, the materials are transported inside small containers (plastic), and the pallets are palletized sets of small containers. In other industries, the unit load can be bigger than pallet size. The trucks should be small to medium (4 to 8 m long) and should have lateral loading capability.

Types of Milk Runs

It is possible to have several types of milk runs depending on the distance between the two most distant points of the route. The local milk-run route services suppliers or customers that are 40 to 400 km away (or approximately six hours' driving time). Many plants or warehouses, however, have suppliers or customers at far greater distances, even overseas. In these cases, it is necessary to extend the milk-run concept.

There can be three types of milk runs:

▲ The local milk run
▲ The far milk run
▲ The local-far milk run with a *cross-dock hub*

The local milk run also can accommodate remote suppliers (see Figures 12.3 through 12.5).

A remote supplier can use a common carrier to transport goods to a hub integrated in the milk-run route. If the frequency of shipment equals the milk run, the hub can be just a cross-dock point for the freight. *Cross-docking* is a logistics practice in which materials are unloaded from an incoming semitrailer, truck, or rail car and loaded onto outbound trailers or rail cars with little or no storage in between. This may be necessary to change the type of conveyance used, to sort material intended for different destinations, or to combine material from different starting points.

In its purest form, this is done directly, with minimal or no warehousing. In practice, many cross-docking operations require large staging areas where inbound materials are sorted, consolidated, and stored until the outbound consignment is complete and ready to

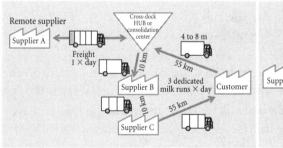

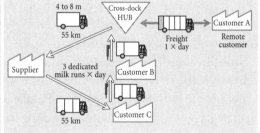

- The local milk run can accommodate remote suppliers

- They need to ship their products daily to a local cross-dock hub facility

- If there is some item customization, the cross-dock hub can be replaced by a warehouse (kitting or sequencing facility)

- Some customers may establish near the plants a consolidation center (for kitting and sequencing) that receives parts from hundreds of remote suppliers

- The local milk run can accommodate remote customers

- A direct delivery with a common carrier is organized from a cross-dock hub to the remote customer

- Usually transport companies can design and implement this type of route very easily

Figure 12.3   The local milk run—source and delivery.

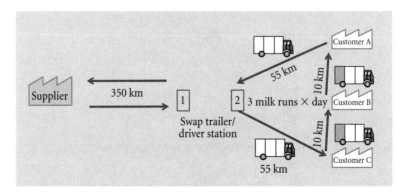

- The truck is a composite of truck + trailer
- Each driver does a maximum work cycle of 8 hours and swaps the trailer at designated stations along the route
- For two drivers with two trucks, the milk run total cycle time will be 8 + 8 = 16 hours
- It is possible to cover distances of 1000 km or more with this system (using more than two drivers)
- It is also possible to use two trucks and swap drivers (instead of trailers)

Figure 12.4 Long-distance (far) milk run.

ship. If the operation takes no more than a day, the hub is usually referred to as a *cross-dock distribution center*. If the operation takes several days or even weeks, the hub is usually considered to be a warehouse.

In the automotive industry you can find hubs that are consolidation centers, in the sense that they prepare sequenced trolleys of parts. This requires storage facilities and warehouse processes to sort parts and make up trolleys. The consolidation center even may operate its own milk-run routes, collecting from several suppliers. The car plant then moves the sequenced trolleys and other small containers directly to the assembly lines or to internal supermarkets. I will discuss this further when I deal with the source-flows domain.

The long-distance (or *far*) milk run is another possible way to shorten the lead time for long-distance transport. The concept can include several drivers who swap trailers or trucks at certain points of the route. This form of milk run is called a *swap-trailer far milk run* and is shown in Figure 12.5.

The alternative to using a swap-trailer far milk run is to use a common carrier that makes the complete loop (a standard long-distance line-haul milk run). Figure 12.6 compares the two approaches. The swap-trailer (or swap-truck) approach reduces the lead time of the order substantially, from 62 to 24 hours—in other words, the order reaches the customer 2.5 times faster.

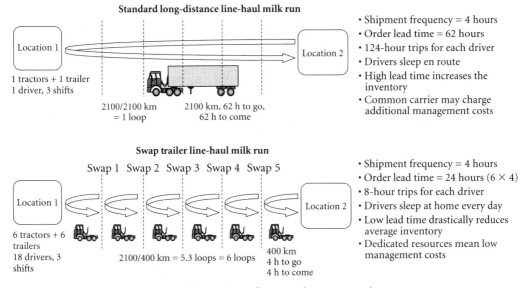

Figure 12.5   Far milk run with a swap trailer.

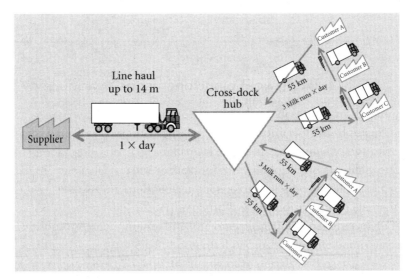

- There is a cross-dock hub located near the customers
- There are several local milk run loops
- The alternative to the milk run would be a direct common carrier delivery from the hub to each customer
- Appropriate for sub-clusters of customers with output that fits in larger trucks
- A cross-dock is a hub where the incoming goods are unloaded, sorted, and loaded to the milk run route (no storage)

Figure 12.6   Local-far milk run with cross-dock delivery.

Using the Different Types of Milk Runs

Here are some guidelines (see Figure 12.7) for using the various kinds of milk runs (keeping in mind that the goal is to reduce transport lead time and increase the frequency of shipments). When a product is needed in multiple truckloads every day,

▲ Local, local-far, or far milk runs can be used. (See Figure 12.6.)
▲ It makes sense for the vendor to take charge of maintaining supplies at the customer end (vendor-managed inventory).

When a product is required only sporadically from a product-specific supplier,

▲ A solution involving daily delivery by a common carrier should be explored.

When the supplier is geographically far from others on a milk-run route,

▲ The cost of making the side trip may not justify it.
▲ A possible solution is for the supplier to make the product available in a sub-warehouse closer to the route traveled on the milk run.

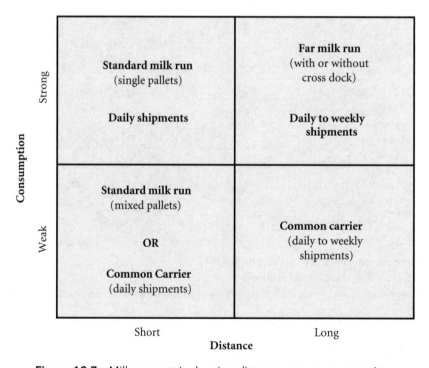

Figure 12.7 Milk-run matrix showing distance versus consumption.

Source Flows

The source-flows domain covers the necessary warehouse operations for handling the incoming of parts until they are stored in the storage points (supermarkets) ready for picking. As you saw in Chapter 11, the new paradigm for source flows (see Table 12.1) is the car assembly supply logistics, the Toyota or logistics way.

> *The targets to achieve in inbound operations are related to the creation of flow and an increase in productivity in all manual logistics tasks.*

Inbound operations include all the activities necessary for receiving and putting away the parts in the supermarkets, as well as for handling the returnable packages and the logistics material waste. The main activities include

▲ Unloading containers from trucks to transit areas
▲ Loading empty returnable containers from transit areas
▲ Checking and sorting full containers into delivery routes to internal supermarkets

Table 12.1   Comparison Between Traditional and Flow Paradigms for Inbound Operations from the Supplier

Traditional Paradigm	Flow Paradigm
Receiving bulk loads of the same part with the minimum possible frequency (usually weekly)	Receiving small loads of the same part with the maximum possible frequency (usually daily but can be up to four times per shift)
Use of disposable packaging (cardboard)	Use of returnable packaging
Use of pallet-sized containers for most of the parts	Use of small plastic containers for most of the parts (transported in pallets of small containers)
Incoming quality inspection	No incoming quality inspection
Lots of pallet transport to and from reserve stock locations	No reserve stock, only supermarkets ready for *mizusumashi* picking
Stacking pallet-sized containers into pallet racking	Linear movements from truck to supermarket (decentralized incoming supermarkets)
Large reserve stock, with the same part stored randomly in several locations to minimize storage space	
Pushing pallet-sized containers to production with the minimum possible frequency (usually daily)	
Passing unpacking and packaging waste disposal operations on to production	

▲ Sorting empty containers by supplier
▲ Delivering and binning containers in supermarkets
▲ Disposing of logistics material waste (e.g., carton, plastic, and other packaging materials)

Flow is achieved by streamlining the flows in order to reduce material waiting time drastically. Productivity is increased by eliminating all non-value-added movements through standard work.

Traditional Inbound Operations Flows

In this section I will analyze the several types of inbound flows operating in a traditional warehouse storing raw materials and components using the example of a vehicle assembly plant. The inbound logistics of such a warehouse are extremely complex because of the different types of raw materials and the large numbers of components. For example, the size of the components ranges from small screws to very big parts such as front windows and bumpers.

In this type of plant, you can identify six main families of flows based on the logistics unit type delivered to the line worker at the border of line. These six families are

▲ *Flow 1.* Bulk containers (bigger than the standard European pallet-sized container) to deliver very big parts such as floor mats and glass windows
▲ *Flow 2.* Large containers (standard European pallet size) to deliver all types of big to small parts
▲ *Flow 3.* Small containers (standard plastic or carton boxes sized 400 × 600 mm) to deliver medium-sized to very small parts
▲ *Flow 4.* Very small containers (very small plastic or carton boxes) to deliver very small parts such as screws and fasteners
▲ *Flow 5.* External *junjo* containers (special containers or trolleys) to deliver sequenced parts coming from external suppliers
▲ *Flow 6.* Internal *junjo* containers (special containers or trolleys) to deliver sequenced parts or kits of parts made internally

Figure 12.8 shows a value-stream map (value-stream mapping is discussed in Chapter 14) of each of the flows using triangles to represent storage points, arrows to represent transport, and other easily recognizable icons. It also shows the line worker at the border of lines. Rectangles with arrows represent the information flow necessary to move and synchronize the supply of materials.

The average daily distribution of containers (unit loads) in the six flows is shown in Figure 12.9. The individual flows are described in Table 12.2.

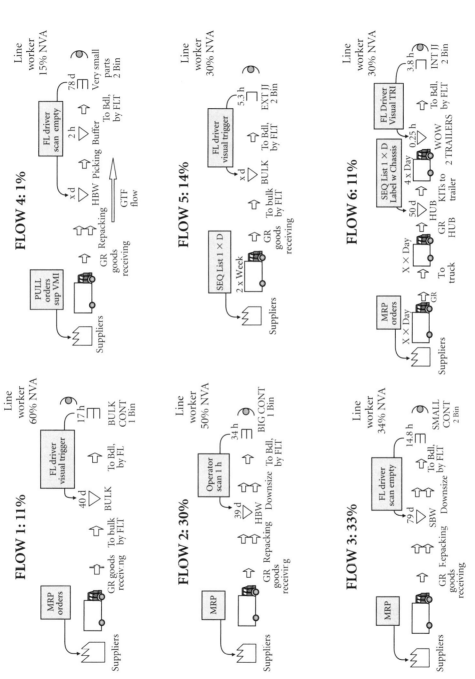

Figure 12.8 Value-stream maps—traditional car assembly supply-chain flows.

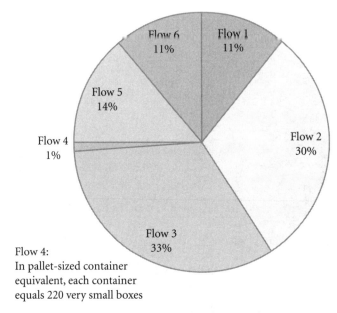

Flow 4:
In pallet-sized container
equivalent, each container
equals 220 very small boxes

Figure 12.9 The average daily distribution of containers in traditional car assembly supply-chain flows.

Table 12.2 Description and Percentage Daily Container Use of the Six Flows

Flow Number	Description	Percentage of Daily Container Use
1	Bulk containers (bigger than the standard European pallet-sized container) to deliver very big parts such as floor mats and glass windows	11
2	Big containers (standard European pallet size) to deliver all types of big to small parts	30
3	Small containers (standard plastic or carton boxes sized 400 × 600 mm) to deliver medium-sized to very small parts	33
4	Very small containers (very small plastic or carton boxes) to deliver very small parts such as screws and fasteners	1
5	External *junjo* containers (special containers or trolleys) to deliver sequenced parts coming from external suppliers	14
6	Internal *junjo* containers (special containers or trolleys) to deliver sequenced parts or kits of parts made internally	11

Flows 5 and 6 are justified by the high number of variants for some types of parts. The number and size of the variants mean that sequenced *junjo* supply is the only alternative because it allows the parts to be presented close to the point of assembly. In this plant, the vehicles to be assembled are trucks, so there is a high number of very large parts that would make it impossible for the worker to move and pick these large parts if they were supplied in bulk containers to the border of line.

Flow 4 is the smallest one because the very small containers are handled inside pallet-sized containers and then put in flow racks at several points of the line. Because these parts are common to many vehicles being assembled at the same time, it is possible to have several flow racks along the line from which the operator can pick a very small container and locate it close to the assembly point.

The main problem areas are flows 1, 2, and 3. In terms of internal logistics, the flows are quite straightforward:

▲   Flow 1 deals with bulk containers coming from suppliers. These are unloaded and put away in a bulk warehouse. Some forklifts are assigned to pick and move the containers from the warehouse to the line on the basis of a visual trigger (this is a nonstandardized decision based on the consumption of the containers on the line). There is no change of bulk container, and a linear movement is required from inward to the line.

▲   Flow 2 uses the same system as flow 1, the difference being that the warehouse is an automated storage and retrieval system (automated warehouse with high bays), and the replenishment signal is sent by computer after a bar code on the container is scanned by the worker on the line. There is no change of bulk container, and a linear movement is required from inward to the line.

▲   Flow 3 is essentially the same system as above, the difference being that the incoming pallets of small containers are stored in an automated storage and retrieval system (automated warehouse with high bays) that is designed for small plastic containers. The small containers are then supplied from the warehouse to the line. Replenishment is by a bar-code scan of empty containers, carried out by the logistics worker, who transports the containers to where they are consumed by means of a special high-capacity forklift.

> *A closer look at the line worker and the border of the line really reveals the consequences of such a straightforward method of supplying the line: The movement of workers is full of* muda, *and the non-value-added time ranges from 34 to 60 percent of the workers' time.*

These three flows all have similar logistics in that they involve the straightforward movement of containers into and out of the warehouses and to the lines. Each warehouse is designed to handle each of the three very specific unit loads (i.e., bulk, big, and small plastic containers). The small plastic containers arrive from the suppliers in a pallet load.

You may have noticed in Figure 12.8 that the amount of inventory is very large (39 to 79 days), but this has more to do with the supplier ordering process than with the logistics methods being used. The orders are calculated by a material requirements planning (MRP) system based on forecasts, not on a logistics pull planning algorithm adapted to each part and transport cycle time. The worker has to do several non-value-adding jobs—making the broken case picking on the line, handling all packaging waste, and in some cases ordering the replenishment of parts.

This is a failure of logistics—materials are not being provided at the point of use and within hand's reach of the operator. What in fact is happening here is that the logistics system is pushing muda *onto the products.*

What you need to consider is the optimization of the whole, not just logistics or production. This means that some changes are needed in the logistics inbound flows so that the materials can be supplied to the workers in the right presentation to eliminate most of their *muda* of movement. You have already encountered this issue when you dealt with organization of the border of line (Chapter 6). Here I will focus on the improvements needed in the source flows.

Creating Flow in Inbound Supply Logistics

Let's continue with the example of the vehicle assembly line. When you look at the non-value-added time spent by line workers, you can see that the worst values are where the bulk and big containers are stored in the border of line. These are the ones that need to be tackled first.

In flow 1, the bulk containers need to be sorted into ergo-pack containers (in which the parts are stored vertically in special trolleys with suitable racks). A sorting operation also needs to be added. This means that some time will be lost, but this loss will be far outweighed by the gains in line-worker time.

In flow 2, the large containers need to be changed to the right size. An analysis of the parts showed that most of them could be placed in small-sized containers. Figure 12.10 shows the effects of the transformation from big to small containers by changing the supplier's provision of big containers to pallets of small containers (palletized small containers). This can take some time, and a temporary right-sizing operation (repacking from big containers to small containers) may be needed to bridge the gap.

A supermarket of small containers was set up close to the assembly line, and a *mizusumashi* transport route was created to supply the boxes in one-hour cycles. This is an

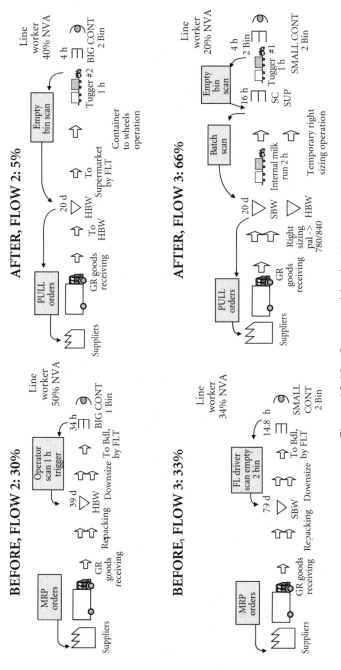

Figure 12.10 Car assembly—logistics.

203

essential part of the solution because changing to the right size greatly reduced the autonomy of the containers in the border of line. The amount of inventory in the warehouses was reduced by a logistics pull planning algorithm (this will be covered in Chapter 13).

The main advantage, however, came from reduction of the non-value-added (NVA) time of the worker in the border of line from an average of 40 to around 20 percent. This was done by rebalancing the line and relocating all part containers. New standard work procedures were drawn up, and the operators received targeted training for one month.

The number of logistics workers was increased by 16 percent, but the number of workers in production was reduced by 33 percent. Overall productivity, including logistics and production, was increased by 29 percent. Other advantages were the reduction of quality rejects and line stops caused by missing parts. The work environment also improved markedly, allowing 5S principles to become a reality.

Eliminating Muda *Through Synchronization in the Supply Chain*

Step 1: Defining Container Size

You have seen that defining the right-sized container to have within hand's reach of the operator is a key factor in eliminating *muda* in the operator's work. It is very important to start from this point. The operator needs the parts in single units (*broken* or *part of a case*, to use the language of logistics). The right-sized container is often the small plastic container but may just as easily be a pallet-sized container or even a bulk container (for very big parts). Sometimes it can be a very big pallet base without any walls (*a container with no walls*). The essential principles of the flow container are that it is easy to handle by the operator on the line and allows broken-case picking in the border of line. Sometimes the picking is done by a machine. This can be efficient, especially if the plant is geared to low-cost automation.

Step 2: Defining the Internal Transport System

Next, you must define the internal transport system. It must operate like a *mizusumashi* and provide high-frequency standard-route transport. *High frequency* means small amounts of many different parts. The water spider's job also must be simplified and rationalized into a standard work procedure.

Step 3: Inbound Operations Flow

Now you need inbound operations to bin the materials in the supermarkets. To build a flow here, you need to use the same containers as on the line. If the supplier is using different containers, why not ask him or her to change? The chances are high that the end of the supplier's assembly or production line is handling the part as a single unit. The movement used in the end of the supplier's line to put the part in a container will be the same movement your worker will have to do to pick the part. You eliminate *muda* from the supply chain when you move in the direction of one-piece flow and one-piece handling. Packing items into a container piece by piece is the same movement as picking from a container piece by piece. The right-sized container should be the most efficient for *both* the customer and the supplier.

You have seen that a water spider can easily handle the small container (and any type of right-sized flow container), so it will not be difficult to apply a similar solution to the two parts of the supply chain. External transport is a constraint and will need to use pallet-sized containers, but this can be a pallet of small containers (palletized containers). This also will fit the most economical use of the space inside the truck. In general, the truck's unit load should be a multiple of the small container, such as a European pallet or a double-sized European pallet. Special cases are also possible, as long as the same size of container suits both the customer and the supplier.

Step 3a: Repacking if Necessary

When there is a mismatch between the container used by the customer and that used by the supplier, a repacking operation is needed in between. This step should be minimized in order to take advantage of all the opportunities in the supply chain for eliminating *muda* but may be necessary as a temporary measure while customer and supplier do not have the same flow strategies (Figure 12.11).

Step 4: Returnable Packaging Between Customer and Supplier

To achieve this level of synchronization, it is necessary to move from disposable or different containers to returnable containers. The disposable container, like the carton box, has many disadvantages. It is a real *muda* generator:

▲   The price of the container is paid by the customer.
▲   Palletized cartons need to be unpacked before the contents can reach the point of use.
▲   The supplier needs to make up cartons and insert dunning.
▲   The customer needs to collapse and bundle the empty cartons.
▲   Bundles of empty cartons need to be shipped to a recycling point.

Returnable containers, on the other hand, offer the following advantages:

▲   There is a cost advantage for both supplier and customer because the cost of packaging and disposal is eliminated (once the returnable packaging has been depreciated).
▲   The materials are usually more substantial (plastic not cardboard), and therefore, the quality of the packaging is much better.

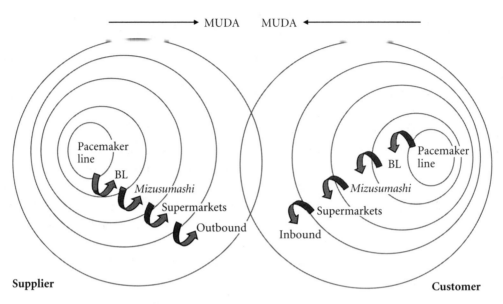

When the customer and the supplier work together to eliminate *muda* in a convergent direction, the result is *muda* elimination in the entire supply chain, from one end to the other.

BL = border of line

Figure 12.11 Where and how *muda* can be eliminated from the supply chain.

▲ The supplier takes responsibility for managing the sorting and storage, which saves time for the manufacturer.

▲ Milk runs reduce storage requirements and the cost of transportation.

▲ The more often a returnable container can be used, the more economical it becomes.

The initial investment in such containers may be shared by both the customer and the supplier, as suggested in Figure 12.12. The total number of containers in the chain depends on the amount of inventory, which is a function of the distance and frequency of transportation—this is why the milk-run concept is so important in accelerating flows. The amount of inventory the supplier needs to hold depends on how flexible the supplier's processes are. This means that the supplier also will have to work on creating production flow through quick changeovers, leveling, and production pull planning.

Elements of a Source-Flow Strategy

A source-flow strategy should be designed at the very beginning of the TFM journey in order to give a clear picture of how to create flow on the source side of the supply chain.

Disposable Containers

- Price is paid by the customer
- Palletized cartons need unpacking before point of use
- Supplier needs to erect cartons and insert dunnage
- Customer needs to collapse and bundle empty cartoons
- Bundles of empty cartoons need to be shipped to recycling

Returnable Containers

- Cost advantage for both supplier and customer
- Packaging quality is much better
- Sorting and storing by supplier needs to be done
- Milk runs reduce the storage requirements and cost of transportation
- The number of times a returnable container can be used is key to its economic value

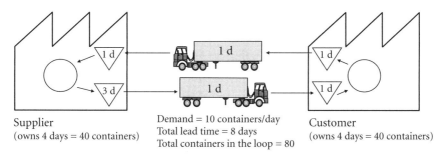

Supplier
(owns 4 days = 40 containers)

Demand = 10 containers/day
Total lead time = 8 days
Total containers in the loop = 80

Customer
(owns 4 days = 40 containers)

Figure 12.12   Advantages of returnable containers and how they are used.

When you call in an order (with daily frequency), you expect the supplier to deliver it quickly. To do this, the supplier must at the very least pick the required cases and put them in the milk run. Then, when you receive them at the other end of the milk run, you can start unloading (perhaps checking and sorting) and putting them away in the right supermarket—preferably using the same returnable packaging.

The elements of a source-flow strategy are

- ▲ Logistics pull planning (going to daily call-off or pull orders or more frequent orders)
- ▲ Improving the system by creating milk runs (transport at least once a day)
- ▲ A returnable-containers policy
- ▲ The organization of stores into supermarkets
- ▲ Incoming operations flow

The last point offers many challenges. You have to find the best transport flows to deliver unit loads to supermarkets for *mizusumashi* use. The chart in Figure 12.13 is an example of a logistics graph (a technique you can use to understand the relationship between all logistics operations handled throughout the system and how to link transport with right-sized flow containers optimized for the operator).

The car assembly industry is a good example here because, as you have already seen, it handles very different logistical containers. Other industries will fit into one of the

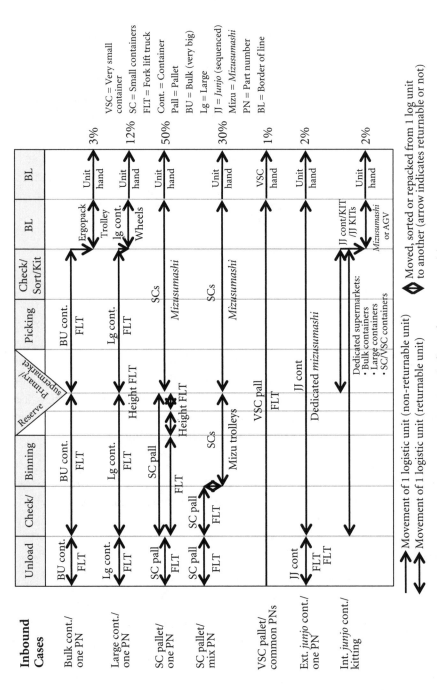

Figure 12.13 Supply flows for car assembly parts.

subgroups of this chart. The graph in the figure shows seven types of flow. The seventh is mainly concerned with building kits or sequenced containers from other part containers. The graph also shows the three main operations before storage (i.e., unload, check/sort, and bin) and the four main operations after storage (i.e., pick, check/sort, border-of-line supermarket, and border-of-line picking).

The storage is divided into *reserve* and *primary* (or *supermarket*). As you continue to implement more solutions to increase the flow, the size of the reserve will go down until eventually in some cases it disappears altogether. When the supplier is very distant, the transport lead time may not allow reserve inventory to be eliminated completely, so it will have to stay. In some situations, however, it is possible to have just a primary location to store the entire necessary inventory. This should be a target to always bear in mind.

CHAPTER 13

External Logistics Flow: Delivery Flows and Logistics Pull Planning

Delivery Flows

The delivery-flows domain involves all the warehouse operations necessary for the delivery of finished goods until they are stored in the retail points, ready for final customer picking. As you saw in Chapter 11, the new paradigm for creating delivery flows is the flow-distribution warehouse, and the best benchmark is the Toyota logistics system for car spare parts.

A worldwide distribution network can be extremely complex. It can include three types of warehouses:

1. Main distribution centers (DCs) receiving goods from plants and delivering to regional DCs, local DCs, and retail stores
2. Regional DCs receiving goods from plants and main DCs and delivering to local DCs and retail stores
3. Local DCs receiving goods from main and regional DCs and delivering to retail stores

In addition to this network of warehouses and located at the beginning of the network, you have the plant finished-goods warehouse that delivers products to main and regional DCs (depending on the location of plants). In some cases the plant finished-goods warehouse is also a main DC.

Creating a flow in the delivery side of the supply chain depends on

▲ Pull planning orders or replenishment orders coming from the final customer pull replenishment signals. These will be treated in the logistics pull planning domain. Daily ordering or daily call-off is essential to create a good flow and reduce material waiting times in all logistic loops of the distribution chain

▲ A policy of daily shipping, with transport organized on the milk-run principle
▲ Creating a flow and improving the productivity of distribution warehouse operations

This chapter deals with how to create a flow and improve productivity within the distribution warehouse across all warehousing operations described earlier. The basic warehouse operations include

▲ Unload (and organize for next steps)
▲ Check and sort (This may include packaging of kits or assortments.)
▲ Put away to storage (This may include putting away from a reserve to the picking location.)
▲ Pick from storage
▲ Check and sort (This may include pricing.)
▲ Load (organizing unit loads and shipping)

The ideal flow inside the warehouse can be defined as follows:

1. There is only one location for each stock-keeping unit (SKU). This location is used to store all the material waiting. When I discussed the storage and warehouse design domain (Chapter 11), you saw that this principle makes it possible to eliminate all movements from the reserve locations to the primary picking locations.
2. The logistics units to be handled flow quickly and directly from the incoming truck to the picking location, with no accumulation of material waiting in the process.
3. The same delivery logistics units flow quickly and directly from the picking location to the shipping truck.
4. All operations are optimized in terms of standard work. (Here you recognize, of course, that *optimized* is not the best word because *muda* elimination is a never-ending story. The goal of standard work is to reduce the *muda* of movement of all the warehouse workers.)

The challenge of turning a traditional warehouse system into this kind of model may look simple. What makes it complex is the *variety* of logistics units to be handled and the *quantities* of inventory that need to be dealt with (ordering in big batches generates a lot of inventory). Excessive inventory of each SKU requires large, single storage and picking locations, and many large locations increase the time it takes to put stock away and also extends the picking cycle time (the put-away and picking face can become physically very large).

Another complicating factor is that the kinds of logistics units can range from full pallets and full cases (returnable or nonreturnable) to single items. A warehouse can receive and ship full pallets, but it also can receive full pallets and ship full cases and individual items. And a warehouse also can deal with a combination of different in and out logistics units. All this variety makes it very difficult to work with a single location and streamline and rationalize all the necessary movements in and out.

> *The first consideration for good storage and warehouse design is to define optimally sized locations and aggregation of storage type.*

The solution will be many smaller warehouses within the one large warehouse. You can end up with the following types of zones (or cells, to make the parallel with line and layout design):

▲ Pallet-sized bins to store pallet loads (putting away and picking of pallets)
▲ Pallet-sized bins to store heavy and big single items
▲ Box-sized bins to store full cases (putting away and picking of pallets)
▲ Box-sized bins to store medium-sized single items
▲ Small-sized bins to store small single items

In this chapter I will assume that the warehouse whose flow we are working on is well profiled and well designed so that it is composed of many cells that have only a single location for put-away (also called *binning*) and picking and that the SKUs inside the cells are organized according to ABC turnover principles of high runners, medium runners, and low runners. These basic design parameters will guarantee many savings in terms of lead time and labor. Let's move to a more detailed analysis of the warehouse operations.

Flow Warehouse Operations

Figure 13.1 shows the logistics graph for a local DC that receives, stores, and ships single-item spare parts for cars. (Figure 13.2 shows the corresponding physical layout.) The diagram includes all the logistics units and how they are handled. The DC has an area of about 10,000 m² and stores 50,000 SKUs. It has two suppliers (two DCs) and serves 50 customers over a region of 120,000 m².

The first thing to notice in Figure 13.1 is the storage design—primary locations only. The logistics unit to be stored is the single item (units). There are three storage cells (three sub-warehouses inside the warehouse) for storing very big parts, medium-sized parts, and small parts. The storage principles used in the design of the warehouse include

▲ Product stored by type (the cells) and turnover (the turnover is single items)
▲ One product-specific storage location per part number (there are only primary locations)
▲ Storage of delivery packages (items are received individually packaged for selling)

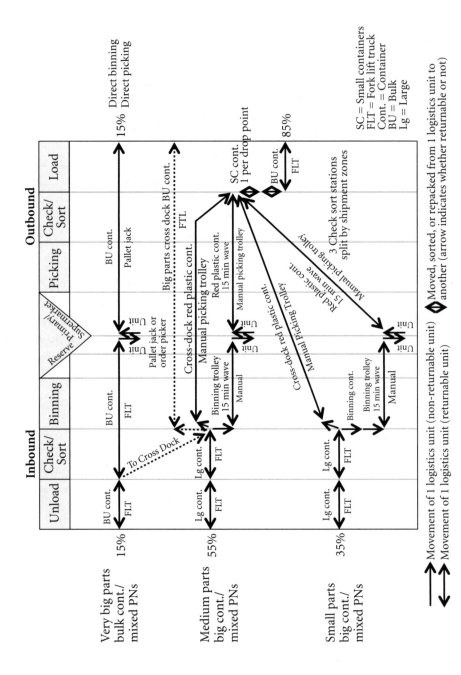

Figure 13.1 Logistics graph for a distribution warehouse.

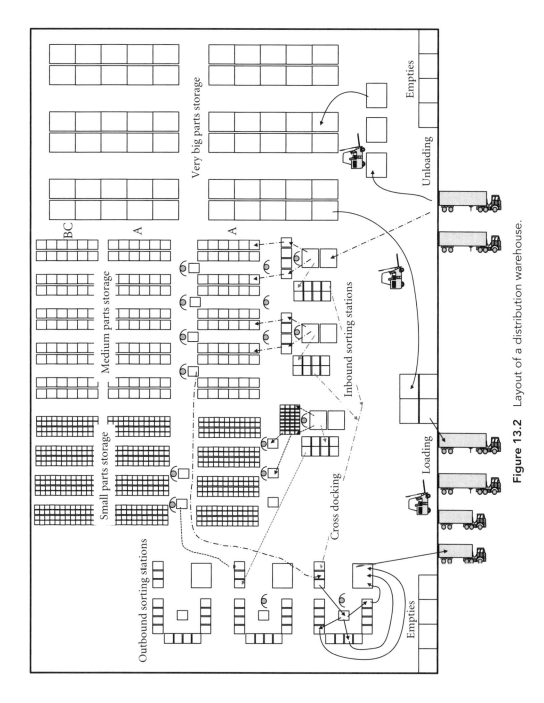

Figure 13.2 Layout of a distribution warehouse.

215

▲ Flexible layouts
▲ Visual management
▲ Control of abnormalities

Flow in Warehouse Cell 1: Large and Awkward Parts

This flow accounts for about 15 percent of the warehouse turnover (lines picked). The typical size of lines picked is very close to one item because of the size of these parts—they are bumpers, exhaust sets, or other big parts such as doors.

The flow sequence is as follows:

1. Unload bulk returnable containers (this includes checking whether there are some medium-sized parts inside and, if so, separating them out). Move containers directly to the cell entry point.
2. Single-part directed binning, first at ground level (using an electric pallet jack) and then at the upper levels (using a pallet order picker).
3. Single-order directed picking of the parts using the same equipment.
4. Loading bulk containers. This includes some arrangement of parts inside the containers to give good unit truck loads.

The picking work is scheduled in periods of 15 minutes by using a leveling box in which the orders are placed. Each slot is filled with orders that represent 15 minutes of picking work (according to the picking standard for the cell). A picking route for each order is displayed on the hand-held PC or paperless warehousing system.

There is also a dotted line in Figure 13.1. This shows that some units are moved directly from the incoming bulk containers to the sorting station for medium-sized parts. This is an initiative by the unloading worker, who knows that the probability of having orders for the high runners is high and so stores those items temporarily for possible cross-docking rather than binning and repicking. In many cases these units will move directly from the sorting station, be picked against customer orders, and then be moved to the loading and shipment area.

This type of flow also can be used in other warehouses that handle full pallets in and out of the warehouse.

This flow can be described as direct primary put-away with direct picking (and a little bit of cross-docking) and can be used in warehouses that handle full pallets using block stacking (single parts stored together in bulk) and a multi-load forklift.

Flow in Warehouse Cell 2: Medium-Sized Parts

This flow accounts for about 55 percent of the warehouse turnover (lines picked). The flow sequence is as follows:

1. Unload big containers (pallet-sized). Look inside and decide if the majority of parts are medium-sized.
2. Move big containers directly to the medium-sized inbound check and sorting cell.
3. Pick parts one by one, read with bar-code scanner, and sort to cross-dock containers and wave binning trolleys. Each wave binning trolley is loaded with a 15-minute workload (according to work standards for the cell). Move binning trolleys to the entry of the appropriate storage cell.
4. Fifteen-minute trolley-directed binning.
5. Fifteen-minute trolley-directed picking. Wave picking orders scheduled in a leveling box for each picker. Move trolleys and cross-dock containers to outbound check and sorting cell.
6. Sort picking batches to small returnable containers for shipping to the customer (there are three cells in Figure 13.2, organized by groups of customers). Put small containers inside bulk containers used for onward transportation.
7. Load bulk containers.

The inbound check/sort station does the sorting to the cross-dock of the large and awkward parts and medium-sized parts. This is done by cross-referencing the line-item information of the incoming lines with the open customer orders. The warehouse management system (WMS) instantly indicates to the cross-dock whether there is a matching line item against a customer order.

This warehouse receives its supplies from suppliers with a lead time of one week and ships products out on a daily basis. There is a good probability that one-fifth of the incoming parts have items that will be shipped on the same or the next day.

Doing away with the need to put away and then repick an item improves overall productivity because it avoids all binning, picking, and sorting.

This type of flow (single items in and out) also can be used for full cases in and out or full cases in and single items out. The inbound check and sorting station should redirect the full cases to the outbound area. The decision on whether to use wave binning would depend on the travel distances of the inbound products requiring put-away and the *muda* of the binning operator.

The configuration of the outbound check and sorting station would depend on what was the best picking strategy. The picking strategy is designed to save the picking operator travel time per line item. There are four possibilities:

1. Single-order picking (picking like a customer in a supermarket, sorting as you go)
2. Batch picking and then sorting into customer orders (picking like a customer in a supermarket who is buying for a group)

3. Progressive order assembly (picking parts of many orders and passing them to another picking cell for consolidation and sorting)

4. Wave picking (picking a group of many orders in a reduced zone) and then consolidating and sorting

The sorting station should be designed to save time and focus the operator on value-added time in sorting. The fact that it reduces the sorting costs makes wave picking a powerful solution. It is well documented that, on average, time spent in picking orders represents 50 percent of warehouse operating costs.

Flow in Warehouse Cell 3: Small Parts

The flow in this cell is quite similar to the flow in the second cell. This flow handles small parts. The only difference is that the inbound sorting is done to small containers, with dunning. The small containers are then loaded onto a manual trolley and taken to binning. This is a good way of eliminating binning errors and increasing binning productivity.

Elements of a Delivery Flow Strategy

A delivery flow strategy needs to be designed at the beginning of the journey of *kaizen* in logistics and supply chains. This will provide a clear picture of how to create flow in the delivery side of the supply chain.

> *Wave picking is the form of picking that saves the most time and also allows the best use of a leveling box to schedule the picking work in batches of 15 minutes.*

Let's take a manufacturing company that produces finished goods. On the delivery side, it interfaces with customers, and including them in the planning of the delivery flow strategy makes good sense. What you are in fact dealing with here is pull logistics loops that include the customer. When the company receives an order, the customer expects it to be delivered quickly. To achieve this, you will have to pick the required items (in their logistics units) and ship them through a milk run. The inward goods process also will have to be improved. In a manufacturing plant warehouse, a process link can be made with the internal *mizusumashi* to include the transport of goods in from the plant as part of their standard work.

The elements of a delivery flow strategy include

1. Incoming operations flow in the plant warehouse according to the internal transport system based on internal *mizusumashi* transportation

2. Vendor-managed inventory (VMI) replenishment of the finished-goods inventory (even if the finished-goods warehouse is located in a distant region) following logistics pull planning procedures

3. Filling of the orders, including picking, sorting, and shipping

4. A milk-run shipping strategy to deliver to customers at least daily

When starting a strategy to implement *kaizen* in logistics and supply chains in a stand-alone distribution warehouse that is not part of a network, you have to look at both ends of the supply chain and define both a source and a delivery strategy that fit the corresponding pull logistics loops. You should start by creating flow in the following areas:

▲ *Logistics pull planning*—sending orders to suppliers with daily deliveries. This will reduce the size of the inventory on hand.

▲ *External transportation*—redesigning the shipment routes according to the milk-run principle and increasing the frequency of shipment while encouraging customers to order on a daily basis. This may seem counterintuitive and a paradox, but it will help to level the picking workload. It also will help customers to reduce their own inventories.

▲ *Storage and warehouse design*—creating warehouse cells and optimized primary locations. The logistics pull planning processes will be used to define the optimal inventory level (OIL) for each SKU.

▲ *Outbound improvement*—organizing picking waves managed with a leveling box as well as checking and sorting stations. Standard work improvement is applied to all manual work.

▲ *Inbound improvement*—organizing checking and sorting stations for cross-docking and/or binning waves. Standard work improvement is applied to all manual work.

▲ *Involving employees and promoting daily* kaizen *activities*—including suggestion systems and *gemba kaizen* workshops.

Logistics Pull Planning

Logistics pull planning deals with the process of deciding when and how much of each product reference to order. This process starts with the final customer needs. The supply chain may have determined that the final product in the final loop of the chain is a stock product (made-to-order SKU) available for immediate delivery. In this case, the final customer just goes to a retail store and buys the product or, alternatively, orders the item and waits for delivery.

Goods Ready to Be Sold

The retailer will have to decide when and how much to order. This decision can be based on a logistics pull planning algorithm.

This supply chain may consist of a retailer, a regional distributor, a central distributor, a main plant, a first-tier supplier, a second-tier supplier, and so on. Each element of the supply chain will have to go through its own pull logistic loops.

This ordering process (also called *inventory management, inventory control,* or *stock replenishment*) is frequently plagued by the whiplash effect (this was discussed in Chapter 11). This is a feature of traditional systems—small changes in the final customer demand will generate demand increases in every loop of the chain. This is also called the *demand amplification effect.*

> The targets to achieve in inbound operations are related to the creation of flow and the increase in productivity in all the manual logistics tasks.

In Figure 13.3 you can see that the retailer bases its order on the expected final customer consumption and so, when deciding how much to buy, will amplify this final customer demand. The regional distributor will amplify these needs when ordering from the central distributor, and the central distributor will do likewise when ordering from the plant.

Why does this happen? There are many reasons for this phenomenon. Batching and the grouping of orders can play a big role in the process, as will the buyer's reaction to and interpretation of small changes in demand, which can result in a decision to over- or under-order.

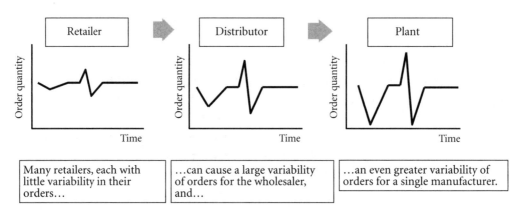

This is an amplification of demand, generated by the increase in the variability of orders as you go upstream in the supply chain

Figure 13.3 The whiplash effect.

The person deciding when and how much to order is often misled by the sales department, in the sense that variability in final customer demand can be created (or influenced) by marketing or sales policies.

Table 13.1 compares two situations in terms of the effect of marketing and sales actions—one in which demand fluctuates a lot (push-type demand, not leveled) and another in which demand is more stable, with less variation (leveled, pull-type demand).

> Monthly sales targets can create an artificial spike at the end of the month because the sales force will try to achieve these targets or the sales forecasts may be too optimistic and thus never be achieved.

It is not the purpose of this book to give a detailed explanation of this issue but just to point out that variation in demand also can be created by the way in which the internal action of the people and processes may influence sales and decisions on when and how much to order.

Table 13.1   The Effect of Marketing, Sales and Order Factors on Push and Pull Types of Demand

Area	Push-Type Demand, Not Leveled	Pull-Type Demand, Leveled
Sales behavior	Instability, with big variability (ups and downs)	Stability, with small variability Close to actual consumption
Sales strategy	Monthly targets Discounts for big orders (single orders) Promotions for the intermediate customer	Weekly targets Discounts for regular and increasing orders Promotions focused on the final customer
Sales forecasts	Unreliable information Optimistic and never achieved No consensus between production and logistics	Reliable information Realistic and achievable Consensus between production and logistics
Order processing	Processed in big batches Includes "noise" (created demand)	Processed in small to unit batches (information flow) No noise—only dealing with real demand, orders, or actual consumption replenishment
Sales force	Order "processor" Pushes the product Non-collaborative Disconnected from manufacturing and product development	Market researcher Sells according to real demand Long-term collaboration with other groups in the supply chain Connected and synchronized closely with manufacturing and product development

Artificial variation in demand can be reduced by focusing on better management of the information flow and reducing its lead time. This can be approached by

▲ Harmonizing plans and forecasts internally into one set of numbers so that all forecasts are prepared to fulfill the same plan

▲ Creating visibility and collaboration across the supply chain (An important goal is for each node to be aware of what is the real end-customer demand and what is the demand created by the supply chain.)

▲ Standardizing the replenishment process according to proven rules that counter the whiplash effect so that every planner follows the same proven standard procedure

▲ Reorganizing responsibilities in the replenishment process and applying (when appropriate) pull VMI systems, in which

   ▼ The customer provides the supplier with real-time data on inventory and demand

   ▼ The supplier takes responsibility for stock replenishment at the customer's site with agreed rules.

Logistics Pull Planning Steps

As you have seen in the internal logistics flow domain, production pull planning involves the following steps:

1. Defining the planning strategy for the product references
2. Planning the capacity on a medium- to long-term basis
3. Order planning—when and how much to order

For a pure pull logistics loop (one that does not involve production or manufacturing), such as ordering from one retail point to a regional warehouse or ordering from a regional warehouse to a central warehouse, the three steps of pull planning have some unique characteristics and are usually easier to implement than production pull planning.

The first step in defining the planning strategy is to decide which product references will be available for immediate delivery and which will have to be ordered.

The first step in defining the planning strategy is to decide which product references will be available for immediate delivery and which will have to be ordered. This tells the customers what they can have during the day (or the next day, depending on the distance) and what items will take longer to deliver (depending on the delivery time of the supplier).

It is also necessary to define the customer-service policy. In the example of the Toyota regional spare parts warehouse serving one region (a country in Europe), you have already seen the following service standards:

▲ Self-pickup (the customer can go to the warehouse to buy parts and immediately take them away)

▲ Same-day delivery (depending on the customer's location, orders received before a certain cutoff time will be delivered on the same day)

▲ Next-day delivery (for orders received after a certain time for a customer located more than a specific distance from the warehouse)

▲ Two days for consumables (the customer maintains an inventory and uses a standard replenishment algorithm to order a replenishment that will be delivered in two days)

In this example, the customer is a car dealer who also will have to set service standards to customers. Because the dealer can be served from the warehouse on the same day, the dealer can maintain a low level of inventory and a high level of service. If the business involves consumables, the customer will need to maintain an inventory that will be replenished every two days.

Planning the capacity of the logistics loop has to do with checking that the distribution warehouse suppliers and the transport network are prepared to handle a forecasted volume of orders.

Planning the capacity of the logistics loop has to do with checking that the distribution warehouse suppliers and the transport network are prepared to handle a forecasted volume of orders. This can be done on a monthly basis using capacity forecasts. The warehouse can send a rolling sales forecast to the suppliers every month, with an additional horizon of two months. Both parties agree that the supplier will have the necessary capacity to supply the anticipated volume under some limits of variation of real demand. The warehouse will agree to comply with the agreed limits. Order planning involves the process of deciding real orders to suppliers (also called *call-off* in the automotive industry).

Order Pull Planning

I have already talked about the traditional replenishment models that work on the basis of the stock reorder point. These can be used on a daily (or continuous) basis. Future stock is calculated by checking the available stock against customer orders on hand and supplier orders in process. As levels of this stock reach the point where it is necessary to reorder, an order is issued covering the lead time for replenishment. The reorder level is calculated on the basis of how much consumption is expected during this lead time.

This daily stock-review algorithm works well when the lead time for supply is short and is close to the stock-review period. For example, when the reorder level is reached, a replenishment order for one day of consumption will be issued and delivered the next day. An order can be issued every day to be delivered on the next day.

If the lead time for supply is greater than one day, the size (and frequency) of the order will depend on what it is. For example, if the supply lead time is five days, each time the reorder level is reached, you issue an order based on the forecasted demand for the next five days. Stock is reviewed daily, but the call-off and delivery will both be weekly.

To summarize, you will have a situation in which

▲ Supply lead time = 5 days
▲ Stock review = once a day
▲ Order size = 5 days (of forecasted demand)
▲ Customer call-off = once a week
▲ Supplier's frequency of shipment = once a week

This situation should be avoided, especially if the supply lead time is really long (e.g., more than 30 days, which happens with the transport of containers from Asia to Europe or America). The forecasting errors involved in ordering and receiving in this way will result in an increase in inventory and a drop in the service level.

Ordering can be done in another way:

▲ Supply lead time = 5 days
▲ Stock review = once a day
▲ Order size = 1 day (what was consumed the day before)
▲ Customer call-off = once a day
▲ Supplier's frequency of shipment = once a day

In this situation, the supplier is distant (it takes five days for the delivery to arrive) but still ships the orders on a daily basis. How the inventory responds can be seen in Figure 13.4.

The model in Figure 13.4 can be used for distances of around 2,000 km, which can be covered in approximately five days by truck. For greater distances and boat transport, where you have lead times of over one month, call-off and shipment can be weekly.

Even with long supply lead times, it is of the utmost importance to order and have the order shipped in a high frequency by the supplier (e.g., daily).

In the Toyota regional warehouse example, you can find a very good example of logistics pull planning. This warehouse is located in a European country (in fact, there are several warehouses in Europe) and receives 25 percent of its goods directly from Japan and 75 percent from the central warehouse in Brussels.

The inventory is managed by the information system. The inventory is monitored on a real-time basis. Every time stock is shipped to a customer, the reorder level is checked. This is a pull-flow model adapted for long-distance supplies.

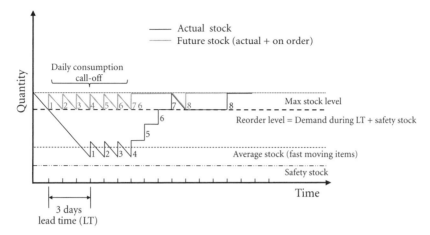

Figure 13.4   Pull planning model.

Customer:
- Checks stock daily (or in real time)
- Orders daily (daily call-of) if future stock is equal to or less than the reorder level

Supplier:
- Ships daily
- Order processing plus shipment equals 3 days (LT)

The reorder level is represented here as fixed. In the model it varies according to a daily rolling demand forecast, with safety stock adjustments when necessary

Fast-moving SKUs (with regular daily consumption) will have an average stock level close to the safety stock plus ½ of the shipment frequency stock equivalent

The shipment frequency is once a day by truck from the central warehouse in Brussels and once a week by boat from Japan. The delivery lead time is 6 days from the central warehouse and 52 days from Japan. The average inventory in the warehouse is 33 days. Urgent orders are delivered by plane. The parts that come directly from Japan are the fast movers (or high runners).

The reorder level is called the *optimal inventory level* (OIP). This level is variable and depends on a forecast method based on rolling demand, which takes into account the lead time and the safety stock. This level is also used to plan the necessary storage capacity in the warehouse.

When the stock reaches the reorder level, this automatically generates an order to suppliers, which is equal to the amount just consumed. Toyota calls this the "sell-one, buy-one system."

The logistics pull planning process is done automatically by the information system. The manual inventory planning tasks of the warehouse are limited to some special cases related to anticipated and infrequent customer orders. This system ensures a good flow of materials and a more functional inventory (lower stock level and higher service).

PART THREE

How to Implement *Kaizen* in Logistics and Supply Chains

CHAPTER 14

Facing the Truth: Analyzing the Current State of the Supply Chain

Now that I have discussed all the important concepts of the Total Flow Management (TFM) pull-flow model—the theory—it is time to go to the *gemba*, the reality of the shop floor, to look at the truth of what is actually happening in the supply chain. Facing the truth means that you look at how the current status of your supply chain compares with the concepts covered in the last several chapters.

In any supply chain, the initiative for a supply-chain design (SCD) process should come from at least one of the companies involved. A supply chain may involve many companies belonging to the same corporation. The main manufacturing company should be the leading company in initiating a Total Flow project and should first involve the companies closest to it on both the delivery and source sides of the supply chain. The *muda* elimination wave generated at this center then will progress to each side of the supply chain. The distribution company closest to the manu-

> *Facing the truth about the flow or lack of it in the supply chain is the first step in starting a change process. It is the first part of supply-chain design (SCD).*

facturing company then should develop its own SCD and involve its own delivery side (the source side will already have been tackled by the preceding initiative).

The design initiative for the source side of the manufacturing company's supply chain would work in the same way—applying the Total Flow model internally and in the company's source, as well as involving its suppliers. Eventually, all parts of the supply chain will be involved in the process and reap the benefits of *kaizen* in logistics and supply chains. The goal in involving people in this way is to create awareness of the opportunities for flow improvement.

Value-stream mapping (VSM) was first described and popularized in *Learning to See: Value-Stream Mapping to Create Value and Eliminate Muda* (Lean Enterprise Institute, 1999)

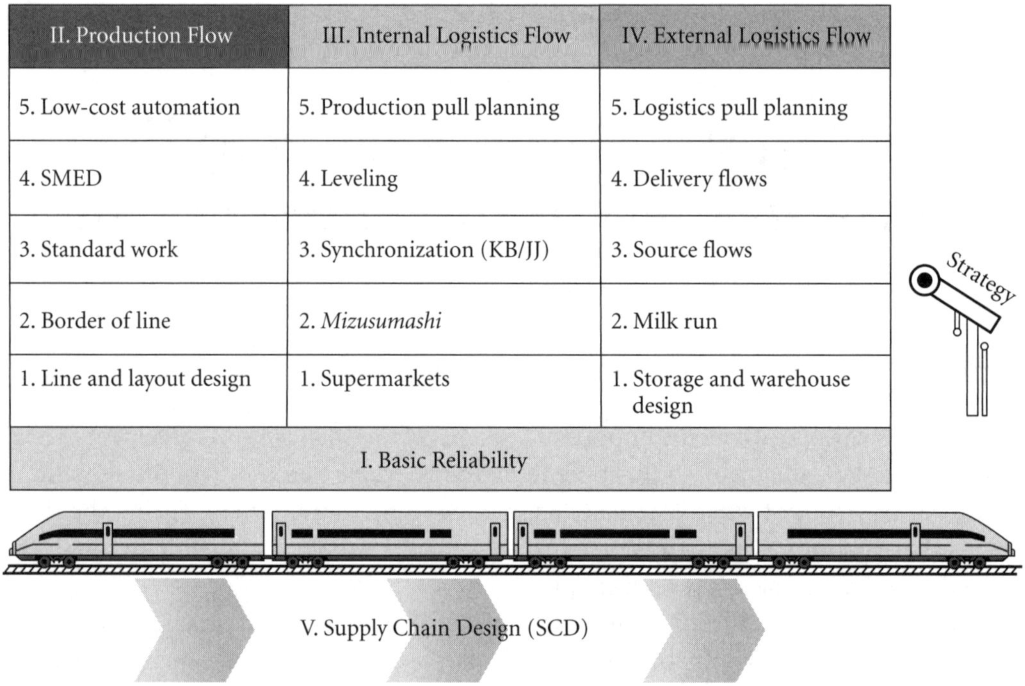

II. Production Flow	III. Internal Logistics Flow	IV. External Logistics Flow
5. Low-cost automation	5. Production pull planning	5. Logistics pull planning
4. SMED	4. Leveling	4. Delivery flows
3. Standard work	3. Synchronization (KB/JJ)	3. Source flows
2. Border of line	2. *Mizusumashi*	2. Milk run
1. Line and layout design	1. Supermarkets	1. Storage and warehouse design
I. Basic Reliability		

V. Supply Chain Design (SCD)

Figure 14.1 The Total Flow Management (TFM) model.

by Mike Rother, John Shook, James Womack, and Dan Jones. The SCD process for every loop of the chain consists of the following steps:

1. *Value-stream mapping*—analysis of current state
2. *Value-stream design*—creating a vision or map of the future state
3. *An action plan*—taking action to change the supply chain

The scope of SCD is the complete supply chain, but it needs to be tackled in incremental steps of value-stream design tasks. The project should begin with a manufacturing company, possibly a product family inside this company. Several value-stream design projects then should extend the SCD process to both the source and delivery sides of the supply chain.

Building Teams and Setting Challenges

The *kaizen* approach is to start with a value-stream design (VSD) exercise by building a team to work on the analysis, design, and action plan. It is a project team given the challenge of redesigning the flow according to the principles of *kaizen* in logistics and supply chains. The focus team for this job should be made up of people from the main departments involved:

▲ *Production.* The leader of the department and the leaders of the sections involved in the value stream.
▲ *Logistics.* As for production.
▲ *Production planning.* The person responsible for this function should be present (it may be someone who reports to the head of production or logistics).
▲ *Maintenance.* The need for reliability means that a large number of the people in this area need to be involved.
▲ *Engineering.* As above. Improving line and layout process design will be a major task.
▲ *Source.* Someone who deals with the suppliers. Purchasing probably will need to be involved.
▲ *Delivery.* Someone who deals with the customers. Sales probably will need to be involved.

When a company wishes to improve its supply chain design, the technique of value-stream mapping (VSM) is used to help people working in various departments to identify and analyze the current state of material and information flow in a visual and participative way.

A total of 7 to 10 people is the right number for this exercise. The team will have to be guided by an experienced value stream designer, someone who has mastered all the concepts covered in this book. This facilitator will conduct an initial training exercise based on simulation games and will guide the team in the tasks team members need to complete.

In some cases, the CEO may be able to delegate this function to a vice president, but the sponsor should be someone who has real influence with the people involved in the exercise. The sponsor should be there at the beginning of the project to challenge the team to create a flow in the supply chain by applying the new aradigm of logistics and supply chain excellence. Maybe in Ohno's words, "All we need to do is look at the time line from customer order to cash collection. . . . And we need to reduce that time line by removing the non-value-added wastes." The sponsor also should come in at the end of team meetings to be briefed on the work being done and should give top priority to the final presentation of the project report.

A key person in the whole exercise is the project sponsor. The sponsor should be a senior manager responsible for manufacturing and logistics, ideally the CEO of the company.

With one or two days of preparation beforehand, a VSD workshop can be completed in two intensive weeks under the guidance of an experienced designer. At the end of each intensive week, team members will present the work they have done. After the workshop, some follow-up will be needed, with a few days of fine tuning, to finish the project and discuss all the implementation details.

Preparing the Current-State Analysis

Start the preparation activities with a *gemba* walk in the chosen supply chain. If the site is a manufacturing one, it must be divided into value streams that make the product families. An initial analysis of pull logistics loops will have to be performed. At this stage, there won't be any, or none that are identified as such, so the first step is actually one of establishing where and how such loops should exist. Some manufacturing facilities can have many logistics loops. Their initial VSD exercise will need to be limited to a feasible number of loops. The nature of the logistics loops and the value-stream families will define the scope of the SCD.

Let's clarify this by looking at some examples. If you are dealing with a car assembly plant, the scope should be the main assembly line. But this line is huge, so the initial project should focus on a section of it—perhaps the section dealing with interior trimming would be a good place to start. All the inbound logistics of the source side for this section should be included in the project. The delivery side, including delivery of the finished product, stems from the logistics loop and so could be left to another project because it involves complex logistics and other, customer-related processes. Thus, in this case, the scope of the initial SCD should be a section of the line together with its supply logistics.

If the preparation work is to profile the operation accurately, the right data are needed. One essential piece of information is a list of the finished goods (by part reference), giving the quantity delivered and how much is held as inventory over a substantial amount of time (one year). A layout drawing is also necessary, along with other information regarding the operations. During the preparation stage, the designer will assess what is needed in order to optimize the work flow during the intensive week. The most important aspects of the preparation stage are

▲ Looking at the product and understanding the bill of materials and the manufacturing processes
▲ Taking a *gemba* walk and understanding the potential pull logistics loops
▲ Choosing the logistics loops to be mapped
▲ Getting some basic information about the logistics loops (e.g., a part quantity analysis, layout drawings, and any other information needed to clarify the previous points)
▲ Choosing the project team

If the company leaders and top management are not involved—moreover, if they do not fully understand the process—then the issues arising during the project will not be addressed, and the project will not be successful. As you saw when you first looked at paradigms and paradigm change, everyone complains when they have to change a habit. This is an unconscious process—it is the brain complaining that current neural connections are being destroyed and that it is experiencing the stress of new ones being formed. To build something new, you have to forget the old. This process must start with the company leadership.

In choosing the project team, it is very important that the real decision makers in the company are involved in the process. The Total Flow Management model underpinning successful kaizen in logistics and supply chains is a big paradigm change.

Mapping the Current State of the Material Flow

The intensive VSM work starts with drawing the current-state map (see Figure 14.3) and having a good look at the *gemba*. The members of the project team are given a brief explanation of the VSM method, the data sheets used to record the value stream, and the icons used in the mapping process. The mapping groups then are organized. One person will record the steps in the process, and others will find the relevant information (mainly by counting material waiting as they go through the process that has been selected for VSM analysis). The operations that are part of the process are recorded on a *process analysis sheet* (shown in Figure 14.2).

The meaning of the icons is as follows:

○ A value-adding operation (Be aware that this is a strategic map, so the level of detail is limited. If a production line or cell already has flow, that whole line will be represented by a circle.)

▽ Material waiting

◇ Quality control or any type of checking

⤵ Transport or movement (All logistics operations are movements or arrows; this means that a VSM in a warehouse will be made of arrows and no circles.)

This exercise may take two to four hours. Then team members will go back to the project room and draw the current-state map on a large sheet of paper on the wall, adding the appropriate icons.

It is not the purpose of this book to describe the VSM exercise in detail (a number of good books are available on this subject, such as *Learning to See*) but to point to the important details that can determine the quality and usefulness of the exercise. The drawing

Page:										◯ Processing (added value)
Area		Process leader								Transportation ⇨
Process		Analyst								◇ Inspection
Takt time		Date								Stock ▽

Item	Description	Icon				Data				Notes
		◯	⇨	◇	▽	Time	Quantity	Distance	Area	
	Total									

Figure 14.2 Process analysis sheet.

of the map should start with the main line or pacemaker process. In many cases it is better to draw a sketch of the main machine or line in the middle of the blank sheet (this is better than just putting a circle because it increases the vision and creativity of team members). The process continues in this way, with the map of the material and information flows drawn from the facts and observations recorded during the *gemba* walk.

The team starts the exercise by following the process flow, starting at the end of the process and walking upstream in the chosen logistics loops.

At this point, you are only recording the basic flow. When this task has been completed, you can add in the main data (the quantities of material waiting and other relevant data, with data boxes below each operation), but be careful not to overload the map with information. Use only the most important. This type of mapping can be extremely useful in giving a clear vision of the flow and its main accumulation points.

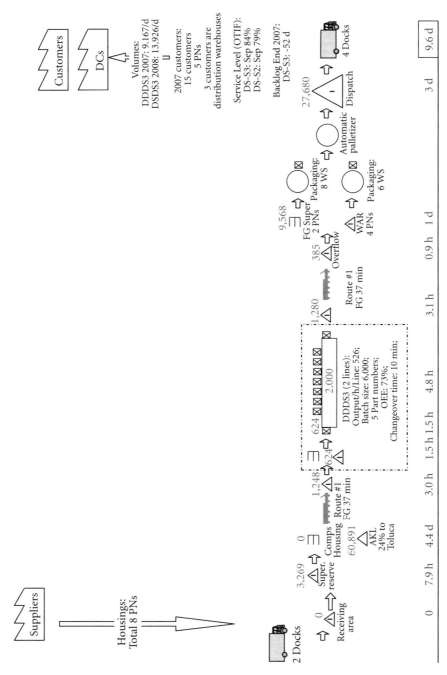

Figure 14.3 An example of a current-state map of the material flow.

235

Mapping the Current State of the Information Flow

Next, you need to map the information flow. To do this, you start with the customer forecasts and orders and map the process of transforming the customer information into production or logistics orders sent to the *gemba* to initiate the movement of materials. This mapping is more difficult because it is not physically visible in the *gemba* (like the material flow) and because it involves many different parts of the organization. A useful technique is to make a preliminary analysis using the following mapping technique.

An important tool at this time, and one that complements the material-flow maps, is the information-flow map. This is easily done by drawing the layout and marking the flows, creating what is also known as a spaghetti diagram.

In an information-flow map (Figure 14.4), the people or functions involved (the "who") are listed vertically. The operations, steps, or processing information (the "does

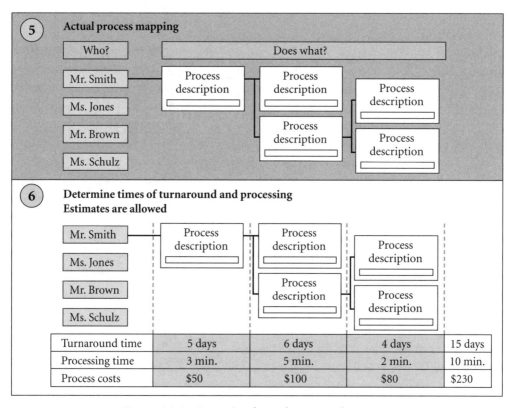

Figure 14.4 Example of an information-flow map.

what") is placed after their names of the people horizontally. This map also computes the lead time of each operation and the total lead time of the entire process.

A summary of the information for this map can be prepared and transferred to the main map. On the main map, the information flow is represented from left to right. Take care not to end up with a very complex map that nobody understands except the information technology (IT) specialist! The level of detail should be "big picture"—the intention here is to show the main steps and their outputs.

The information-flow map should show clearly the capacity-planning process—the steps used to check, discuss, and decide on capacity issues (e.g., using forecasts and having a monthly meeting to discuss alignment between capacity and forecasted load). It also should show the order-execution process (from customer information to production and supplier orders).

Once the current-state map has all the important data on it (and some important key performance indicators as well—e.g., defect rates and changeover times), it is complete. The most important types of data are

▲ Customer demand data (These are necessary to calculate the *takt* time.)
▲ Material waiting quantities (checked on the *gemba*)
▲ Customer-service-level data (on-time delivery data)
▲ Operations data:
  ▼ Machine overall efficiency of key equipment (with a Pareto diagram detailing losses for the main machines)
  ▼ Manpower efficiency (if possible, also with a Pareto diagram detailing losses)
  ▼ Machine changeover times
  ▼ Machine or operation opening (or working) times

If there are no data on efficiency and changeovers, some additional time will have to be spent collecting this information on the *gemba*. This should be done by organizing data observation teams to go to the *gemba* and observe the operations for at least two hours, validating their observations by talking to the operators. The result of this exercise will be an estimate of efficiency and changeover times, as well as the main causes for loss of efficiency.

You may need to do the same thing to collect data on customer service. To understand what's happening on the *gemba*, go to the sales office and talk to the salespeople.

Understanding the Current-State Process

Waste Observation and Awareness Exercises

You can now use the current-state map for the last step—that is, achieving a full understanding of what is happening along the value-stream flow and what the key issues are.

The purpose of the VSM exercise is to interpret what is going on and to create a common understanding for stakeholders. The information on the map is used to calculate the total lead time, as well as the value-added time. Calculating the value-added time usually generates a lot of discussion. It is not worth spending too much time on this—a rough estimate will be fine. Just consider the total value-added operations time for each of the units. These times may include some *muda*, but compared with the total lead time, the size of this time is minimal. This is why I say that a simple estimate will do, because the total lead time will be far bigger than the worst estimate you may arrive at. There will be huge quantities of material waiting all through the flow.

The value-added time can be an estimate of the sum of the unloading, binning, picking, and loading operations.

For a warehouse map, this calculation may be more difficult. The value-added time can be an estimate of the sum of the unloading, binning, picking, and loading operations. Just consider these tasks because they are the ones that are necessary to fulfill the logistics function in the supply chain (to make goods available to users all over the globe).

The final current-state map will look like the map in Figure 14.5, which is the map from Figure 14.3 with all the information now added.

The next steps will be to provide basic training for the operators and supervision in all the TFM pillars and to fill out the TFM scorecards.

Kaizen Reliability Training and Scorecard Audit

The typical training for *kaizen* in logistics and supply chains consists of a quick explanation of the main *kaizen* concepts in each TFM pillar followed by a simulation game that shows how these concepts work in a physical environment. There is a simulation game for each pillar. After this, the participants are invited to fill in the TFM scorecards. These scorecards present a number of questions that evaluate how the concepts have been applied and developed for the logistics loops being analyzed. It is a kind of audit performed by the people taking part in this evaluation of the current state of the supply chain.

Training Step 1: Basic Reliability

The first pillar to present in the training is that of basic reliability (discussed in Chapter 4). The five domains of this pillar are

▲ *Kaizen* foundations
▲ Manpower reliability

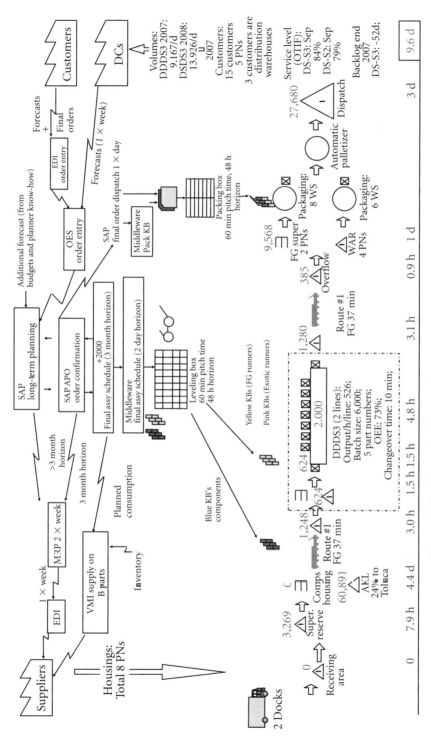

Figure 14.5 Example of a complete current-state value-stream map.

▲ Machine reliability
▲ Materials reliability
▲ Methods reliability

The simulation games used for training in this pillar are the *5S Game* and the *R Game*. For the 5S Game, you use two briefcases containing Lego parts inside. Each briefcase has all the parts needed to assemble a small house. You ask two participants to play the game, each of whom is given a briefcase. The participants are told that they have to assemble the house with one hand, but it must be their non-preferred hand (the left hand for those who are right-handed, and vice versa). You let them get ready and then time the exercise until the house is completely finished. The winner always gets the 5S briefcase.

The R Game consists of 10 cardboard pieces that can be used to assemble a big letter *R* (like a jigsaw puzzle). The participants are divided into several teams of two or three people and are asked to assemble the *R* in 15 minutes. It is very rare for a team to finish the game in 15 minutes. It is quite difficult to assemble the *R* without any instructions, although the task appears to be simple because the parts are big and there are only 10 of them. Then you get the teams to do it again, this time giving them a standard (a shadow board). This time the results are a bit better. You go through the game twice more, with better standards (better shadow boards). Finally, you challenge the teams to put the *R* together in one second. They can do this by using single-minute exchange of dies (SMED) principles (everybody holds two or three pieces above the right place and just drops the pieces). This game is useful to show the power of visual standards.

After team members have been introduced to the concept of basic reliability and have played the games, they proceed to fill in the scorecards. Figures 14.6 and 14.7 show the scorecards used for the five domains. There are seven items to be evaluated in each domain. Each scorecard applies to one specific pull logistics loop that has already been mapped. The scorecards can be used by small teams to review each domain or to review one logistics loop. From the scorecards, you can then calculate the basic reliability score and make a top-five list of the main issues that need to be addressed. The complete set of scorecards for this pillar can be found in Appendix D.

Training Step 2: Production Flow

The second pillar in the order of training is production flow (discussed in Chapters 5 through 7). The five domains of this pillar are

▲ Line and layout design
▲ Border of line
▲ Standard work

I. Basic Reliability – *Kaizen* Foundations

No.	*Kaizen* Foundations	How to Score	Comments	Score
I.1.1	Quality first	Check degree of belief/commitment of key leadership. Ask if they believe in bring market in, next operation is customer, upstream management. Ask what have they done to implement it or what they intend to do.		
I.1.2	Focused teamwork	Check degree of belief of key leadership. Ask if they believe in involving people, don't judge/don't blame, *kobetsu* teamwork. Ask what have they done to implement it or what they intend to do.		
I.1.3	Process and results	Check degree of belief of key leadership. Ask if they believe in focus on process improvement through SDCA and PDCA. Ask what have they done to implement it or what they intend to do.		
I.1.4	*Gemba* orientation	Check degree of belief of key leadership. Ask if they believe in go tc *gemba*, check *gembutsu*, speaking with data. Ask what have they done to promote it or what they intend to do.		
I.1.5	*Muda* elimination	Check degree of belief of key leadership. Ask if they believe in eliminate 3 Ms, 7 flow *mudas*, 8 equipment losses, other *mudas*. Ask what have they done to promote it or what they intend to do.		
I.1.6	Visual standards	Check degree of belief of key leadership. Ask if they believe in develop standard work, visual management, standard management. Ask what have they done to implement it or what they intend to do.		
I.1.7	Pull flow thinking	Check degree of belief of key leadership. Ask if they believe in create material and information flow, pull from market. Ask what have they done to implement it or what they intend to do. Make the evaluation on the basis of the answers.		

Company: _____
Analyst: _____

Logistic Loop: _____
Date: _____

Avg Score: _____

na: not applicable
0: very insufficient
1: insufficient
2: sufficient
3: good
4: very good

Figure 14.6 Sample basic reliability scorecard.

I. Basic Reliability—Summary

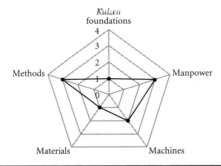

No.	Basic Reliability – Top 5 Issues
1	
2	
3	
4	
5	

Figure 14.7 Sample summary basic reliability page of the scorecard.

▲ SMED
▲ Low-cost automation

The simulation game used here is the *Plug Game*. In this game, teams of participants design a one-piece-flow line using an electrical plug. The assembly work content of the game is 90 seconds and 10 operations. The participants are invited to do the following exercises:

▲ Draw the process graph.
▲ Create a functional layout.
▲ Design a one-piece-flow line.
▲ Simulate an actual one-piece-flow line.

This is a rather good game because all the production-flow concepts can be shown and tried out by the participants.

The team then fills in the scorecards (Figures 14.8 and 14.9). Each domain has seven items to be evaluated. Each scorecard applies to one specific pull logistics loop that has

II. Production Flow – Line and Layout Design

No.	Line and Layout Design	How to Score	Comments	Score
II.1.1	Process layout	Degree of operations integration into assembly cells or lines that include all the necesary operations.		
II.1.2	Material flow inside cells or line	Degree of one-piece flow implementation.		
II.1.3	Low-speed cells/ lines	Degree of speed measured by cell/line cycle time. Few large, high-speed versus several low-speed cells/lines.		
II.1.4	Daisy line layout design	Degree of separation between manual work and machine automated work. Degree of non-isolated manpower. Degree of daisy layout design.		
II.1.5	*Shojinka* level	Operators' degree of multi-skills, handling multi-operations.		
II.1.6	*Mura* line balancing	Degree of line balancing according to the line cycle. Degree of variation of work cycle between different product references.		
II.1.7	*Gemba* workstation design	Degree of *muda* elimination principles applied during line design. Degree of *gemba* checking using cardboard engineering.		

Company: _____ Logistic Loop: _____

Analyst: _____ Date: _____ Avg Score: _____

na: not applicable
0: very insufficient
1: insufficient
2: sufficient
3: good
4: very good

Figure 14.8 Sample production-flow scorecard.

243

II. Production Flow—Summary

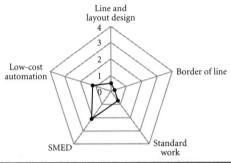

No.	Production Flow – Top 5 Issues
1	
2	
3	
4	
5	

Figure 14.9 Sample production-flow summary scorecard.

already been mapped. You can ask small teams to review each domain or to review a single logistics loop. From the scorecards, team members calculate the production-flow score and make a top-five list of the main issues to be addressed. The complete set of scorecards for this pillar can be found in Appendix D.

Training Step 3: Internal Logistics

The third pillar in the order of training is that of internal logistics flow (covered in Chapters 8 through 10). The five domains of this pillar are

▲ Supermarkets
▲ *Mizusumashi* system
▲ Synchronization (*kanban* or *junjo*)
▲ Leveling
▲ Production pull planning

The simulation game used here is the *Pull-Plug Game*. This builds on the previous one-piece-flow game, from which you already have one assembly line that has been designed and tried out. Now you add all the necessary internal logistics: supermarkets for the parts, finished-goods stores, transportation and planning, and a scheduling system. The participants are invited to

1. Calculate the *takt* time.
2. Draw up the *standard work sheet* (SWS) for the assembly line.
3. Using the SWS, prepare the assembly line for simulation.
4. Draw the future VSM (pick from stock and make to stock).
5. Draw the physical layout that reflects the future map.
6. Create the water spider operation list and standard work sheet.
7. Prepare the logistics system in the classroom, and develop the route and equipment used by the water spider (in other words, prepare the *gemba* for the simulation).
8. Program the leveling box according to level 5 of leveling.
9. Simulate the pull-flow logistics system for 15 minutes (not forgetting to pace the *mizusumashi* cycle).

Most of the concepts in internal logistics flow can be shown to and tried by the participants.

The team then fills out the scorecards. Figures 14.10 and 14.11 show the scorecards used for the five domains of internal logistics. There are seven items to be evaluated in each domain. Each scorecard applies to one specific pull logistics loop that has already been mapped. You can ask small teams to review each domain or to review one loop. At the end of the exercise, team members calculate the internal logistics score and make a top-five list of the main issues to be addressed. The complete set of scorecards for this pillar can be found in Appendix D.

Training Step 4: External Logistics

The fourth pillar is that of external logistics flow (covered in Chapters 11 through 13). The five domains of this pillar are

- Storage and warehouse design
- Milk run
- Source flows
- Delivery flows
- Logistics pull planning

III. Internal Logistics Flow – Supermarkets

No.	Supermarkets	How to Score	Comments	Score
III.1.1	Flow racks	Degree of implementation. For small containers or pallets of small containers.		
III.1.2	Ground storage on wheels	Ground storage on wheels for trolleys or rollers. Degree of implementation of trolleys or rollers.		
III.1.3	Ease of picking and supply	Degree of ease in picking or supplying the supermarkets. Check organization according to consumption and other relevant criteria.		
III.1.4	Bought components supermarkets	Degree of implementation of number of bought components ready to supply to the cells/lines. Check PFEP (plan for every part).		
III.1.5	Border of line supermarkets	Degree of separation between supply path and consumption path. General organization of border of line supermarkets.		
III.1.6	Finished product supermarkets	Degree of implementation of finished product supermarkets. Check the applicability of logistic cells or end of line supermarkets.		
III.1.7	Visual management of supermarkets	Degree of visual management and 5S of supermarkets.		

na: not applicable
0: very insufficient
1: insufficient
2: sufficient
3: good
4: very good

Company: _____
Analyst: _____

Logistic Loop: _____
Date: _____

Avg Score: _____

Figure 14.10 Sample internal logistics flow scorecard.

III. Internal Logistics Flow—Summary

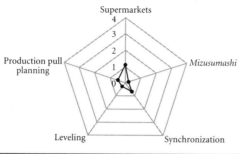

No.	Internal Logistics Flows – Top 5 Issues
1	
2	
3	
4	
5	

Figure 14.11   Sample internal logistics flow summary scorecard.

The simulation game used for the training of this pillar is the *Beer Game*. This game demonstrates the whiplash effect that takes place in traditional supply chains and consists of the amplification of demand from the final customer to the last supplier through the several elements of the supply chain. The game demonstrates that standard pull planning procedures and leveling are the keys to stable supply chains. The participants are invited to simulate

▲   A supply chain that consists of a finished goods warehouse, a main distribution center, a regional distribution center, and a local distribution center (the final customer buys from the local distribution center). There are no rules for this game; the participants must rely on common sense.

▲   The same supply chain, but this time using some pull planning rules.

▲   This game allows the participants to try out the very important concepts of pull planning.

▲   Team members then fill in the scorecards (Figures 14.12 and 14.13). There are seven items that need to be evaluated for each domain. You can ask small teams to review each domain.

IV. External Logistics Flows – Storage and Warehouse Design

No.	Storage and Warehouse Design	How to Score	Comments	Score
IV.1.1	Storage profiling	Degree of clear operations profiling studies that justify the layout of storage and layout (example: PQ analysis or product family analysis).		
IV.1.2	Product stored by type and turnover (storage cells)	Degree of cell layout implementation according to storage profiling. Example 1: Layout divided by customer logistic cells. Example 2: Layout divided by high runners, medium runners, and low runners.		
IV.1.3	One product-specific storage location per part number	Degree of existence of 1 primary location only for each SKU. Degree of space utilization for each location.		
IV.1.4	Storage of delivery packages	Degree of no repacking of individual SKUs.		
IV.1.5	Flexible layouts	Degree of separation of inbound and outbound operations (via different working timetables or different alleys). Existence of machine capacity for binning and picking.		
IV.1.6	Visual management	Degree of visual management standards in the warehouse (identification of location addresses and other visual standards).		
IV.1.7	Abnormalities control	Degree of daily measurement and control of abnormal situations (such as missing products, wrong quantities, wrong locations, wrong packaging, wrong identification).		

Company: _____
Analyst: _____

Logistic Loop: _____
Date: _____   Avg Score: _____

na: not applicable
0: very insufficient
1: insufficient
2: sufficient
3: good
4: very good

Figure 14.12 Sample external logistics flows scorecard.

IV. External Logistics Flows—Summary

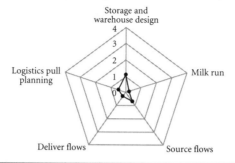

No.	External Logistics Flow – Top 5 Issues
1	
2	
3	
4	
5	

Figure 14.13 Sample external logistics flows summary scorecard.

At the end of the exercise, team members calculate the external logistics scores for both the source side and the delivery side of the supply chain and make a top-five list of the main issues to be addressed for each side. The complete set of scorecards for this pillar can be found in Appendix D.

Defining the Main KPIs of the Current State

At this point of the exercise, the team will have a full understanding of the current situation and how far they are from (or close to) the new paradigm of *kaizen* pull flow, the TFM model. I call this *facing the truth*, and it is only possible by going to the *gemba*, drawing up the map of the current state, and doing the simulations to really understand the paradoxical elements of the TFM model. Without going through this process, the team will not see, understand, or feel what the trainer is talking about. Learning to see can only be achieved through experience (at this point, through the simulations).

Everyone will now also be aware of the main KPIs of the supply chain, which are

- ▲ The total lead time (and inventory)
- ▲ The service levels (for the several logistics loops)
- ▲ Efficiency and quality

When the team has reached agreement about the current situation, the facing-the-truth process is complete. The team then can proceed to the next step—to establish the vision and design based on applying principles of *kaizen* in logistics and supply chains.

CHAPTER 15

Establishing the Vision: Designing the *Kaizen* Pull-Flow Supply Chain

Now that you have completed the value-stream map showing the current state of the supply chain and understand how the supply chain works, you can begin putting together the value stream map of the future state—the state you intend to implement. This is called *establishing the vision of kaizen in logistics and supply chains.*

You have reached the point where it's time to be creative and innovative. You need to use your awareness of the current situation and the concepts you have assimilated to design the new pull-flow supply chain, creating flow in the points of the chain that have the most *muda* of material waiting. You also need to increase the overall levels of productivity, quality, and service. You can now start to develop the vision.

You do this by drawing a value-stream map of the future state, a layout-vision map (to complement the future state map), an implementation plan, and a cost-benefit analysis. Together these elements make up a complete business case for implementation of *kaizen* in logistics and supply chains.

Beginning the Value-Stream Future Map: Creating Production Flow

The first steps in creating a value-stream future map involve the design of production flow:

1. Starting with a blank sheet, the project team begins with line and layout design. The goal is to create as much one-piece flow as possible by integrating all the operations in the assembly or production lines. By designing one-piece flow lines, you are radically simplifying and streamlining the production process. The first step is to look at the

pacemaker process (which defines the capacity of the logistics loop and usually starts the production schedules) to see what other operations, downstream or upstream, you can integrate into it.

2. Next, the team needs to look at the border of line. Where are the parts located? What types of containers are they kept in? How is the number of options for the same type of part handled?

3. In terms of border of line, you start by considering the number of *kanban* supermarkets you can have in the border of line (by checking the available space) and the feasibility of locating the containers in these supermarkets within hand's reach of operators.

4. You know that a production line with all the parts in *kanban* supermarkets in the border of line is the best solution because it allows free scheduling of the line without having to check or pick components located elsewhere. Limitations of space often prevent this. The alternative is to design *junjo* supply areas in the border of line so that the parts and options are supplied in the sequence of assembly or production. You look at the required parts and make two groups, one with *kanban*-supplied parts and the other with *junjo*-supplied parts. The *junjo*-supplied parts will have an entry point in the line that is as close as possible to the hand's reach of workers (frontal supply, if possible).

5. Next, you look at standard work. The exact form this takes will depend a lot on the solutions to one-piece-flow integration in the border of line. You also must consider *shojinka* (the concept of having all workers in the same area free of obstacles—also called *daisy-line design*). If the operators in the current lines work in separated islands, this needs to be changed by redesigning and rebalancing the lines.

6. The next step is to check the single-minute exchange of dies (SMED) or flexibility of the line—its ability to handle variety and product changeovers. The ideal solution is zero setup. This will help the flow tremendously because you will not be obliged to work with a batch, and you can level the schedule to please the customer, smooth the demand to suppliers, and work with a fixed crew on the line.

7. Here you may find a situation of fast cycle times and high levels of automation. This is the worst situation if changeover time is also high. One possibility worth exploring is to divide the line in two, three, or even four lines. If you have one line that has a cycle time of 10 seconds, then you can split it into two lines with a cycle time of 20 seconds or even three lines with a cycle time of 30 seconds. This could be a feasible way of dedicating lines to product families and balancing the operations better (the losses created by line balancing diminish with the increase in cycle time). You could have all operators working in the same area with a very good level of standard work (which means less *muda* and higher productivity).

8. In some situations, the level of available technology or the extremely high capital expenditure already committed will make it impossible to integrate operations in this

way and divide the lines in two. Then the only solution will be to optimize the border of line, make improvements in the standard work, and reduce changeover time. A high changeover time means many losses in line efficiency, and reducing it should be the main target. Such a reduction plan will have a huge impact on internal logistics (leveling and production pull planning).

9. Finally, you should look at the opportunities for improving productivity through low-cost automation.

The purpose of creating production flow is to have fully integrated one-piece flow operations with high worker productivity and high flexibility in changeovers. In practice, it is very rare to find such lines or machines. Usually you find manual lines with low worker productivity and fast changeover times or automatic lines with high worker productivity and high changeover times. Searching for ways to apply the five domains of production flow will lead to the optimal solution in terms of productivity and flexibility so that you can introduce effective internal logistics.

> The purpose of creating production flow is to have fully integrated one-piece flow operations with high worker productivity and high flexibility in changeovers.

There will be an inventory at the end of the logistics loops. This inventory is the result of the total lead time and the size of the batch or production order. Creating one-piece flow and achieving zero changeover time will reduce the inventory at the end of the logistics loop dramatically.

Here I must once again mention car assembly lines. In some situations, it's possible to integrate some subassemblies into the main line, but most often you find that these opportunities have already been explored. The weak point in most assembly lines is poor standard work owing to badly planned borders of lines. You find that big containers are used all over the line, and the workers are doing logistics work (e.g., picking far away with bad ergonomic design and walking a lot). They also deal with wasted packaging materials and carton disposal. Here production flow is best achieved by focusing on improving the border of line and standard work through an internal logistics flow that delivers small containers with high frequency.

Fine-Tuning the Map

The results of the analysis and discussions should be entered in the future-state and future-layout maps by using sketches and high-level design solutions or concepts. After rethinking production flows, it is advisable to look again at basic reliability. Doing this will give you a new design for good line layout; you now need to check how reliable it will be.

> *Although basic reliability is the first pillar, the best time to look for improvement opportunities is after working through the production-flow pillar.*

The top five issues listed in the scorecards will point to areas where Improvements are needed. Issues such as high scrap rates, frequent machine breakdowns, or other instances of poor reliability of manpower, materials, or methods will have to be addressed. The team will define a number of subprojects to tackle the main issues, including subprojects or workshops on reducing changeover time. Chapter 16 explains how these subprojects can be tackled through *kaizen* workshops.

Identify Clear Internal Logistics Loops

Internal logistics is the next key area to work on. The starting point for applying this pillar of improvement is an analysis of the border of line, which has already been done. The first point to consider is supermarkets—those needed to supply the *kanban* supermarkets and the *junjo* areas in the border of line. You already know what types of flow containers are needed (i.e., small boxes, trolleys, or containers on wheeled bases). You now must decide what types of supermarkets are needed and approximately where they will be located.

After this, you can check the *mizusumashi* domain. You will need to establish *mizusumashi* shuttle lines between the supermarkets and the border of line. A starting point for deciding the *mizusumashi* pitch time is usually 20 or 60 minutes. During this time, the production line should be able to process a certain amount of *kanbans* (logistics units or logistics output). The size of the *kanbans* can be one single item (one finished workpiece) or the number of finished goods inside a small plastic container or pallet-sized container. It is important to calculate the cycle time of one *kanban*. For example, the cycle time can be five minutes; this means that in 20 minutes, the water spider will have to take four containers to the end of the line. (Remember, the leveling box will schedule the finished-goods *kanbans* along the line in periods of time that are equal to the *mizusumashi* pitch time.)

The shuttle lines keep the parts and products flowing between stores and lines or machines—they are the factor that links the customer *takt* time with the production cycle time.

The next question is what size the supermarkets should be. This will depend on which synchronization method (either *kanban* or *junjo*) is chosen. When you have defined the supermarkets and the *mizusumashi* lines, you can make an initial estimate of supermarket sizes and the information-flow circuits for supplying or replenishing needed parts.

When you have decided which of the different types of *kanban* loops (these are part of the synchronization domain) you wish to use, some quick calculations will give you the size of the supermarkets and also clarify the flow of the *kanban* cards (which record the physical movements of the water spider).

You also must determine the *junjo* or sequenced flows. For example, if you have a subassembly that is part of a sequence of the final assembly, you will need to define the circuit of the information flow (where the subassembly will receive the *junjo* order from and when).

The synchronization system must be balanced by the leveling and pull-flow solutions devised for each section of the line. The standard logistics models presented in the explanation of the leveling domain will need to be adapted for each particular situation. By using the internal logistics planning tools presented in Chapters 9 and 10, it will be possible to design a customized solution for each scenario. These tools include

> *Establishing the* mizusumashi *shuttle line is one of the more important domains of internal logistics flow.*

- ▲ The *kanbans*
- ▲ The logistics box
- ▲ The leveling box
- ▲ The batch-building box
- ▲ The line sequencer

The aim is to use these tools to design the information flow that will achieve the best synchronization. The input will be the production orders that need to be leveled and synchronized in a seamless and physical way. All these tools are real objects that are used by the water spider and line workers and that allow the production system to react to real pull signs.

Production Pull Planning

In order to be a *pull* supply chain, however, the system needs the *right kind* of input, and this has to do with production pull planning. The three steps of pull planning will have to be addressed. These steps are to plan the

- ▲ Strategy (at the finished-goods level and also down to the component level at the bill of materials)
- ▲ Capacity (in terms of logistics and production)
- ▲ Execution (what orders to start on the pull production system)

In planning strategy, you have to look at the finished goods references and decide which will have a made to order or made to stock strategy. You use the capacity-planning process to reach a solution (or improve an existing one) for using forecasts and contracts between production and logistics. Planning execution consists of calculating pull algorithms for the replenishment of finished-goods inventories (preferably stored in supermarkets) and for making product references to order.

Once the supermarkets and the *mizusumashi* lines have been defined, you can use the three tools just listed to design the information flow, starting from the customer orders. The new information-flow map now can be drawn and discussed.

Create a Source Flow Strategy

One of the main types of *muda* found in any company is the materials or parts inventory that comes in from suppliers. If you are talking about a manufacturing company, then this material waiting can be found in the materials and parts inventory. If you are talking about a distribution warehouse, this material waiting can be found in the total inventory held by the warehouse.

In both cases, this material waiting is the end result of a logistics loop that begins with the way in which orders to suppliers are calculated and issued. In the preceding section of this chapter I considered internal logistics; now I will examine the source logistics loops. The difficulty with source logistics loops is that part of the loop takes place at the supplier. You can make decisions on how you order internal supplies (logistics pull planning), and you can decide how you will receive the parts (inbound source flows) until they are stored in the supermarkets, but you can't (easily, at least) decide how a supplier will process your order or the supplier's picking and outbound delivery flows. You may or may not be able to influence transport depending on whether or not it is included in the price of the parts.

The supply chain design team should include people who know and have connections with suppliers (usually the purchasing department). Their first task is to analyze the source logistics loops without involving the suppliers.

The first thing to look at is the information flow of the orders sent to suppliers.

This analysis should result in a profile of the suppliers' logistics loops showing all the locations of all the suppliers on a map and identifying both the types of goods supplied and the type of logistics unit used (i.e., containers or packaging). Each logistics loop then can be studied in more detail, with the analysis focusing on an important supplier of several parts.

The current state map will show clearly what the current process is, and you should be able to understand why you have a certain amount of inventory waiting in the source warehouse. The supplier orders are probably being calculated on the basis of a material resource planning (MRP) system and are probably too big. You should check the order call-off frequency (this is the average number of days after which you repeat an order for the same part). Here the solution should be quite straightforward. You can use a pull-planning algorithm to check the impact of orders on the inventory. This type of pull algorithm makes a

It is also important to create a flow in the inbound processes of unloading, checking, sorting, and binning the parts until they are available in the warehouse.

daily call-off (to start with) and is fundamental in creating a flow in the source flows. A simulation can be done for some parts of the loop based on the total lead time of the logistics loop, and the effect on inventory can be calculated. This is also a good opportunity to reexamine how the lead time is calculated.

Here the analysis can focus on the several types of logistics flows. The new paradigm is the car assembly supply flows presented in Chapter 12. You can use the logistics graph for the different types of parts flow and devise a way to reduce lead time and increase productivity.

You also can use the lead-time calculations to look at transport. Here you need to check how the daily call-off orders will be conveyed to the plant. If the shipment frequency is weekly and the call-off is daily, then the orders will wait for one week before they get

shipped. The transport lead time will depend on the distance to be covered and the mode of transport (e.g., air versus road). This lead time can be reduced by looking at waiting times in the transport route itself. The milk-run truck is the best mode of transport because it allows high shipment frequencies and an optimized

The shipment frequency and the transport lead time are key points to consider.

transport lead time (see Chapter 12). A milk run route can be operated by the company or subcontracted outside. The first option is the best because the company then can standardize the work of the driver (or drivers) and achieve the minimum transport lead time.

With all these data and ideas for improvement, the team can draw up a source improvement strategy and have a clear picture of what to ask and how to involve the suppliers. Another element probably will be the right sizing of containers (as a result of the border of line and standard work improvements), and this must be included in the source strategy. Involving the suppliers in the optimization of the source logistics loops will be a key issue from this point on.

It also will be necessary to address the top five issues identified in the scorecards because these issues may have a direct impact on the relevance and success of the strategy.

Create a Delivery Flow Strategy

At the opposite side of our value stream, you see the inbound delivery flows. Here you consider the position of the supplier (just as in the source flows). You receive the orders from the customers, and you have to quickly pick and ship the goods. What happens if your customers are not implementing a TFM strategy? They probably will order from you in the same way that you were ordering from your suppliers. This means MRP-generated orders based on forecasts and higher-than-necessary daily call-off orders. They also will be using the push type of container (which they can move quickly to their production lines, transferring all the *muda* onto the line workers).

The best solution is when the shipment frequency matches the call-off frequency.

Here again, it is important to have a clear view of the logistics loops. What often happens is that the manufacturing company delivers to distribution warehouses in distant locations (in other countries), which can belong to the same corporation but are formally separate companies. In this situation, the loop begins in the distant warehouse. It comes into the plant and goes through the assembly, transport, and other cross-dock warehouses along the route to its final destination. Here the warehouse will be ordering with a call-off frequency of perhaps one month (based on forecasts). In a situation such as this, you may need to redefine the logistics loop and break it into two or more smaller loops.

When the logistics loop is a simple sequence of order processing, picking, and shipping, it will be necessary to streamline the order-fulfillment process. You may want to look at the final warehouse inbound flows as well. The incoming containers from production into the final warehouse can be cross-docked to the customer outbound check/sort stations without being stored. And you can do much to improve the productivity of the plant warehouse by applying the tools presented in Chapter 13. The picking work will be critical. You can design wave picking (in waves of 15 minutes) using a leveling box. You also can adapt your order picking to use the containers the customer requires and check whether these containers are the same type and size as the ones you are using for your production lines.

The delivery flow strategy should include plans for involving customers.

If the customer order call-off frequency is less than daily, you can propose a daily delivery service, perhaps conducting a pilot project to show the customer the advantages to be reaped by reducing material waiting inventories. This naturally leads to discussion of shipment frequencies and transport lead times. The milk run system also can be a useful way to reduce transport lead time.

Start devising a delivery strategy, and the best way of involving your customers will become evident. At first, you may simply improve your internal delivery flows (inbound and outbound from your finished-goods warehouse), but then other pilot projects involving customers will become apparent.

These solutions will have to be checked against the top five issues identified in the scorecards analysis, and a clear connection will have to be established. The improvement strategy should completely eliminate the top five issues.

Finalizing the TFM Supply-Chain Design Strategy

Using Mock-Ups

During the supply chain design phase, it is possible to build some mock-ups of the new solutions to gauge what they would really be like and to test them out. A mock-up will put an end to all the theoretical discussions. This was the method used by Taiichi Ohno. Some extra time will be needed for this, but it may be a crucial exercise in getting the team to believe in the new paradigms.

Building a mock-up of a new production or assembly line (or just a section of the line) out of cardboard, wooden pallets, and plastic tubing is not difficult. It is also possible to build mock-ups of supermarkets and *mizusumashi* trains or even check/sort stations for repacking. Designing repacking stations can involve endless discussions about manpower, with some people saying that they need a lot of manpower and others saying the opposite. A mock-up simulation will show what actually happens and put an end to the debate.

Similarly, pull planning can be tested with computer simulations, and it's advisable to do so. The programs don't need to be complex—it's possible to demonstrate pull planning algorithms very easily with Excel, for example.

Defining the Vision

The future state vision will be summed up in two documents: the *vision map* (using the value-stream icons) and the *layout vision map* (representing the new layout and the new flows). In some cases, the layout vision map will give you a better idea of the improvements to be made, but it will have to be complemented by at least an *information flow map* (the material flow map can be replaced by the layout flow map).

In the end, the team must put together all the new concepts and ideas and reach a common understanding of how the vision will work. The solution will have to be shared and approved by everybody on the team. This is essential for a smooth implementation. Calculation of the total lead time will establish the most important target key performance indicator.

Putting It into Practice

The first step in implementing the vision is to define a series of subprojects that both cover it and tackle it step by step. You can plot subprojects or workshops on the vision map with *kaizen* bursts or clouds (Figure 15.1). This process should be quite easy—it simply consists of a list of subprojects to be done within a certain time frame and in a certain order.

For each project/workshop shown by a bubble, it is necessary to clearly define who the project leader and the members of the focus action group will be. I have already talked about the focus group of any change project in Chapter 13—its members should be the people who will have to change their daily habits as a result of the introduction of new standards. They need to be involved in the change process and go through the awareness and improvement phases. They need to be aware of the issues to be solved, and they must be part of the detailed design and implementation work. I will talk more about this in Chapter 16.

A complete business case for the project will require a cost-benefit analysis. For this, you will need a list of investment expenses and benefits. The project should pay for itself in less than one year. Here I say the project, not the subprojects, because the aim is to optimize the entire supply chain, not just parts of it.

The main quantifiable key performance indicators are

▲ Reduction of inventory
▲ Improvement of productivity
▲ Improvement of quality
▲ Improvement of customer service

I can also mention here other improvements that are less easy to quantify, such as ergonomic factors, safety, the quality of the work environment, and the morale and motivation of the employees. The improved competitiveness of the company in terms of getting new orders also is another factor to be considered.

If the return on investment is longer than one year, something is wrong. Usually this means too much capital expenditure was allowed in the vision for the system.

The final part of the cost-benefit analysis is the *return on investment* (ROI) calculation. Capital expenditure is the easy way to make improvements but is also the path that will be followed by most of your competitors. If a technological upgrade is really needed and the advantages to the flow and other TFM features are obvious, then it can be included.

When the ROI is higher than one year, the vision will have to be reviewed and perhaps divided into stages. The basic rule is that each stage should be paid for in less than one year. At the end of that year, the vision should be

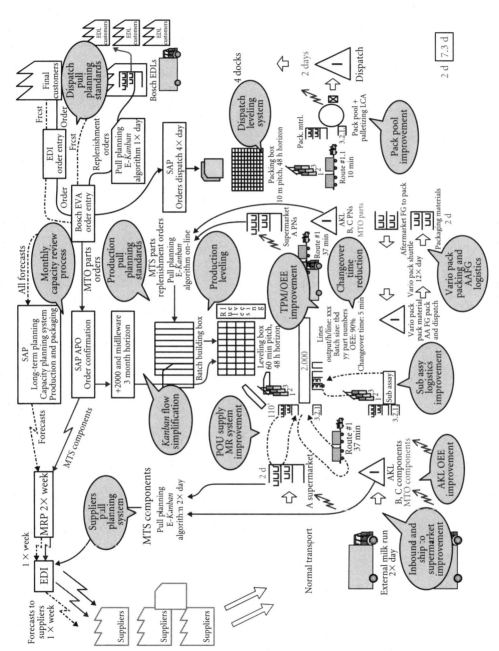

Figure 15.1 Vision map with *kaizen* clouds.

reevaluated. The learning that has taken place during that time will ensure a more accurate and realistic understanding of opportunities and solutions—it typically will lead to a very different, more realistic solution from what was originally planned.

CHAPTER 16

Taking Action:
The Power of the *Kaizen* Way

Introducing the *Kaizen* Foundations Approach

A project to implement excellence through *kaizen* in logistics and supply chains is a transformational effort that will involve many people, some from several functions within the company and others from different companies that are part of the source and delivery sides of the supply chain. At the Kaizen Institute, we usually advise companies to start this type of project by preparing people for the challenge of change. We do this by holding a *kaizen* foundations seminar.

Chapter 1 introduced the concept of *kaizen*—change for the better—and I spoke about the importance of commitment to *kaizen* principles. Let me recall these eight *kaizen* principles:

- ▲ Safety first
- ▲ Quality focus
- ▲ *Gemba* orientation
- ▲ Waste elimination
- ▲ People development
- ▲ Visual standards
- ▲ Good process, good results
- ▲ Pull-flow thinking

The one-day *kaizen* foundations seminar is for everyone in the company, to explain the principles and concepts of *kaizen*. This seminar includes some *muda* awareness exercises and explains the main *kaizen* improvement tools. It is also a very good opportunity to present the vision of *kaizen* in logistics and supply chains for the company. The purpose of the seminar is to prepare people for the challenge of implementing the vision and to give them an opportunity to reflect on their own attitudes toward the changes needed in everyone's work habits.

Before this seminar is held, you will have worked with the main executives to determine the current status, create a strategic vision (including a pull-flow strategy), and draw up a list of subprojects to implement. You will already have an estimate of the costs and benefits of the plan and the approval of the company's management to start implementation. It's time to take action.

The *Gemba Kaizen* Workshop

As far as possible, you will use the *gemba kaizen* workshop format. This is a proven format that involves the right people in examining and changing their own work habits.

For a successful project, several different *gemba kaizen* workshops are usually needed. These include

▲ The single-minute exchange of dies (SMED) workshop
▲ The standard work workshop
▲ The *kobetsu* workshop
▲ The line design workshop

The *gemba kaizen* workshop is a highly standardized way of initiating improvement that yields the desired results within a short time frame. The workshop consists of preparation days, intensive days, and follow-up days.

SMED Workshop

The SMED *gemba kaizen* workshop is the one most often needed when implementing *kaizen* in logistics and supply chains. Flow relies on quick changeovers, and you have seen in Chapter 7 that the Wilson formula for batch sizes depends on the changeover time. A quick changeover means small batch sizes, which, in turn, mean flow improvement. In some cases, the time taken for changeover (often because of high product variety and small orders) is the main cause of losses in machine efficiency.

The best way is to start with a *gemba kaizen* workshop with a pilot machine. The workshop needs to have the elements listed in Table 16.1.

The complete SMED workshop, including preparation, intensive days, and follow-up, can last two to three months. The workshop is finished only when all the planned actions are implemented and people are trained in the new method. Once the workshop has been completed and the changes have been implemented, tested, and refined, the team can discuss how to deploy the new process on other machines.

Table 16.1   Elements Needed for a SMED *Gemba Kaizen* Workshop

The challenge	To reduce changeover time in order to achieve a certain target (the first workshop should aim to achieve a reduction of at least 50 percent)
The *kaizen* coach	An experienced trainer in SMED workshops
The team	The workers who actually do the changeover work Their supervisor Representatives of the main internal suppliers (e.g., people from maintenance, die preparation, quality control, and others) A team of seven to nine persons is a good size
The team leader	The supervisor of the area or someone on the team who has leadership skills
The schedule	The *kaizen* coach and the team leader work together in preparation for the workshop The team works together during the intensive days (three to five days) as well as during the follow-up days

It is advisable not to break up the intensive days into several weeks because spending these days together will strengthen the spirit and effectiveness of the team (Table 16.2). The final presentation at the end is also very important. On the afternoon of the last intensive day, the team will give a presentation to management and other invited guests, showing what they have achieved (including a demonstration of the new changeover) and explaining all the plans for improvement.

Table 16.2   Structure of Intensive *Gemba Kaizen* Days

Day 1	Presentation of the challenge by top management Presentation of the SMED methodology by the *kaizen* coach Participants observe the *gemba* and watch a changeover video Changeover work study
Day 2	Exploration of potential improvements Preparation of trial 1 of improved changeover Execution of trial 1
Day 3	Analysis of trial 1 Further improvement of the method Preparation of trial 2 Preparation of action plan Preparation of presentation to management Delivery of presentation Execution of trial 2

If the changeover is fairly long or complex, this agenda can be spread over four or five days. The start of the follow-up should be planned for the week immediately after the intensive week. The follow-up days can be broken in half-days or two-hour sessions to be done on a weekly basis.

Standard Work Workshop

The standard work *gemba kaizen* workshop is useful to eliminate *muda* of workers' movements and improve the efficiency of all types of manual work. (In fact, a SMED workshop is actually a special form of standard work in the sense that its goal is to improve the efficiency of the manual changeover work.)

In fact, all the manual work in a warehouse, such as loading or unloading trucks, checking, sorting, binning, or picking, can be improved using standard work.

The standard work approach can be applied in production or assembly lines where one-piece flow is already a reality, but workers still have a lot of *muda* of walking and other movements that do not add value. It also can be applied to maintenance work and to warehouse work. All the manual work in a warehouse, such as loading or unloading trucks, operating check/sort stations, and binning or picking, can be improved using standard work.

The aims of this workshop are to

▲ Reduce worker waiting time and simplify worker movements (improve and shorten the worker flow)
▲ Reduce material waiting and movement inside cells or workstations (improve and shorten the material flow)
▲ Improve teamwork
▲ Establish a 5S culture to create excellent workplace organization
▲ Improve line and cell productivity

Like the SMED workshop, the standard work workshop includes preparation time, intensive days, and follow-up days. The team consists of the workers who usually do the job that is to be improved during the workshop, their supervisors, and some representatives from the support functions such as maintenance, process engineering, quality control, and so on.

The main tasks for the workshop include

▲ Introduction to the concepts
▲ Quantification of the *muda* and value-added elements of the total time
▲ Visual awareness based on time measurements and observation

▲ List of opportunities for *muda* elimination

▲ List of worker *muri* (difficulties) and *mura* (variability)

▲ Discussion and definition of the action plan

▲ Implementation of the action plan

▲ Cleaning and inspection of the layout and work environment

▲ Standardization and training of workers' movements

Kobetsu *Workshop*

Kobetsu is a Japanese word that means "focused." The *kobetsu gemba kaizen* workshop is used to improve an important issue affecting flow. This may be a quality problem (e.g., high scrap rates) or issues of machine efficiency such as breakdowns. It can be any type of problem that affects the basic reliability of manpower, machines, materials, or methods. The most common application of this workshop, however, is to reduce quality defects and to improve machine overall equipment effectiveness (OEE).

Participants in the workshop use the plan, do, check, and act (PDCA) method to tackle big issues. This method can be applied to any type of reliability problem or improvement opportunity found in the current-state analysis, and it should be applied when you find low OEE or major problems of quality in the flow.

Let me describe the challenges and targets for a *kobetsu kaizen* workshop held to improve machine OEE (Table 16.3). This type of workshop can be organized in two intensive weeks (preparation and follow-up days are also needed). The people to involve are the maintenance and production operators and their supervisors. It is important to go to the

> *The increase in productivity is usually between 20 and 40 percent, especially if the starting point of OEE is around 50 percent (a value often found in real-life cases).*

gemba with them and create a strong awareness of the OEE issues and their impact on the company's performance.

This type of workshop can have a big impact on machine efficiency. The increase in productivity is usually between 20 and 40 percent, especially if the starting point of OEE is around 50 percent (a value often found in real-life cases).

Line Design *Workshop*

The line design *gemba kaizen* workshop is usually necessary when the value-stream design is implemented. In the future state vision, you defined a high-level design of the lines based on the concepts of line and layout design. The line design workshop looks at the detailed

Table 16.3 Elements of a *Kobetsu* Workshop

Challenges and Targets	Tasks
Week 1	
Reduce losses in machine availability (breakdowns), machine performance (micro-stoppages and low speed), and machine quality (defects and rework). Involve operators in basic inspection and maintenance tasks. Improve OEE of the line or cell.	Concepts training: Quantify OEE (awareness through observation, calculation of OEE, and setting up a visual control in the machine). List top 10 losses (for the bottleneck machine or module). Start countermeasures to reduce main losses. Clean and inspect the machines. Solve main machine issues (restore basic machine conditions).
Week 2	
Involve workers in machine inspection and maintenance. Improve machines in terms of cleanliness and access to maintenance points. Implement maintenance visual standards. Improve OEE of the line or cell.	Concepts training: Week 1 audit. Eliminate equipment leaks, dirtiness, and contamination sources. Improve access to equipment inspection and maintenance points. Establish inspection, cleaning, and maintenance standards (using visual management). Follow up on OEE losses and implement more countermeasures.

design of the lines (and, in many cases, the complete layout). This requires the building of mock-ups. In some cases, a small mock-up is built and tested as part of defining the future state vision, but this is a very limited application of the idea, meant only to show how a part of the line would work with the new concepts. The line design workshop builds and tests a complete mock-up in order to test all the details before you start building the actual line.

The *kaizen* team for this workshop should be the people who are responsible for designing and building new lines and layouts—the process engineers. The team leader should be a senior engineer or even the head of the section. Other participants can be people from production (the users) and logistics.

It is very important to have the process engineers involved in this type of work because they need to learn how to design lines and layouts along production flow principles. There is a big difference between a line designed according to *kaizen* principles and a line designed and built in the traditional way.

When you are dealing with storage and warehouse design, it is very important that the logistics engineers participate in the profiling and design work in order to decide the characteristics of the logistics storage cells. The probability that people will successfully implement what they themselves have designed is very high. In storage design, making mock-ups of sections of shelves and types of bins will help to produce a better solution.

The line design workshop builds and tests a complete mock-up in order to check all the details before starting to build the actual line.

The mock-ups are made from cardboard cartons, wood from pallets, plastic tubing, tape, and other fasteners and connectors. When the mock-up is ready, it will be necessary to perform several test runs with the operators, measuring times. This testing serves to perfect standard work and the workstation layout so that operators can focus on adding value.

The line design workshop creates the blueprints for the new line. During construction, the team can meet for follow-up sessions. When the construction is finished, the training of the operators can start. The line design team should coach and support the line until the operators are fully trained and the line is performing according to the plan.

Specialized Subprojects

Near the beginning of this chapter I mentioned that part of the *kaizen* preparation work with management is to create a list of subprojects to tackle. The list of subprojects also includes other, less standardized improvement work that can be done with a less concentrated allocation of time and with fewer people. Here are some implementation guidelines for the following types of subprojects:

▲   Implementing supermarkets
▲   Implementing *mizusumashi* shuttle lines
▲   Implementing leveling
▲   Implementing pull planning
▲   Implementing supplier milk runs
▲   Implementing right-sized containers

Each subproject needs to have a project leader and a small team. The schedule of work should be defined based on the targets of the subproject and the overall time frame for implementation. I will also discuss the importance of job instruction, work standards, and resistance to change during project implementation.

Logistics Implementation

The physical implementation of the solutions envisioned for internal logistics is done in smaller teams. Here you are dealing with designing and building supermarkets and *mizusumashi* shuttle lines, possibly in many different areas of the plant. One method is to work in smaller, independent teams of two to three people who do not have to follow a rigid schedule organized around the *gemba kaizen* workshop or event.

Supermarkets are usually designed and built using flow racks and small plastic containers (although if the parts are big, you will have to use trolleys or wheeled bases). To have the supermarkets in operation as quickly as possible, you also may have to do some repacking to achieve right-sizing (while talking to suppliers about changing the inbound packaging or container).

The supermarkets can be sized by using the algorithms presented in Appendix A. As soon as the supermarkets and borders of lines are ready, you can start testing the *mizusumashi* lines. The unit of supermarket *mizusumashi* border of line will work like a production cell (you can visualize it as a cell divided in two parts that are separated by a long distance so that the operator has work to do at one end and then rides a small train and goes to work at the other). As soon you have one line ready, the test can begin. In fact, the implementation plan should allow for building and testing the *mizusumashi* lines one by one. It is best to avoid building a big batch of supermarkets and only then testing everything.

The *mizusumashi* train (an electric locomotive with wagons) will need a lot of testing because the number and configuration of the wagons may result in what I call the "snake effect"—when the train moves, it may swing from side to side like a snake. This is not good for either safety or speed. The answer is to change the geometry of the wheels (e.g., the width of the axles, the distance between the axles, the connection between the wagons, or other parameters). The best solution is to buy a train that has already been tested. If this proves difficult (because the wagons will need some customization to suit this purpose), it may be possible to benchmark an existing train system elsewhere.

> *It is vital that the* mizusumashi *worker follows his or her standard work and synchronizes his or her work with the established pitch.*

It is also possible to build mock-ups of *mizusumashi* cells. This may be useful when training a large number of logistics engineers in *mizusumashi* lines. The water spider will have to do much moving of both material and information. As laid down in the future-state map, the water spider will have to start from a leveling box and move *kanbans* between the leveling box and the various border of lines and supplier supermarkets. It is vital that the *mizusumashi* worker follows his or her standard work and synchronizes his or her work with the established pitch. Developing these habits will require a lot of training. If the pitch time varies and is not maintained at the nominal value (e.g., 20 minutes), the flow may be broken and will not work as intended.

The water spider train driver must be a very reliable and responsible worker. Some companies chose the water spider from their best logistics or production workers as a gateway to future leadership positions. The initial month of operation is critical in terms of training. The implementation team needs to keep moving with the train and improving the standard until the driver is fully trained and following the pitch time like a clock.

For synchronization and leveling, it will be necessary to make up the leveling box and the *kanban* cards (these can be plastic credit card types of cards produced on a special printer).

Pull Planning

The work of building supermarkets, creating *mizusumashi* shuttle lines, synchronization, and leveling can be done with small teams of people mainly from logistics and production. The work to be done in production pull planning will have to focus on the planning department. The people involved in transforming customer orders and forecasts into production orders are the ones to change their working procedures and habits here.

> *The people involved in transforming customer orders and forecasts into production orders are the ones to change their working procedures and habits here.*

This can be a tough task, especially if there is a well-established information system already in place. My experience is that the planning team has a lot of influence in the planning of the new system, and the human factor is always present when they have to decide the capacity in a given time.

Here again, it will be necessary to work with the planners in small teams and make computer simulations (the software equivalent of physical mock-ups) to try out and test the pull planning algorithms. Many enterprise resource planning (ERP) packages offer the possibly of testing new models, and most of them have pull algorithms. Another possibility is to use an Internet-based pull planning package to do the testing.

It is possible to have everything working except the pull planning. It is also possible to have the leveling, synchronization, *mizusumashi*, and supermarket systems running perfectly but still have the planning being done using the old MRP logic. Of course, the result will be a lot of *muda* at the warehouse at the end of the loop. The new pull solution will be complete only when the planning procedures are changed in line with the rest of the process.

Pull planning also includes capacity planning, and here the team will include not only the planners but also people from production and logistics. This subproject will involve all the necessary work of checking and adapting capacity to forecasted demand, including checking the size of supermarkets and other data-profiling work.

External Logistics

The subprojects dealing with external logistics probably will start with the source side. Here it is the company that probably will have the greater power because it is the buyer or customer. From this position it is easy to change logistics pull planning (the way orders are calculated and sent to suppliers). The transportation and inbound work subprojects are also easy to start.

The focus teams should be the buyers, who will have to do a lot of work with the suppliers to change containers (e.g., right-sizing and use of returnable containers). It is best to include the suppliers on the implementation team (starting with a pilot subproject) whenever possible.

On the source side of external logistics, you can divide the subprojects into four types:

▲ Logistics pull planning (involving planners)
▲ Inbound improvement (involving logistics—warehouse personnel)
▲ Milk run (involving logistics, third-party transport company, and suppliers)
▲ Containers (involving purchasing and suppliers)

As I've said before, the subprojects involving milk runs and containers are best done by involving suppliers. The milk run lines depend almost completely on the third-party transport company (if there is one). Here you can make a parallel with a *mizusumashi* line. In fact, you need the supplier supermarket, the customer border of line supermarket, and the *mizusumashi* person. In external logistics, the supplier supermarket belongs to several outside companies, the water spider may belong to an external contractor, and only the border of line belongs to the company starting to implement *kaizen* in logistics and supply chains.

Because of this added complexity, you may need to go more slowly and include the external people who are involved in the pull logistics loops.

Other Important Implementation Points

A very important aspect of any change process is training people to follow new standards and acquire new habits. If the company has good *gemba* supervisors, this work goes much better. Supervisors' ability to provide training is a very important factor in the success of any projects to implement *kaizen* in logistics and supply chains. If the company does not train its supervisors in this way, it will be necessary to start the change process by giving them Training Within Industry (TWI) training, more specifically the Job Instruction (JI) module. TWI was a service run from 1940 to 1945 by the War Manpower Commission of the U.S. Department of War. The purpose of TWI was to provide consulting services to war-related industries whose personnel were being conscripted into the U.S. Army at the same time as the War Department was issuing orders for additional material. It was apparent that the shortage of trained and skilled personnel at precisely the time they were most needed would impose a hardship on industries and that only improved methods of job training would address the shortfall.

Toyota learned TWI after World War II and now is training its supervisors in JI. The supervisors are then responsible for training the workers in new operations and performing new and improved standards until they acquire new working habits.

When new production or logistics cells and lines are set up, it is extremely important that the workers are trained using the JI method. The subproject teams need to bear this in mind and involve supervisors in the training. These supervisors should already be trained in TWI.

> *The shortage of personnel trained and skilled in pull-flow standards is exactly the issue that needs to be addressed here.*

Resistance to change is very likely during implementation. This is why it is important to work with focus groups—the people who will actually have to change their own work habits. I have already discussed the importance of involving focus groups in the detailed design phase. By analyzing data and looking at the types of *muda* that are targeted for elimination, the members of these groups can develop a strong awareness of the actual situation and the need to change for the better. Giving them the opportunity to take part in the detailed design phase will help to minimize resistance to change during implementation.

However, this tactic will not completely eliminate resistance to change because it will be impossible to involve every worker in the design phase. The implementation teams must be prepared to deal with resistance.

At some point the CEO or other representative of senior management will call the implementation team, complaining about the process and saying that the operations are a mess. This is when the implementation team will need to go back to the basic *kaizen* principles discussed in Chapter 1 and ask for management's trust and confidence that the right process will give the right results.

When I was a young process engineer in my first job, I once complained to my boss that a certain project was too difficult. He just told me that if it was easy, he would not have needed an engineer to do it. In a Total Flow paradigm-change project, you can say the same thing—if it was easy, anybody could do it, including your competitors. Stress is a part of life, and it is the only way to progress. At the end of the process, the company will have a unique pull-flow system that will perform much better than the previous one and certainly much better than that of the competitors, but to get to that point, the company will have to go through the stress of dealing with the difficulties on the way.

Many of these difficulties, however, will simply be negative emotions based on fear of the unknown and not really physical difficulties at all. This is why the company needs to have a strong commitment to change and the determination to go ahead and implement the new system. The *kaizen* foundation seminars given at the beginning of the process also will help to disarm resistance to change. Of course, the fact that the project is initiated at the highest level in the company also helps.

CHAPTER 17

The *Kaizen* Pull-Flow Life of Company A

In Chapter 2, I talked about the history of Company A and about its no *kaizen*, no pull-flow life. This company experimented with many types of *kaizen* tools and got good improvement results for many years, but it never really changed its planning system from a push to a pull system. Even more important, the company was convinced that it already had a pull system because it operated a two-bin system to supply some parts to the assembly lines and used hourly batches. The argument was, "We already have very small hourly batches that are pulling the preassemblies, with one day of delay, and we have the two-bin system pulling the parts from the warehouse." The mental block caused by this fixed mindset was the company's number one obstacle to progress.

At the end of 2004, Company A was showing the following key performance indicators (KPIs):

Total inventory coverage (raw materials + work in process + finished goods)	50 days
Internal defects rate	12,000 parts per million (ppm)
Customer service level	93 percent
Achievement of the assembly production schedule	50 percent
Productivity	70 parts per operator
Final efficiency of assembly line	75 percent

One of the main issues was the assembly schedule accuracy—only 50 percent. This was proof that the synchronization system was not working well. Only 50 percent of the scheduled products could be assembled as promised within the scheduled time. For all the others, some part or other was missing at the time it was needed, so the schedule had to be changed. This had an impact on both line efficiency and customer service (both KPIs were insufficient).

The company's leaders thought they had nothing else to learn, that they had mastered all types of kaizen and Lean tools because they had a lot of training (classroom, by the way).

What was perhaps even more important than the results was the attitude of some of the people in leadership positions in the company. They had the support of a big corporate continuous improvement (CI) team, and they thought that all the *kaizen* tools were already working within the company. Of course, to recognize *muda*, you need a growth mind-set and a strong understanding of the *kaizen* principles. You also need some knowledge and experience in practical pull-flow systems and Total Flow model.

There were more and more signs that a big change of paradigm was needed. Every year it was becoming harder to achieve the targeted results. The corporate CI team pointed out that the degree of compliance with *kaizen* scorecards was low (one audit of the current state against *kaizen* scorecards found a score of 28 percent). Gradually, the company began to understand and accept that a change of paradigm had to take place.

The gemba reality was a bit different— muda was visible everywhere.

The *Kaizen* Pull-Flow Project Planning Phase

Then a new manager was appointed, with responsibility for finance and logistics. This manager decided to get together with the leaders of production and engineering to do something different and innovative. The first step was to convince the CI corporate team to let them contact outside experts. This turned out to be a hard job—it took about a year until the new manager succeeded.

At the beginning of 2005, the company began the planning phase of a pull-flow project. This consisted of

▲ Analyzing the current state using value-stream mapping
▲ Defining a future state vision
▲ Organizing a project to implement pull flow based on the TFM model

The design project team consisted of the heads of the production, logistics, engineering, maintenance, and continuous improvement departments, as well as some key deputies. The external experts were two *kaizen* coaches from the Kaizen Institute, and the team leader was the production manager. The team mapped the flows of one of the most important product families, analyzing the current way of doing things and the existing *muda* and identifying opportunities for improvement. Figure 17.1 shows Company A's current state map.

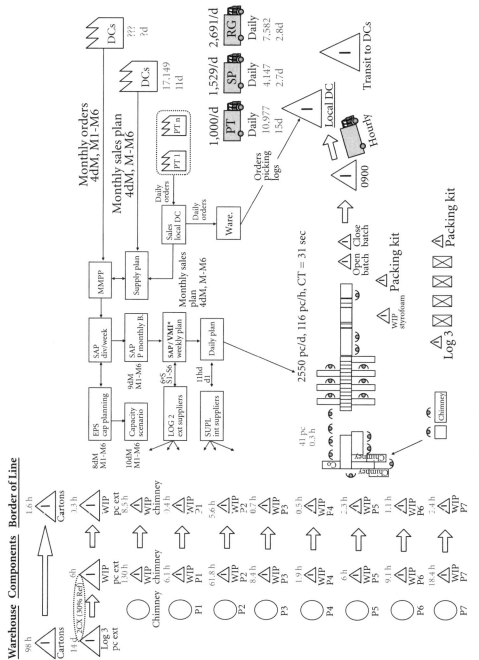

Figure 17.1 Company A's current state map.

The main issues were summarized as follows:

- ▲ Too much finished goods inventory (15 days)
- ▲ Dysfunctional finished goods inventory (final customer-service level of 93 percent)
- ▲ Order planning based on sales forecasts
- ▲ Planning department overloaded with planning tasks, especially at the end of the week (preparing next week's plan)
- ▲ Low fulfillment of the assembly schedule (50 percent)
- ▲ Poor assembly line efficiency (operators isolated from each other, backsupply, supply of big pallet-sized containers, bad operator standard work, line balancing not very good)
- ▲ Many line stops and schedule changes owing to lack of parts and many difficulties in line supply and synchronization
- ▲ Big inventory of bought materials and parts
- ▲ A lot of management time dedicated to daily fine-tuning and crisis management, lots of stress, and no time for *kaizen*

Next, the team received training using the TFM simulation games and applied the scorecards in order to fully understand the TFM concepts and be able to redesign the current system into a practical pull-flow system. The team's recognition and acceptance that the situation could be improved drastically were a surprise to everybody, and a sense of hope and challenge began to emerge.

The team began to discuss the future state vision map by looking at the final assembly lines. (These were the lines that had previously been diagnosed as not having a big potential for improvement—an expert from the corporation had said that the improvement potential was only 3 percent.) Everybody was anxious to understand how, using the *kaizen* eyes, the evident types of *muda* could be eliminated.

The design team spent four days on current state mapping and training activities and another three days on designing the future state vision. Another two days were dedicated to planning the implementation. The whole project planning phase was done in nine days spread over a period of one month. The first implementation phase took 10 months.

Let's now look at how other features of the project and the implementation proceeded.

Finished Goods Assembly Lines

The team started applying the production flow concepts of line design, border of line, standard work, single-minute exchange of dies (SMED), and low-cost automation. Although the line had a conveyor, it quickly became evident that real one-piece flow had not been achieved. There were small batches (resulting from accumulation because of different worker speeds and other line issues). It also was evident that the workers were too separated from each other and that the supply of parts was done from behind.

The lines could be classified as fast cycle time lines with isolated worker islands. The cycle time was 30 seconds. Setup time was about 5 minutes because there was a changeover in a small press die at the beginning of the line and also because it was difficult to change the parts.

It was evident that a leaner line could be designed to have a lower cycle time and more efficient standard work. This line should have

▲ Less variety of product references
▲ Small containers within hand's reach and in a fixed location
▲ Better balancing
▲ Zero changeover and low-cost automation

The first workshop after the planning phase was dedicated to designing a detailed line and building a mock-up of it. A test of the mock-up showed a productivity increase of 25 percent. Figure 17.2 shows a comparison between the old and new lines.

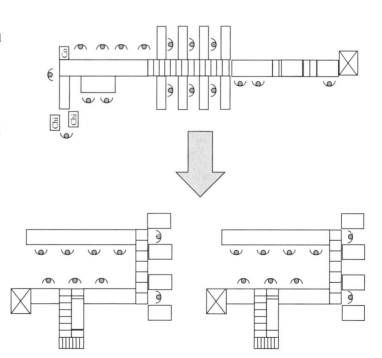

Figure 17.2   Evaluation of assembly lines.

It is also vital to define the characteristics of the border of line supermarkets. In this case, about half the parts needed for assembly could be supplied using *kanbans*. The border of line was designed accordingly with flow racks. There was no space for the rest of the parts because of the extremely large number of variants (the total number of finished-goods references was 607). The high variety of parts had to be supplied using a *junjo* (sequenced) system. Another difficulty was the size of the parts—in some cases (even when there were only four or five variants), the part had to be classified as a *junjo* part.

A new line was then designed with a cycle time of 60 seconds (this meant having two lines instead of one, and zero changeover time was achieved by moving the small press upstream into the process).

Having *junjo* parts meant that the synchronization system had to be totally foolproof; otherwise, the wrong sequence would be supplied to the line and the company would have the old problem of stoppages and assembly schedule changes.

On the basis of the line design and tests conducted on the mock-up, two new lines were ordered from an equipment supplier. The space occupied by these new lines was 70 percent of the space occupied by the single old line. Part of the materials used to build the new line, including the conveyor, came from the old line.

Changes to the Planning System

Finished Goods Pull Planning and Leveling

Company A's current state map showed two types of customers—a product distribution center (PDC) within the country and several PDCs abroad. Both types of customers provided monthly forecasts. The planners of Company A managed the stock in the domestic PDC (parts distribution center) but had no inventory information about the stock in the PDCs abroad. In all PDCs, production planning relied on the monthly forecasts sent by the sales department.

The main steps of the process were

1. Maintain a monthly master production schedule (MPS) based on forecasts.
2. Use this monthly plan to decide monthly capacity.
3. Use this monthly plan to decide the weekly assembly schedule (one week frozen).
4. Use the weekly assembly schedule to decide the daily assembly schedule.
5. Use the weekly assembly schedule to synchronize subassemblies and internal suppliers.
6. Use the monthly plan to order from external suppliers.

This was a typical "plan from plan from plan," material resource planning (MRP)–based process (the name *master production schedule* says it all) starting from the monthly demand forecasts.

The first change was to use the forecasts only to do the monthly capacity planning exercise (see Figure 17.3). The second was to apply a pull planning algorithm on a daily basis to compare a certain replenishment level with the current stock of finished goods so that when the amount of actual stock fell below the replenishment level, a replenishment order was generated. This change was applied only in the domestic PDC (the same solution could be adapted later for the foreign PDCs).

In this way, the planning system was divided into two sections—capacity planning and order planning. The order planning system now functioned as a daily vendor-managed inventory.

The new order planning process can be summarized as follows:

1. Calculate replenishment needs every day.
2. Maintain a production order list that includes the replenishment needs and PDC orders.
3. Transform the production order list into *kanbans*.
4. Assign *kanbans* to production each day using a logistics box.

With this system, the source of the planning data was no longer forecasts, but rather real pull orders. The daily assembly schedule then was decided by freezing one day of production on the logistics box. The *kanbans* were sorted every day to a leveling box. The rules for leveling were

1. Fill the day with the available *kanban* orders.
2. If the quantity of orders is not enough to fill the contracted capacity (the production-logistics contract), anticipate some made to order (MTO) orders from the PDCs abroad.
3. If the quantity is still not enough, make some made to stock (MTS) high runners, up to a defined maximum stock level.
4. If the quantity is still not enough, stop the process (this results in working less time).
5. If the quantity of orders is too much for the day, postpone some MTO orders (if this is possible in view of the final delivery date).
6. If the quantity is still too much, delay some MTS high runners down to a defined minimum stock level.
7. If the quantity is still too much, increase capacity by working during weekends for the MTO orders.

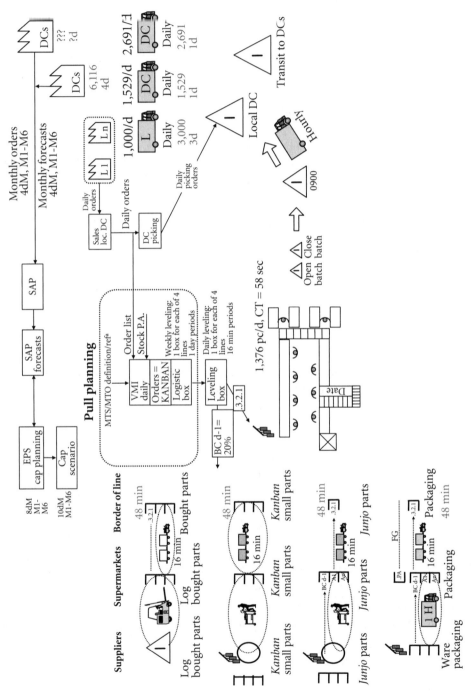

Figure 17.3 Implementation of the future state vision during the first year of the project.

This leveling ensured a stable daily schedule for production. The extreme solutions of having to stop the line or doing overtime during weekends were rarely needed.

Supermarkets and Mizusumashi *Lines*

Three types of *mizusumashi* shuttle lines were established—one for the bought parts, another for the subassemblies, and another for the finished goods and packaging. All these lines handle both *kanban* and *junjo* parts. A sequencer was prepared for each line, and from this sequencer, the *mizusumashi* picks the information needed for the next cycle. This information consists of a picking list for the *junjo*-supplied parts. Each internal supplier receives the *junjo* list every four hours, during which time they have to produce only four trolleys (one trolley is for a 16-minute batch, and 16 minutes is the *mizusumashi* pitch time). Every time the *mizusumashi* picks one trolley of *junjo* parts, the internal supplier has to make up the next one on the list.

For the *kanban* parts, the process is simpler and consists of simply exchanging empty containers for full containers in the supermarkets.

Each water spider has supermarkets available in each supplier with an area for *kanban* parts (the high runners) and a lane for *junjo* parts (with four sequenced trolleys or containers). According to the information received every cycle, the *mizusumashi* picks one sequenced trolley (or containers) and delivers the line in sequence.

Implementing Other TFM Tools

During construction of the new assembly lines, all supervisors were trained in the Job Instruction (JI) module of the Training Within Industry (TWI) program, and a training plan was prepared for the workers. A major training drive was held during the initial startup month until the workers got used to the new standard work. The productivity of the line began to grow steadily and reached the target increase of 27 percent after the initial training month. The company held a daily *kaizen* meeting between workers and supervisors at an information corner close to the line so that the workers could see the results of their efforts on output, productivity, quality, and compliance with the schedule.

The logistics pull planning subproject changed the way orders were sent to suppliers. The previous system was to issue weekly or monthly call-off orders, together with a six-week forecast. The forecast information was increased to eight weeks but otherwise stayed much the same, so the suppliers were able to do their own capacity planning. The weekly and monthly call-off connected to the master production schedule was eliminated and transformed into a daily call-off based on the results of a pull planning algorithm. In the new system, the parts inventory was checked on a daily basis, with an order generated (typically equal to the daily consumption) if the inventory was below the replenishment level.

At the same time, a pilot local milk run was established with suppliers who were located less than six hours' travel time from Company A. Most of the suppliers were already making some deliveries every day, so it was not difficult to arrange daily shipments of orders. For some distant suppliers, the shipping frequency remained one week.

Summary of the Subprojects

Tables 17.1 through 17.3 provide a summary of the actions taken in each domain of the TFM pillars.

Table 17.1 Production Flow Actions

Line and layout design	Main assembly lines were redesigned to create one-piece flow (in a U shape, with all workers close to each other).
	The line-balancing loss was reduced by
	• Working with the cycle time doubled (from one 30-second line to two 60-second lines)
	• Reducing the product variety (from all product references in one line to a small number of high runners in one line and the other references in the other line)
Border of line	Redesign of the lines included the redesign of all the containers supplied to the line.
	Frontal supply was implemented by using flow racks.
	The supply method for each part was defined (either *kanban* or *junjo*).
	Junjo supply was used for the biggest parts or parts with many variants that needed a lot of space in the line frontal storage.
Standard work	Workers' movements were analyzed and improved by trials done on a mock-up line.
	Standard work sheets were drawn for all workstations.
	Supervisors were trained in JI, and workers were trained very carefully during the startup month.
SMED	The line was transformed from a 5-minute changeover line to a zero-changeover line. This was made possible by
	• The new system of parts supply based on *kanban* and *junjo*
	• Relocating a small press to the internal supplier upstream
Low-cost automation	Some operations in the line that handled heavy parts or were ergonomically difficult were automated—mainly the testing and packaging operations at the end of the line. Potential still remains for more improvement in the lines through low-cost automation.

Table 17.2   Internal Logistics Flow Actions

Supermarkets	Three types of supermarkets were designed and built: • One type in front of each internal supplier • Another in the warehouse for bought parts • Another for finished goods and packaging materials The two first types (for parts) were divided into *kanban* supermarkets and *junjo* supermarkets. *Kanban* was applied to the parts classified that way in the border of line. *Junjo* supermarkets consisted of a lane for each reference with a sequence of four trolleys or containers. Each trolley is consumed every 16 minutes (this means that the available *junjo* parts cover about 64 minutes of assembly). The sequence list is received in advance every four hours. The supermarkets were designed for very easy and quick picking (using flow racks and visual management).
Mizusumashi shuttles	Three types of *mizusumashi* trains were designed and built. The pitch time is 16 minutes for each train. The standard work was thoroughly tried out in order to eliminate *muda* during the 16 minutes of operation. The *mizusumashi* take the information from sequencers (the *junjo* picking lists), travel to supermarkets, pick the parts, deliver parts to the assembly line, and pick empty containers (to be delivered next cycle).
Synchronization	Since *kanban* synchronization is the best solution, it was explored to the maximum. Having as many parts as possible waiting to be assembled in the border of line is the optimum. However, this affects the size of the picking face for operators. To optimize this, some parts need to be supplied in sequence. The decision between *kanban* or *junjo* was based on a compromise between simplicity of the supply process, worker efficiency, and the amount of inventory (*kanban* requires more inventory, but the 16-minute supply cycle ensures that the maximum *kanban* inventory is three cycles, or 48 minutes). The mixed (*kanban* and *junjo*) synchronization system was tested exhaustively on the *gemba* to make sure that the system of *mizusumashi*, supermarkets, and suppliers was operating like clockwork. This *gemba* testing is essential.
Leveling	A logistics box was implemented to plan the finished-goods *kanbans* (decided in the pull planning process). A leveling box also was implemented to schedule the daily activity.

(continued on next page)

Table 17.2 Internal Logistics Flow Actions *(continued)*

	The rules to operate both the logistics box and the leveling box were defined.
	The daily leveling of the load (fixed daily quantity) and product mix were established. The daily order mix ensured that the high runners were completed on a daily basis.
Production pull planning	A pull planning algorithm was run daily for:
	The replenishment of daily consumption in the domestic PDC (a vendor-managed inventory system)
	The orders coming from the other PDCs abroad

Table 17.3 External Logistics Flow Actions

Storage and warehouse design	The parts warehouse was redesigned to include supermarkets and reserve storage close by (a logistics cell).
	The first logistics cell was established to serve the assembly lines improved in the project.
	Further cells will be added to serve other internal customers.
	The logistics cells were organized to minimize the picking and binning work.
Milk run	A pilot milk-run line was implemented to deliver the logistics cell on a daily basis. This means that the parts in this milk run are ordered and received on the same day.
Source flows	The inbound flows of unloading, checking/sorting, and binning containers to the logistics cells were defined and improved.
	A plan was made to eliminate incoming quality control.
	A check/sort station was designed with improved standard work.
	Some containers had to be right-sized in the check/sort station, but a plan was made to right-size all containers at the supplier.
	Six months after the startup, 95 percent of the containers were supplied in the right size.
Delivery flows	The outbound flows to the PDC were streamlined by using finished-goods *mizusumashi*.
	The management of the finished-goods warehouse is subcontracted to a third party. Because of this, the *mizusumashi* leaves the finished goods in an unloading area in the warehouse. The project didn't improve the process up to the picking face of the finished goods.

Table 17.3   External Logistics Flow Actions *(continued)*

Logistics pull planning	A pull planning algorithm was started with the suppliers (daily call-off based on parts consumption).
	Vendor-managed inventory (VMI) was started in the domestic PDC—the inventory was managed by Company A, and a pull planning algorithm was started with the domestic PDC.
	The foreign PDCs kept sending their monthly orders as before.
	The capacity-planning process was improved.
	A logistics-production contract was established.

Results and Ongoing Strategy

The design work for the supply chain was done in January 2005, producing an initial plan for 2005. At the end of the year, the project had been implemented in half the assembly lines. The next year, 2006, was dedicated to completing implementation in all the final assembly lines. Table 17.4 shows the evolution of the main KPIs from the end of 2004 to the end of 2006.

Company A had embraced a new operations system paradigm; the results just given show what a breakthrough had been achieved from the stagnation during 2000–2004.

> *By the end of 2005 (at the end of the first year of TFM implementation), it became clear that new horizons could be seen for the supply chain based on the pull-flow possibilities discovered.*

Table 17.4   Evolution of the Main KPIs for Company A from 2004 to the End of 2006

KPI	2004	End of 2006
Total inventory coverage (raw materials + work in process + finished goods)	50 days	30 days
Internal defects rate	12,000 ppm	5,750 ppm
Customer-service level	93 percent	98.5 percent
Achievement of the assembly-line production schedule	50 percent	92 percent
Productivity	70 parts/operator	94.5 parts/operator
Efficiency of final assembly line	75 percent	101 percent

The project breathed new life into Company A's strategy for improvement. By the end of 2005, the company had defined a new strategy to cover the next seven years until the end of 2012. This strategy was divided into the following components:

▲ *Pull-make strategy.* This strategy made use of all the tools in the production and internal logistics flow domains. The first two years of implementation focused mainly on the final assembly. The system has still to be extended to all the internal suppliers. The goal is to have all the type 2 and type 3 logistics loops (discussed in Chapter 2) perfected with *kaizen* tools.

▲ *Pull-deliver strategy.* This strategy took all the tools in the external logistics flow domain and applied them to the delivery side of the supply chain. The first two years focused on the domestic PDC. The goal is to have all foreign PDCs embrace VMI. The plan also includes extending the model to the PDCs and perfecting the type 1 logistics loop (from final customer order to final customer delivery and satisfaction). This will result in improvements to all aspects of transport and operation of the PDCs.

▲ *Pull-source strategy.* This strategy took all the tools in the external logistics flow domain and applied them to the source side of the supply chain. The first two years focused on the bought parts for the final assembly lines and the suppliers involved. The plan includes extending the model to all suppliers and creating logistics cells in the warehouse for all parts.

Company A is now certain that every year will be a better year in terms of *kaizen* results. The company is confident about the future because it has begun to deploy a clear model—and one that all employees fully support. The *kaizen* pull-flow system is no longer simply a theoretical model or a dream but very much a reality—a reality coming out of practical *gemba* activities that make the company more competitive every day.

PART FOUR

Appendices

Calculations for Transport *Kanban* Loops

Supporting Excel files used to generate some of the diagrams can be downloaded from the Kaizen Institute's website (www.kaizen.com).

In the discussion on the internal logistics flow pillar and the synchronization domain (Chapter 9), I talked about six types of *kanban* loops (recognized by the different types of *kanban* cards used for each type of *kanban* loop) (Figure A.1). In this appendix I give more information about the first three types of *kanban* loops that do not include production in the logistics loop. *Kanban* loops 1 and 2 are delivery and source *kanban* loops, respectively. *Kanban* loop 1 is simply the customer orders converted into *kanban* cards. *Kanban* loop 2 is the method of ordering the materials and parts from the purchased component supermarket to the suppliers, which starts with a logistics pull planning algorithm (explained in Chapter 13).

Kanban Loop 1: Transport Delivery *Kanban*

This *kanban* works in the logistics loop involving the final customer. It is just a subset of the customer order. If the company is managing the finished goods inventory at an outside location (vendor-managed inventory [VMI]), then a logistics pull planning algorithm can be used to calculate replenishment needs. Because the source and delivery sides of any company in the supply chain are mirrors of each other (my company is a supplier in the delivery logistics loop and a customer in the source logistics loop), the company can use the algorithms explained for *kanban* loop 2 (transport source *kanban*) in a VMI situation. Figure A.2 provides a summary of *kanban* loop 1.

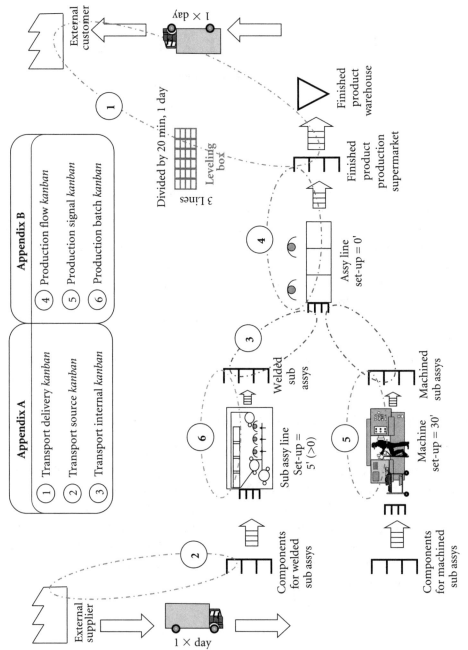

Figure A.1 Six types of *kanban* loops.

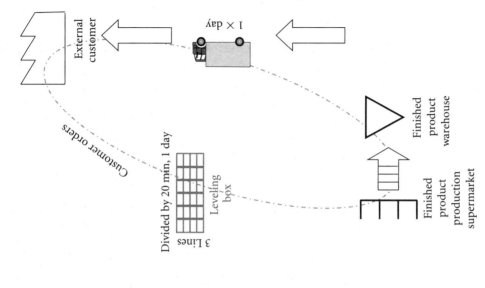

- Customer is an external customer (also called the company direct customer)

- Supplier is a finished product supermarket (or even a final assembly line in some cases)

- Transport is by truck

- Typical transport frequencies are 1 to 5 days, but can be 30 days or more (international deliveries)

- Delivery lead time can vary a lot around the average

- It is a *kanban* calculated based on the production orders

- The *kanban* is just a multiple of the production order (the production order divided by the container size)

- It is a *kanban* used to start the pull flow cycle

- This *kanban* comes from the leveling box

- The operation of the system is explained in detail in the logistics pull planning chapter

Figure A.2 *Kanban* loop 1: transport delivery *kanban*.

293

Kanban Loop 2: Transport Source *Kanban*

Figures A.3 through A.6 explain a possible process for establishing a *kanban* system with an outside vendor.

Order Size Calculations: A Word of Advice

A word of advice is necessary regarding order-size calculations. You will notice that in the parameter calculations, the order size is equal to the order level (the replenishment level). This works very well when the shipment frequency (SF) and the lead time are one day or less, but when these two parameters are higher than one day, the size of the generated inventory will be too big. The order size will have to be recalculated using the sell-one, buy-one approach or by determining demand according to the shipment frequency. (For example, if the SF is one day, you order one day's worth of sales or one day of estimated demand. If the SF is five days, you can order daily, but you know that you will receive a batch of five days' worth of orders.)

- Customer is a purchased components supermarket
- Supplier is an outside (external) supplier
- Transport is made by truck, usually with no standard work cycle (meaning there is not a fixed schedule for the delivery)
- Typical transport frequencies are 1 to 5 days, but can be 30 days or more (international deliveries)
- Delivery lead time can vary a lot around an average when the external supplier has a lot of internal *muda*

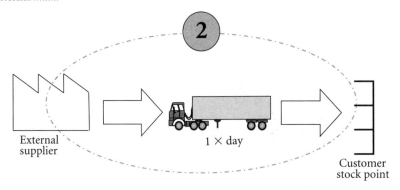

Figure A.3 *Kanban* loop 2: transport source *kanban* (a).

1. Calculate *kanban* parameters:

	Parameters	Formula	Units	Part A	Part B	Part C	Observations
a	Average demand		parts/hour	15	5	2	
b	Average leadtime		hours	1	1	5	
c	Demand variation		%	10%	10%	20%	Estimate according to daily variation
d	Leadtime variation		%	10%	10%	20%	Estimate according to daily variation
e	Cycle stock	a x b	parts	15	5	10	
f	Safety stock demand variation	c x e	parts	2	1	2	
g	Safety stock leadtime variation	(e + f) x d	parts	2	1	2	

i	Order level	e + f + g	parts	19	7	14
h	Order size	g	containers	19	7	14

- The order size and order level can be calculated in number of containers (ex: pallets)
- If pallet size is 9 parts for part A, then we order 2 pallets when we reach the level of 2 pallets
- Then the *kantan* can be 9 units (1 pallet) and order level 2 *kanbans*

2. Make *kanban* documents:

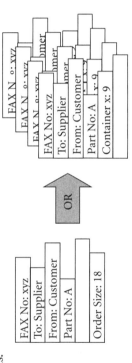

FAX No: xyz
To: Supplier
From: Customer
Part No: A

Order Size: 18

OR

FAX No: xyz
To: Supplier
From: Customer
Part No: A
Container x: 9

Figure A.4 *Kanban loop 2: transport source kanban* (b).

295

3. Operation:

- Place *kanban* on the order level point in the physical stock
- If the parts are inside a container, a *kanban* card can be made for each container and all parameters can be calculated in number of containers
- In this case it is possible to make a order building box to place each *kanban* and mark the order level on the box

Order level

FAX No: xyz
To: Supplier
From: Customer
Part NO: A
Order level: 18
Order size: 18

A	B	C
A		
A	B	C

Or

Kanban ordering box

A

Order building box

Figure A.5 *Kanban* loop 2: transport source *kanban* (c).

3. Operation (continued):

- Make a ordering box (to collect *kanbans* that reached the order level)
- Send to supplier (define the frequency; example: every 2 hours)

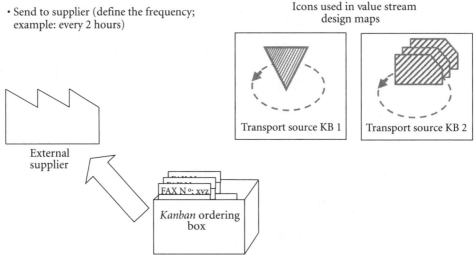

Icons used in value stream design maps

Transport source KB 1

Transport source KB 2

External supplier

FAX N°: xyz

Kanban ordering box

Figure A.6 *Kanban* loop 2: transport source *kanban* (d).

Kanban Loop 3: Transport Internal *Kanban*

Kanban loop 3 is explained in Figures A.7 to A.9.

The calculations of bin size in fact give the size of the supermarket for each stock-keeping unit (SKU). The units of calculation are expressed in number of parts. The number of containers is shown in the results cell.

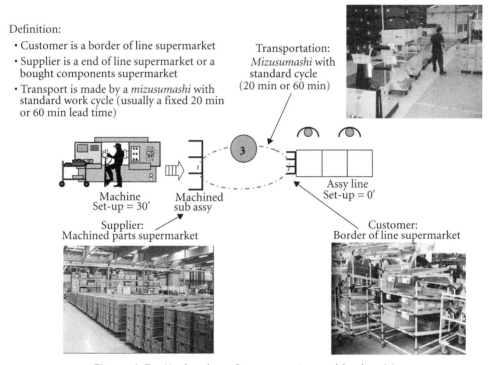

Definition:
- Customer is a border of line supermarket
- Supplier is a end of line supermarket or a bought components supermarket
- Transport is made by a *mizusumashi* with standard work cycle (usually a fixed 20 min or 60 min lead time)

Transportation:
Mizusumashi with standard cycle (20 min or 60 min)

Machine
Set-up = 30'

Machined
sub assy

Assy line
Set-up = 0'

Supplier:
Machined parts supermarket

Customer:
Border of line supermarket

Figure A.7   *Kanban* loop 3: transport internal *kanban* (a).

1. Each *kanban* is attached to one small container

   (chosen to eliminate *muda* of operator picking in the border of the line)

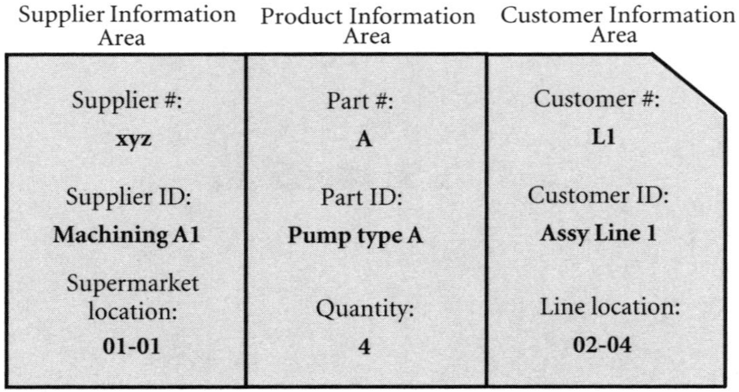

Supplier Information Area	Product Information Area	Customer Information Area
Supplier #: **xyz** Supplier ID: **Machining A1** Supermarket location: **01-01**	Part #: **A** Part ID: **Pump type A** Quantity: **4**	Customer #: **L1** Customer ID: **Assy Line 1** Line location: **02-04**

2. Calculate *kanban* parameters

	Parameters	Formula	Units	Part A	Part B	Part C	Observations
a	Average demand		parts/hour	30	15	5	
b	Average leadtime		hours	1	1	1	*Mizusumashi* cycle
c	Demand variation		%	10%	10%	20%	
d	Leadtime variation		%	0%	0%	0%	Standard *mizu* cycle=no delays
e	Container size (KB)		parts/KB	4	4	2	
f	Cycle stock	a x b	parts	30	15	5	
g	Safety stock demand variation	f x c	parts	3	2	1	
h	Safety stock leadtime variation	(f+g) x d	parts	0	0	0	
i	Bin size	(f+g+h) x 2+e	parts	70	38	14	Customer supermarket size
	Bin size	i / e	containers	18	10	7	Customer supermarket size

Input cell
Intermediate calculations cell
Result cell

Figure A.8 *Kanban* loop 3: transport internal *kanban* (b).

298

3. Operation:

- The *mizusumashi* stops every cycle at all border of line supermarkets
- Collects empty containers (with *kanban* fixed tags)
- Goes back to the supplier supermarket
- Collects full containers (replacing empty with full)
- Goes back to the border of line supermarket
- Supplies full containers and collects empty containers
- The *kanbans* are attached to the containers

Icon used in value stream design maps

Transport internal KB

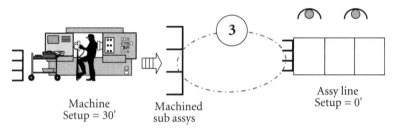

Machine
Setup = 30'

Machined
sub assys

Assy line
Setup = 0'

Figure A.9   *Kanban* loop 3: transport internal *kanban* (c).

Calculations for Production *Kanban* Loops

Supporting Excel files used to generate some of the diagrams can be downloaded from the Kaizen Institute's website (www.kaizen.com).

In the discussion on the internal logistics flow pillar and the synchronization domain in Chapter 10, I talked about six types of *kanban* cards (Figure B.1). In this appendix I give more information about *kanban* loops 4 to 6, which include production in the logistics loop. The big difference between logistics loops with and without production is that an economic order quantity (EOQ) type of calculation will be required to optimize the utilization of the pacemaker machines or lines in the loop. In *kanban* loop 4, the changeover time is zero, and this implies that the order or batch size can be zero. In *kanban* loop 5, the changeover time is larger than zero, and a batch size that optimizes machine utilization must be calculated. *Kanban* loop 6 is similar to *kanban* loop 5—the difference is in the format and use of the *kanban* cards. In *kanban* loop 5, only one card is used, representing the batch size. In *kanban* loop 6, there is one card per container and a batch-building box.

Kanban Loop 4: Production Flow *Kanban*

This *kanban* works in a logistics loop that includes a production or assembly line with zero changeover (or setup) time (Figures B.2 through B.4).

302

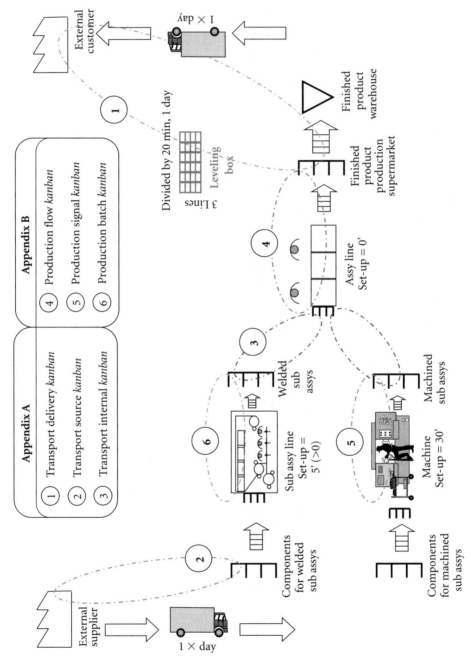

Figure B.1 Six types of *kanban* loops.

Appendix A

① Transport delivery *kanban*

② Transport source *kanban*

③ Transport internal *kanban*

Appendix B

④ Production flow *kanban*

⑤ Production signal *kanban*

⑥ Production batch *kanban*

External customer

1 × day

Finished product warehouse

Finished product production supermarket

Divided by 20 min, 1 day

Leveling box

3 Lines

Assy line
Set-up = 0'

Welded sub assys

Machined sub assys

Sub assy line
Set-up = 5' (>0)

Machine
Set-up = 30'

Components for welded sub assys

Components for machined sub assys

External supplier

1 × day

3. Operation:

- *Kanbans* are located on supermarket on each container (usually in front of the assembly or production line)
- Consumption at supermarket frees *kanban*
- *Kanban* is sent to one line with zero set-up capability (means it has flexibility to work with very small batches or even batches of 1 piece)
- *Kanban* goes to a sequencer at the beginning of the line
- *Kanban* is produced in FIFO according to the sequencer order
- The border of line has all the necessary components to start production

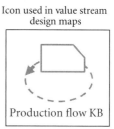

Icon used in value stream design maps

Production flow KB

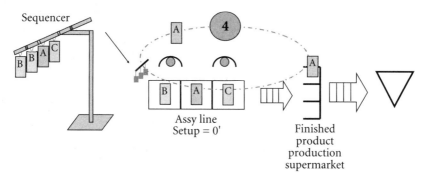

Figure B.2   *Kanban* loop 4: production flow *kanban* (a).

1. Each *kanban* is placed in one small container

(chosen to eliminate *muda* of operator picking in the border of the line)

Supplier Information Area	Product Information Area	Customer Information Area
Supplier #: **L1**	Part #: **A**	Customer #: **S1**
Supplier ID: **Line A1**	Part ID: **Pump type A**	Customer ID: **FP supermarket 1**
Sequencer location: **L1-WS1**	Quantity: **4**	Supermarket location: **01-02**

Input cell
Intermediate calculations cell
Result cell

2. Calculation of *kanban* parameters

	Parameters	Formula	Units	Part A	Part B	Part C	Observations
a	Part work content		min/part	4	4	4	sum of all workstations
b	Container size (KB)		parts/KB	4	4	2	
c	Average demand		parts/hour	30	15	5	
d	Demand variation		%	10%	10%	20%	
e	Transport average leadtime		hour	0.3	0.3	0.3	consider 2 *mizu* cycles
f	Line average leadtime	a x b / 60	hour	0.3	0.3	0.1	Leadtime of 1 *kanban*
g	Leadtime variation		%	10%	10%	10%	Machine stoppage time
h	Cycle stock	c x (e + f)	parts	17	9	3	
i	Safety stock demand variation	d x h	parts	2	1	1	
j	Safety stock leadtime variation	(h+ i) x g	parts	2	1	1	

l	Bin size	(h+i+j) + b	parts	25	15	7	Customer supermarket size
m	Bin size	i / b	containers	7	4	4	Customer supermarket size

Figure B.3 *Kanban* loop 4: production-flow *kanban* (b).

3. Operation:

- *Kanbans* are located on supermarket on each container (usually in front of the assembly or production line)
- Consumption at supermarket frees *kanban*
- *Kanban* is sent to one line with zero set-up capability (means it has flexibility to work with very small batches or even batches of 1 piece)
- *Kanban* goes to a sequencer at the beginning of the line
- *Kanban* is produced in FIFO according to the sequencer order
- The border of line has all the necessary components to start production

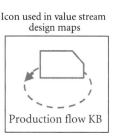

Icon used in value stream design maps

Production flow KB

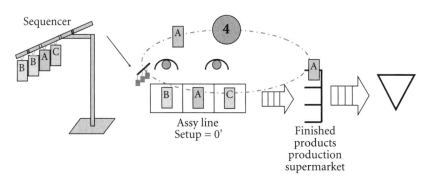

Figure B.4   *Kanban* loop 4: production flow *kanban* (c).

Kanban Loop 5: Production Signal *Kanban*

Kanban loop 5 is explained in Figures B.5 through B.8. There is only one *kanban* (in triangular form) per stock-keeping unit (SKU), and the quantity on the *kanban* card is the same as the batch size.

The calculations of batch size are based on the following EOQ concepts:

▲ A certain number of product references is assigned to each machine (dedicated to the machine).

▲ The unit cycle times are used to calculate the total production time (production or value-adding time).

▲ The time available for changeover is then calculated by subtracting the production time and the stoppage time (except changeover) from the machine opening time.

▲ Using the unit changeover time, you calculate the possible number of changeovers. This result is used to calculate the batch size.

Definition:

- Customer is an end of line supermarket
- Supplier is a production or assembly line with product reference changeover (set-up time greater than 0)
- Transport of signal order (triangular *kanban*) to the beginning of the line is made by a *mizusumashi* or using other means
- The sequencer should be a physical device in order to have visual control of line performance
- There is only one *kanban* for each product reference

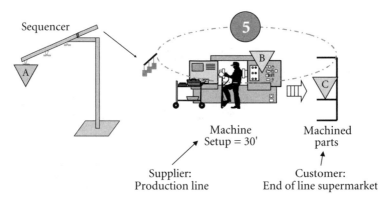

Figure B.5 *Kanban* loop 5: production signal *kanban* (a).

1. Each *kanban* is placed in the reorder level point (in the supermarket)

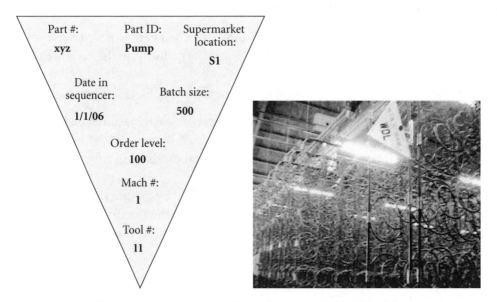

Figure B.6 *Kanban* loop 5: production signal *kanban* (b).

2. Calculation of kanban parameters

Supplier pacemaker machine:

- It is necessary to have machine OEE data, namely:
  - Opening time
  - Unavailability time (stoppages)
  - Setup time (real)
- Batch size and order level are printed on the kanban
- The maximum size of the customer supermarket is the sum of batch size and order level

Time for producing the demand	632
Opening time	860
Available time	228
% Stoppage time	15%
Stoppage tim/day	129

Average time for setup	99
Average setup time per SKU	5
No Refs	5

Possible # setup/day	19.8
Possible EPE—Every product every (days)	0.3

Input cell
Adjustment cell
Checking cell

Prod. code	Product identification ref. name	Demand (parts/day)	Cycle time (min)	Production time (min)	Batch size (parts)	Batch size (days)	Real # Setup/day	Machine time (min)	Transport time (min)	Leadtime (min)	Takt time (min)	Max LT (min)	Order level (parts)
008C528	Component 1	438	1.3	569	438	1.0	1.0	569.4	60	634.4	2.0	634.4	323
008C539	Component 2	18	1.3	23	180	10.0	0.1	234.0	60	299.0	47.8	634.4	13
008C533	Component 3	13	1.3	17	130	10.0	0.1	169.0	60	234.0	66.2	634.4	10
008A970	Component 4	10	1.3	13	100	10.0	0.1	130.0	60	195.0	86.0	634.4	7
008A749	Component 5	7	1.3	9	70	10.0	0.1	91.0	60	156.0	122.9	634.4	5
		486		632			1.4						
							3.6						

Real EPE (days)

Figure B.7 Kanban loop 5: production signal kanban (c).

3. Operation:

- *Kanban* is located on supermarket on the order level point. There is only one *kanban* for each part number (triangular shape)
- Consumption at supermarket frees *kanban* (when stock reaches order level)
- *Kanban* is sent to one production line (dedicated to a fixed number of part numbers). Because the line has set-up time, the *kanban* indicates what is the batch size
- *Kanban* goes to a sequencer at the beginning of the line
- *Kanban* is produced in FIFO according to the sequencer order
- The border of line has all the necessary components to start production

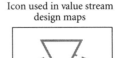

Icon used in value stream design maps

Production signal KB

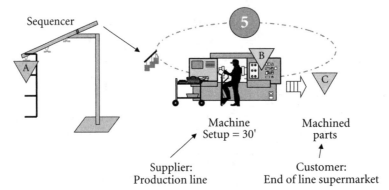

Figure B.8 *Kanban* loop 5: production signal *kanban* (d).

Kanban Loop 6: Production Batch *Kanban*

Kanban loop 6 is explained in Figures B.9 through B.12. There is one *kanban* card for each container. The *kanbans* accumulate in a batch building box until the batch size is reached for each reference.

The calculations for batch size are based on the EOQ concept of optimizing machine utilization and are similar to those for *kanban* loop 5 (production signal *kanban*).

Definition:

- Customer is an end of line supermarket
- Supplier is a production or assembly line with product reference changeover (set-up time greater than 0)
- Transport of *kanbans* to the beginning of the line is made by a *mizusumashi* or using other means
- The batch building box should be a physical device in order to have visual control of line performance
- The product is inside a standard container, each one with a *kanban* inside

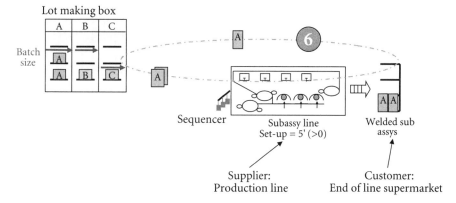

Figure B.9 *Kanban* loop 6: production batch *kanban* (a).

1. Each *kanban* is placed in the order level point (in the supermarket)

Supplier Information Area	Product Information Area	Customer Information Area
Supplier #: **L1**	Part #: **A**	Customer #: **S1**
Supplier ID: **Line A1**	Part ID: **Pump type A**	Customer ID: **FP supermarket 1**
Batch box location: **L1-BB1**		
Sequencer location: **L1-WS1**	Quantity: **4**	Supermarket location: **01-02**

Figure B.10 *Kanban* loop 6: production batch *kanban* (b).

2. Calculation of *kanban* parameters

Supplier pacemaker machine:

Time for producing the demand	632
Opening time	860
Available time	228
% Stoppage time	15%
Stoppage tim/day	129

Average time for setup	99
Average setup time per SKU	5
No refs	5

Possible # setup/day	19.8
Possible EPE—Every product every (days)	0.3

- It is necessary to have machine OEE data, namely:
  - Opening time
  - Unavailability time (stoppages)
  - Setup time (real)
- Batch size and order level are printed on the *kanban*
- The maximum size of the customer supermarket is the sum of batch size and order level

Input cell
Adjustment cell
Checking cell

Prod. code	Product identification ref. name	Demand (parts/day)	Cycle time (min)	Cycle time (min)	Production time (min)	Batch size (days)	Real # Setup/day	Machine time (min)	Transport time (min)	Leadtime (min)	Takt time (min)	Max LT (min)	Total # cont	Batch # cont
008C528	Component 1	50	438	1.3	569	111	4.0	143.8	60	208.8	2.0	208.8	5	3
008C539	Component 2	50	18	1.3	23	5	4.0	5.9	60	70.9	47.8	208.8	1	1
008C533	Component 3	50	13	1.3	17	3	4.0	4.3	60	69.3	66.2	208.8	1	1
008A970	Component 4	50	10	1.3	13	3	4.0	3.3	60	68.3	86.0	208.8	1	1
008A749	Component 5	50	7	1.3	9	2	4.0	2.3	60	67.3	122.9	208.8	1	1
			486		632		19.8							
							0.3							

Real EPE (days)

Figure B.11 *Kanban* loop 6: production batch *kanban* (c).

3. Operation

- *Kanbans* are located on supermarket on each container (usually in front of the assembly or production line)
- Consumption at supermarket frees *kanban*
- *Kanban* is sent to one line that needs to build a batch to be efficient. *Kanban* goes to a lot-making box
- A batch of *kanbans* goes to a sequencer at the beginning of the line
- The batch of *kanbans* is produced in FIFO according to the sequencer order
- The border of line has all the necessary components to start production

Icon used in value stream design maps

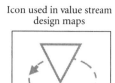

Production signal KB

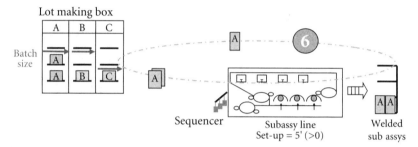

Figure B.12   *Kanban* loop 6: production batch *kanban* (d).

Two Types of Pull Planning Algorithms

Logistics Pull Planning Algorithms

Figure C.1 shows a basis for an algorithm that can be used to calculate supplier orders. This algorithm is presented purely as an example to serve for simulations. Each practical case should be thoroughly tested and simulated before the algorithm is put into practice. Fine-tuning will be necessary based on the reality of each case.

It is also advisable to take a look at the current enterprise resource planning (ERP) system running in the company and check what types of logistics pull planning algorithms are available and what type of parameterization is possible. The following algorithm serves as a basis for quick experimentation using a spreadsheet. It must be tested for improvements and to be sure that it covers all possible scenarios before it is eventually implemented.

The transport *kanban* calculations presented in Appendix B are also based on logistics pull planning (logistics in the sense that no production exists in the logistics loop) and should be checked (mainly the calculations for the transport source *kanban*).

Calculating the Logistics Pull Planning Algorithm

The following calculations need to be done for each product each time the product is sold:

1. Calculate stock level (SL):
   SL = current stock + supplier orders in process

2. Calculate reorder level (RL):
   RL = AS3M × OIL

   where AS3M = average daily sales for the last three months (moving average with daily updates), and OIL = optimal inventory level

The following calculations need to be done for each product reference each time a product is sold:

- *Calculate SL:* Stock level = current stock + supplier orders in process

- *Calculate RL:* Reorder level = AS3M * OIL

- *Calculate AS3M:* Average daily sales last 3 months (moving average with daily update)

- *Define OIL:* Optimum inventory level (in days):
  - OIL = 0, means MTO make to order product (no stock)
  - OIL = Total replenishment lead-time + safety stock (% demand variation + % lead-time variation)
  - Special cases can have a special OIL with a higher safety stock or a seasonality correction

- *Calculate SO:* Supplier order = RL – SL
  - Generate a list of SOs
  - Identify product line, delivery date, and OIL policy

Figure C.1 Logistics pull planning algorithm (a).

▲ OIL = total replenishment lead time + safety stock (percent demand variation + percent lead-time variation).

▲ OIL = 0 when it is a make-to-order (MTO) product; that is, no stock will be built.

Where a seasonality correction is required, OIL can have a higher safety stock.

3. Calculate supplier order (SO):
SO = RL – SL

▲ Generate a list of SOs.

▲ Identify product line, delivery date, and OIL policy.

Production Pull Planning Algorithms

Figure C.2 shows a basis for an algorithm that can be used to calculate production orders. This algorithm is presented purely as an example to serve for simulations. Each practical case should be thoroughly tested and simulated before the algorithm is put into practice. Fine-tuning will be necessary based on the reality of each case.

It is also advisable to take a look at the current ERP system running in the company and check what types of production pull planning algorithms are available and what type of parameterization is possible.

The following calculations need to be done for each product reference each time a product is sold or consumed

- *Calculate SL:* Stock level = current stock – current customer orders (up to 10 days logistics box horizon) + production orders in process

- *Calculate RL:* Reorder level = AS3M * OIL

- *Calculate AS3M:* Average daily sales last 3 months (moving average with daily update)

- *Define OIL:* Optimum inventory level (in days):

  - OIL = 0, means MTO make to order product (no stock)

  - OIL = Total replenishment lead-time + safety stock (% demand variation + % lead-time variation)

  - Special cases can have a special OIL with a higher safety stock or a seasonality correction

- *Calculate NPO:* Needed production order = RL – SL

- *Calculate BS:* Batch size = AS3M * EPEI

- *Define EPEI:* Every product every interval (in days):

  - EPEI = 0 day, means no need of batch because the machine or line has "zero changeover" (flexibility)

  - EPEI = 1 day, means make a batch of 1 day (usually used for high runners)

  - EPEI = 5 day, means make a batch of 5 day (usually used for medium low runners)

  - An EPEI should be defined for each product reference based on the "production batch *kanban*" calculations explained in Appendix B

- *Calculate CPO:* Corrected production order:

  - If NPO is equal or bigger than BS then CPO = NPO

  - If NPO is smaller than BS then CPO = BS

  - Identify "CPO for customer order" (part of CPO to fulfill customer order) and "CPO for stock" (part of CPO to fulfill OIL or batch policy)

  - Identify product line, delivery date, OIL, and batch size policy

Figure C.2   Logistics pull planning algorithm (b).

The following algorithm serves as a basis for quick experimentation using a spreadsheet. It must be tested for improvements and to be sure that it covers all possible scenarios before it is eventually implemented.

The production *kanban* calculations presented in Appendix B are also based on production pull planning (production in the sense that production, with or without changeover time, exists in the logistics loop) and should be checked (mainly the calculations for the production batch *kanban*).

Calculating the Production Pull Planning Algorithm

The following calculations need to be done for each product each time the product is sold or consumed:

1. Calculate stock level (SL):
   SL = current stock – current customer orders (up to 10-day logistics box horizon) + production orders in process

2. Calculate reorder level (RL):
   RL = average daily sales for the last three months (moving average with daily updates) (AS3M) × optimal inventory level (OIL)
   ▲ OIL = total replenishment lead time + safety stock (percent demand variation + percent lead-time variation).
   ▲ OIL = 0 when it is a make-to-order (MTO) product; that is, no stock will be built.
   ▲ Where a seasonality correction is required, OIL can have a higher safety stock.

3. Calculate needed production order (NPO):
   NPO = RL – SL

4. Calculate batch size (BS):
   BS = AS3M × EPEI
   ▲ Define every product every interval (EPEI) expressed in days.
   ▲ EPEI = 0 days when no batch is required because the machine is totally flexible; that is, it required zero changeover time.
   ▲ EPEI = 1 day when one batch of the same product will be produced every day (usually used for high runners).
   ▲ EPEI = 5 days when one batch of the same product will be produced every five days (usually used for medium or low runners).
   ▲ EPEI should be defined for each product based on the production-batch *kanban* calculation explained in Appendix B.

5. Calculate corrected production order (CPO):
   ▲ If the NPO is equal to or greater than the BS, then CPO = NPO.
   ▲ If the NPO is smaller than the BS, then CPO = BS.
   ▲ Define the CPO for customer order (part of CPO to fulfill customer order).
   ▲ Define the CPO for stock (part of CPO to fulfill OIL or batch policy).
   ▲ Define product line, delivery date, OIL, and batch-size policy.

Total Flow Management (TFM) Scorecards

- Basic reliability
- Production flow
- Internal logistics flow
- External logistics flow

Figure D.1 TFM scorecards.

No.	*Kaizen* Foundations	How to Score	Comments	Score
I.1.1	Quality first	Check degree of belief/commitment of key leadership. Ask if they believe in bring market in, next operation is customer, upstream management. Ask what have they done to implement it or what they intend to do.		
I.1.2	Focused teamwork	Check degree of belief of key leadership. Ask if they believe in involving people, don't judge/don't blame, *kobetsu* teamwork. Ask what have they done to implement it or what they intend to do.		
I.1.3	Process and results	Check degree of belief of key leadership. Ask if they believe in focus on process improvement through SDCA and PDCA. Ask what have they done to implement it or what they intend to do.		
I.1.4	*Gemba* orientation	Check degree of belief of key leadership. Ask if they believe in go to *gemba*, check *genbutsu*, speaking with data. Ask what have they done to promote it or what they intend to do.		
I.1.5	*Muda* elimination	Check degree of belief of key leadership. Ask if they believe in eliminate 3 Ms, 7 flow *mudas*, 8 equipment losses, other *mudas*. Ask what have they done to promote it or what they intend to do.		
I.1.6	Visual standards	Check degree of belief of key leadership. Ask if they believe in develop standard work, visual management, standard management. Ask what have they done to implement it or what they intend to do.		
I.1.7	Pull flow thinking	Check degree of belief of key leadership. Ask if they believe in create material and information flow, pull from market. Ask what have they done to implement it or what they intend to do. Make the evaluation on the basis of the answers.		

na: not applicable
0: very insufficient
1: insufficient
2: sufficient
3: good
4: very good

Company: _____ Logistic Loop: _____
Analyst: _____ Date: _____ Avg Score: _____

Figure D.2 Basic reliability—*kaizen* foundations.

No.	Manpower Reliability	How to Score	Comments	Score
I.2.1	General level of 5S and housekeeping	Degree of 5S of workstations and work areas.		
I.2.2	Turnover, punctuality, and absenteeism	Degree of reliability of the workers present according to the work timetable.		
I.2.3	Supervisor skills	Degree of capability of supervisors in terms of Job Instruction (teaching) and job relations (maintaining good work relations and solving HR problems).		
I.2.4	Operator skills	Degree of specialization, as opposed to multi-skills.		
I.2.5	Motivation	General degree of people motivation according to company recent history and current status.		
I.2.6	Compensation	General level of salaries and compensation schemes. Type of bonus or incentives.		
I.2.7	Teamwork habits	Degree of practice of working in improvement teams.		

na: not applicable
0: very insufficient
1: insufficient
2: sufficient
3: good
4: very good

Company: _____ Logistic Loop: _____
Analyst: _____ Date: _____ Avg Score: _____

Figure D.3 Basic reliability—manpower.

No.	Machines Reliability	How to Score	Comments	Score
I.3.1	Machine 5S	General level of 5S regarding equipment maintenance. Degree of machine 5S.		
I.3.2	Equipment capacity	Degree of obvious availability of machine capacity.		
I.3.3	Maintenance support	Degree of availability of maintenance support.		
I.3.4	Equipment reliability	Degree of availability of equipment uptime.		
I.3.5	Changeover times	Degree of variability in changeover times. Importance of changeover times in the availability of machine uptime.		
I.3.6	Use of space	Degree of availability of space.		
I.3.7	Machine standards	Existence of basic standards for cleaning, inspection, and service of machines.		

Company: _____ Logistic Loop: _____
Analyst: _____ Date: _____ Avg Score: _____

na: not applicable
0: very insufficient
1: insufficient
2: sufficient
3: good
4: very good

Figure D.4 Basic reliability—machines.

No.	Materials Reliability	How to Score	Comments	Score
I.4.1	General 5S in stores	General level of 5S in storage areas. Degree of storage 5S.		
I.4.2	Materials availability	Degree of materials availability when needed.		
I.4.3	Materials quality	Degree of reliability regarding the quality of materials.		
I.4.4	Inventory information reliability	Degree of reliability of stock control systems.		
I.4.5	Materials accessibility	Degree of easiness to identify and release materials from storage.		
I.4.6	Materials synchronization	Degree of reliability of the materials planning systems.		
I.4.7	Incoming inspection	Degree of effectiveness of incoming quality inspection.		

na: not applicable
0: very insufficient
1: insufficient
2: sufficient
3: good
4: very good

Company: _____
Analyst: _____

Logistic Loop: _____
Date: _____

Avg Score: _____

Figure D.5   Basic reliability—materials.

No.	Methods Reliability	How to Score	Comments	Score
I.5.1	Basic work instructions/ standards	Degree of information regarding variations in working methods.		
I.5.2	Product work content variations	Degree of variation of methods from operation to operation and from product to product.		
I.5.3	Working environment variation	Degree of environmental variation (temperature, humidity, etc.).		
I.5.4	Working cycle variability	Degree of variation of working cycle time for each operator.		
I.5.5	Quality requirements variation	Degree of variation in quality requirements from operation to operation.		
I.5.6	Basic work content load leveling	Degree of stability in working loads and timetables.		
I.5.7	Safety and ergonomics	Degree of existence of obvious *muri* situations (extremely difficult and variable work methods that pose a threat in terms of ergonomics and safety).		

na: not applicable
0: very insufficient
1: insufficient
2: sufficient
3: good
4: very good

Company: _____ Logistic Loop: _____
Analyst: _____ Date: _____ Avg Score: _____

Figure D.6 Basic reliability—methods.

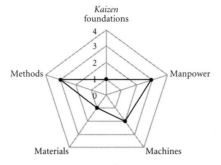

No.	Basic Reliability–Top 5 Issues
1	
2	
3	
4	
5	

Figure D.7   Basic reliability—summary.

No.	Line and Layout Design	How to Score	Comments	Score
II.1.1	Process layout	Degree of operations integration into assembly cells or lines that include all the necessary operations.		
II.1.2	Material flow inside cells or lines	Degree of one-piece flow implementation.		
II.1.3	Low-speed cells/lines	Degree of speed measured by cell/line cycle time. Few large, high-speed versus several low-speed cells/lines.		
II.1.4	Daisy line layout design	Degree of separation between manual work and machine automated work. Degree of non-isolated manpower. Degree of daisy layout design.		
II.1.5	*Shojinka* level	Operators' degree of multi-skills, handling multi-operations.		
II.1.6	*Mura* line balancing	Degree of line balancing according to the line cycle. Degree of variation of work cycle between different product references.		
II.1.7	*Gemba* workstation design	Degree of *muda* elimination principles applied during line design. Degree of *gemba* checking using cardboard engineering.		

Company: _____   Logistic Loop: _____   na: not applicable
Analyst: _____   Date: _____   Avg Score: _____   0: very insufficient
1: insufficient
2: sufficient
3: good
4: very good

Figure D.8 Production flow—line and layout design.

No.	Border of line	How to Score	Comments	Score
II.2.1	Back vs. frontal supply	Degree of maximizing frontal supply as compared to back supply.		
II.2.2	Big vs. small containers	Degree of use of small containers.		
II.2.3	Fixed vs. flow containers	Degree of use of flow containers (containers less than 10 kg or placed on roller bases with wheels).		
II.2.4	Use of kitting	Use of kitting. Degree of organization of parts inside one finished unit container. Degree of use of the concept of kitting.		
II.2.5	Dunning	Degree of organization of parts inside containers.		
II.2.6	Single feed of parts	Degree of use of individual part presentation to the operator.		
II.2.7	Racks and container layout	Degree of placement near the point of use.		

Company: _____   Logistic Loop: _____
Analyst: _____   Date: _____   Avg Score: _____

na: not applicable
0: very insufficient
1: insufficient
2: sufficient
3: good
4: very good

Figure D.9 Production flow—border of line.

325

No.	Standard Work	How to Score	Comments	Score
II.3.1	Standard operations times (SOT)	Degree of use of standard operation times and process capacity sheets.		
II.3.2	Quality of standard operation times	Degree of *muda*-free SOT.		
II.3.3	Efficiency improvement targets	Degree of efficiency measurement and establishment of improvement targets.		
II.3.4	Standard work sheets	Degree of use and display of SWS to visualize operator movement *muda*.		
II.3.5	Improvement sheets	Degree of use and display of improvement sheets (before/after display with results).		
II.3.6	Training plans	Degree of use and display of operators' training plans.		
II.3.7	Use of job instruction	Degree of use of breakdown sheets and TWI JI method for operator training.		

Company: _____ Logistic Loop: _____

Analyst: _____ Date: _____ Avg Score: _____

na: not applicable
0: very insufficient
1: insufficient
2: sufficient
3: good
4: very good

Figure D.10 Production flow—standard work.

No.	SMED	How to Score	Comments	Score
II.4.1	Changeover measurement	Degree of measurement of changeover times.		
II.4.2	Changeover reduction targets	Degree of use and display of SMED targets.		
II.4.3	SMED standard work sheets	Degree of use and display of changeover standard work sheets.		
II.4.4	Separation between internal and external set-up	Degree of use and display of this type of solution.		
II.4.5	Conversion of internal to external set-up	Degree of use and display of this type of solution.		
II.4.6	Reduction of internal set-up	Degree of use and display of this type of solution.		
II.4.7	Reduction of external set-up	Degree of use and display of this type of solution.		

na: not applicable
0: very insufficient
1: insufficient
2: sufficient
3: good
4: very good

Company: _____ Logistic Loop: _____
Analyst: _____ Date: _____ Avg Score: _____

Figure D.11 Production flow—SMED.

No.	Low-cost Automation	How to Score	Comments	Score
II.5.1	Low-cost automation checklist	Degree of utilization and display of the LCA checklist.		
II.5.2	LCA targets for process flow	Degree of LCA targets and action plans for LCA implementation.		
II.5.3	LCA experts team	Degree of existence and development of a dedicated team of experts for LCA implementation.		
II.5.4	Time-saving devices	Degree of implementation of this type of device.		
II.5.5	Automation of machine time	Degree of implementation of machine time automation.		
II.5.6	Automation of machine time with *poka yoke*	Degree of implementation of machine time automation with *poka yoke*.		
II.5.7	Automation of unloading time	Degree of implementation of unloading time automation.		

na: not applicable
0: very insufficient
1: insufficient
2: sufficient
3: good
4: very good

Company: _____ Logistic Loop: _____
Analyst: _____ Date: _____ Avg Score: _____

Figure D.12 Production flow—low-cost automation.

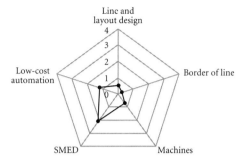

No.	Production Flow – Top 5 Issues
1	
2	
3	
4	
5	

Figure D.13   Production flow—summary.

No.	Supermarkets	How to Score	Comments	Score
III.1.1	Flow racks	Degree of implementation. For small containers or pallets of small containers.		
III.1.2	Ground storage on wheels	Ground storage on wheels for trolleys or rollers. Degree of implementation of trolleys or rollers.		
III.1.3	Ease of picking and supply	Degree of ease in picking or supplying the supermarkets. Check organization according to consumption and other relevant criteria.		
III.1.4	Bought components supermarkets	Degree of implementation of number of bought components ready to supply to the cells/lines. Check PFEP (plan for every part).		
III.1.5	Border of line supermarkets	Degree of separation between supply path and consumption path. General organization of border of line supermarkets.		
III.1.6	Finished product supermarkets	Degree of implementation of finished product supermarkets. Check the applicability of logistic cells or end of line supermarkets.		
III.1.7	Visual management of supermarkets	Degree of visual management and 5S of supermarkets.		

na: not applicable
0: very insufficient
1: insufficient
2: sufficient
3: good
4: very good

Company: _____   Logistic Loop: _____
Analyst: _____   Date: _____   Avg Score: _____

Figure D.14 Internal logistics flow—supermarkets.

No.	Mizusumashi	How to Score	Comments	Score
III.2.1	Separation between production and logistics operators	Degree of separation between production operators and logistics supply operators. Use of local *mizusumashi* with trolley.		
III.2.2	High-frequency standardized *mizusumashi* trains	Degree of implementation of logistics trains for small containers, trolleys, and rollers. Minimum frequency usually 60 minutes.		
III.2.3	*Mizusumashi* automated guided vehicles (AGV's) for KIT supply	Degree of AGV used only for sequenced supply of 1-piece kits.		
III.2.4	*Mizusumashi* standard work sheet	Degree of use of SWS showing frequency, tasks, times, and route.		
III.2.5	*Mizusumashi* schedule control	Degree of control of *mizusumashi* timetable. Related to route time variability control.		
III.2.6	*Mizusumashi* ergonomics	Degree of fulfillment of ergonomic rules for the *mizusumashi*, regarding loads and *muda* of operation.		
III.2.7	Visual management	Degree of visual management and 5S of *mizusumashi* trains.		

Company: _____   Logistic Loop: _____
Analyst: _____   Date: _____   Avg Score: _____

na: not applicable
0: very insufficient
1: insufficient
2: sufficient
3: good
4: very good

Figure D.15   Internal logistics flow—*mizusumashi*.

331

No.	Synchronizations (*Kanban, Junjo*)	How to Score	Comments	Score
III.3.1	Border of line supply with *kanban* system	Degree of implementation of internal delivery *kanban* system.		
III.3.2	Border of line supply with unit *junjo* (sequenced)	Degree of implementation. First, a check has to be made for any opportunities to implement this type of synchronization method.		
III.3.3	Border of line supply with kit *junjo* (sequenced)	Degree of implementation. First, a check has to be made for any opportunities to implement this type of synchronization method.		
III.3.4	*Kanban* movements made by *mizusumashi*	Degree of integration of the *kanban* system with *mizusumashi* tasks.		
III.3.5	Monthly check of *kanban* parameters	Degree of review of *kanban* parameters according to forecasted demand.		
III.3.6	Effectiveness of synchronization method	Degree of effectiveness of the synchronization method in preventing material shortages and guaranteeing just in time delivery to the border of line.		
III.3.7	*Kanban* visual management	Degree of visual management of the system to ensure that everyone can easily monitor the *kanban* status and instructions.		

na: not applicable
0: very insufficient
1: insufficient
2: sufficient
3: good
4: very good

Company: _____
Analyst: _____

Logistic Loop: _____
Date: _____   Avg Score: _____

Figure D.16   Internal logistics flow—synchronization (KB/JJ).

No.	Leveling	How to Score	Comments	Score
III.4.1	Leveling on the pacemaker cells/lines	Degree of leveling used, according to 5 Toyota levels.		
III.4.2	Order *kanbans* for leveling	Use of a procedure to transform customer or replenishment orders into *kanbans* (either small batch or unit *kanbans*).		
III.4.3	Logistics box concept for volume leveling	Use of a procedure to plan a constant daily work load on the pacemaker cells/lines, according to line capacity defined for the month.		
III.4.4	Leveling box concept for mix leveling	Use of a procedure to plan the exact sequence of products to be started on the cells/lines.		
III.4.5	Leveling standards	Degree of visual management and standardization of leveling procedures.		
III.4.6	Integration of leveling with *mizusumashi*	Degree of integration of leveling with *mizusumashi* tasks. Leveling information should be the starting point of *mizusumashi* work cycles.		
III.4.7	Use of leveling in the border of line supply	Use of leveling for *mizusumashi* supply to border of line.		

Company: _____   Logistic Loop: _____
Analyst: _____   Date: _____   Avg Score: _____

na: not applicable
0: very insufficient
1: insufficient
2: sufficient
3: good
4: very good

Figure D.17   Internal logistics flow—leveling.

No.	Production Pull Planning	How to Score	Comments	Score
III.5.1	Planning strategy for finished product	Degree of definition of MTS (make to stock) or MTO (make to order) for the finished product.		
III.5.2	Planning strategy for parts	Degree of definition of MTS (make to stock) or MTO (make to order) for parts.		
III.5.3	Capacity planning of the pacemaker cells/lines	Degree of capacity planning using forecasted demand to ensure required capacity in time for production.		
III.5.4	Logistics–production contract	Use of a formal meeting between logistics and production to agree to the forecasted capacity and product mix.		
III.5.5	Execution planning for MTS part numbers (PNs)	Use of pull algorithms for MTS products, based on frequent inventory replenishment algorithms.		
III.5.6	Execution planning for MTO PNs	Use of pull algorithms for MTO PNs, based on fixed customer orders (not forecasts).		
III.5.7	Leveling information coming from the market	Use of leveling information to determine acceptable delivery variations. This information should be included in the orders that will be used for leveling.		

na: not applicable
0: very insufficient
1: insufficient
2: sufficient
3: good
4: very good

Company: _____ Logistic Loop: _____
Analyst: _____ Date: _____ Avg Score: _____

Figure D.18 Internal logistics flow—production pull planing.

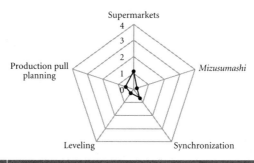

No.	Internal Logistics Flow – Top 5 Issues
1	
2	
3	
4	
5	

Figure D.19   Internal logistics flow—summary.

No.	Supermarkets	How to Score	Comments	Score
IV.1.1	Storage profiling	Degree of clear operations profiling studies that justify the layout of storage and layout (example: PQ analysis or product family analysis).		
IV.1.2	Product stored by type and turnover (storage cells)	Degree of cell layout implementation according to storage profiling. Example 1: Layout divided by customer logistics cells. Example 2: Layout divided by high runners, medium runners, and low runners.		
IV.1.3	One product-specific storage location per part number	Degree of existence of one primary location only for each SKU. Degree of space utilization for each location.		
IV.1.4	Storage of delivery packages	Degree of no repacking of individual SKUs.		
IV.1.5	Flexible layouts	Degree of separation of inbound and outbound operations (via different working timetables or different alleys). Existence of machine capacity for binning and picking.		
IV.1.6	Visual management	Degree of visual management standards in the warehouse (identification of location addresses and other visual standards).		
IV.1.7	Abnormalities control	Degree of daily measurement and control of abnormal situations (such as missing products, wrong quantities, wrong locations, wrong packaging, wrong identification).		

na: not applicable
0: very insufficient
1: insufficient
2: sufficient
3: good

Company: _____   Logistic Loop: _____
Analyst: _____   Date: _____   Avg Score: _____

Figure D.20 External logistics flows—storage and warehouse design.

No.	Milk Run	How to Score	Comments	Score
IV.2.1	Frequent shipment policy	Degree of existence of frequent shipments in the logistics loop (on a daily basis).		
IV.2.2	Local milk run operations	Degree of existence of local milk run operations (dedicated trucks and routes).		
IV.2.3	Far milk run operations	Degree of existence of far milk run operations (dedicated trucks and routes).		
IV.2.4	Local–far milk run operations	Degree of existence of local–far milk run operations (dedicated trucks and routes).		
IV.2.5	Milk run standard work	Degree of evidence of existence and improvement of milk run standards.		
IV.2.6	Milk run schedule control	Degree of control of fulfillment of the transportation schedules.		
IV.2.7	Truck utilization	Degree of utilization of truck capacity through load optimization.		

Company: _____
Analyst: _____

Logistic Loop: _____
Date: _____   Avg Score: _____

na: not applicable
0: very insufficient
1: insufficient
2: sufficient
3: good
4: very good

Figure D.21   External logistics flows—milk run.

No.	Source Flows (Inbound)	How to Score	Comments	Score
IV.3.1	Unloading operations	Degree of organization of unloading operations. Degree of flow (small amount of materials waiting time to be unloaded).		
IV.3.2	Check/sort operations	Justification for the check/control operations. Ideal state is no incoming quality control and sorting justified to obtain higher binning productivity and cross docking. Evaluate use and extension of cross docking to outbound.		
IV.3.3	Binning operations	Degree of effectiveness (reduced material waiting to be binned) and efficiency of binning operations (movements of workers against standard targets).		
IV.3.4	Leveling of binning operations	Use of leveling (or *heijunka*) box to control binning operations. Implies wave binning in standard pitch cycles.		
IV.3.5	Flow of returnable containers	Degree of effectiveness and efficiency in handling of returnable containers (5S and streamlined flow).		
IV.3.6	Inbound KPIs	Degree of existence of inbound KPIs (lines/man-hour, etc.).		
IV.3.7	Inbound standard work	Degree of improvement activities performed in all inbound operations (check evidence of value stream projects, *gemba kaizen* workshops, and other improvement activities).		

na: not applicable
0: very insufficient
1: insufficient
2: sufficient
3: good
4: very good

Company: _____
Analyst: _____

Logistic Loop: _____
Date: _____   Avg Score: _____

Figure D.22   External logistics flows—source flows.

No.	Delivery Flows (Outbound)	How to Score	Comments	Score
IV.4.1	Customer service flow policy	Existence of a frequent delivery service policy. Delivery lead times should be the minimum possible according to reliable milk run operations.		
IV.4.2	Picking operations	Degree of efficiency of binning operations (movements of workers against standard targets).		
IV.4.3	Leveling of picking operations	Use of leveling (or *heijunka*) box to control binning operations. Implies wave picking in standard pitch cycles.		
IV.4.4	Check/sort operations	Justification for the check/control operations. Ideal state is no outbound quality control and sorting justified to obtain higher picking productivity and cross docking from inbound. Must have sort operations in case of wave picking.		
IV.4.5	Loading operations	Degree of efficiency of the loading work of the milk run operator (implies an effort to use truck capacity effectively and make the loading an efficient operation).		
IV.4.6	Outbound KPIs	Degree of existence of outbound KPIs (lines/man-hour, etc.).		
IV.4.7	Outbound standard work	Degree of improvement activities performed in all outbound operations (check evidence of value stream projects, *gemba kaizen* workshops, and other improvement activities).		

na: not applicable
0: very insufficient
1: insufficient
2: sufficient
3: good
4: very good

Company: _____ Logistic Loop: _____
Analyst: _____ Date: _____ Avg Score: _____

Figure D.23 External logistics flows—delivery flows.

339

No.	Logistics Pull Planning	How to Score	Comments	Score
IV.5.1	Planning strategy for product references (PR)	Degree of definition of MTS (make to stock) or MTO (make to order) for the product references.		
IV.5.2	Capacity planning of storage cells	Degree of capacity planning using forecasted demand and OIL (optimum inventory levels) to set up the needed storage capacity in time for consumption.		
IV.5.3	Sales–warehouse contract	Use of a formal meeting or process between sales and warehouse for the definition of the forecasted capacity and how to deal with variations in the mix.		
IV.5.4	Execution planning for MTS PRs	Use of pull algorithms for MTS products based on frequent inventory replenishment algorithms.		
IV.5.5	Inventory accuracy	Degree of accuracy of the inventory and effective use of continuous inventory checking practices.		
IV.5.6	Service KPIs	Existence of OTIF (on time delivery in full) measurement and targets for OTIF improvement.		
IV.5.7	Inventory KPIs	Existence of inventory coverage (or inventory rotation) measurement and targets for inventory reduction.		

na: not applicable
0: very insufficient
1: insufficient
2: sufficient
3: good
4: very good

Company: _____   Logistic Loop: _____
Analyst: _____   Date: _____   Avg Score: _____

Figure D.24   External logistics flows—logistics pull planning.

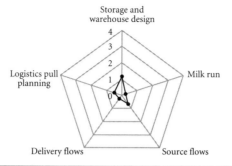

No.	External Logistics Flow – Top 5 Issues
1	
2	
3	
4	
5	

Figure D.25   External logistics flows—summary.

Bibliography

Barker, J. (1993). *Paradigms: The Business of Discovering the Future.* New York: HarperBusiness.

Dweck, C. S. (2006). *Mindset: The New Psychology of Success.* New York: Random House.

Forrester, J. (1961). *Industrial Dynamics.* Cambridge, MA: MIT Press.

Graupp, P., and Wrona, R. J. (2006). *The TWI Workbook: Essential Skills of Supervisors.* New York: Productivity Press.

Imai, M. (1986). *Kaizen: The Key to Japan's Competitive Success.* New York: McGraw-Hill.

Imai, M. (2012). *Gemba Kaizen: A Commonsense Approach to a Continuous Improvement Strategy.* New York: McGraw-Hill.

Ohno, T. (2013). *Taiichi Ohno's Workplace Management.* New York: McGraw-Hill.

Rother, M., Shook, J., Womack, J., and Jones, D. (1999). *Learning to See: Value-Stream Mapping to Create Value and Eliminate Muda.* Cambridge, MA: Lean Enterprises Institute.

Sekine, K., Arai, K., and Talbot, B. (1992). *Kaizen for Quick Changeover: Going Beyond SMED* (trans. by B. Talbot). Portland, OR: Productivity Press.

Shingo, S. (1985a). *A Revolution in Manufacturing: The SMED System.* Stamford, CT: Productivity Press.

Shingo, S. (1985b). *Zero Quality Control: Source Inspection and the Poka-Yoke System* (trans. by A. P. Dillion). Portland, OR: Productivity Press.

Shingo, S. (1989). *A Study of the Toyota Production System: From an Industrial Engineering Viewpoint.* Portland, OR: Productivity Press.

Smalley, A. (2004). *Creating Level Pull: A Lean Production-System Improvement Guide for Production-Control, Operations, and Engineering Professionals.* Cambridge, MA: Lean Enterprises Institute.

INDEX

Absenteeism, 49
Action plans,
    263–274
    defined, 230
    gemba kaizen workshops, 264–269
    kobetsu, 267, 268
        line-design, 267–269
        SMED (single-minute exchange of
            dies), 264–266
        standard work, 266–267
    kaizen foundation approach and,
        263–264
    other implementation points, 272–274
    specialized subprojects, 269–272
        Company A, 284–287
        external logistics, 272
        logistics implementation, 270–271
        pull planning, 271–272
Andons, 70
Apple, 7
Assemble-to-order strategy, 163–164
Automated guided vehicles (AGV), 133
Autonomous quality control, 70
Autonomy, of small containers, 74

Barker, Joel, 5
Basic reliability/basic stability, 40, 45–56
    change capability, 45–46
    creating *kaizen* mindset, 46

Basic reliability/basic stability (*Cont.*):
    four *M*s, 40, 48–56
    identifying critical *muda* variables, 46–48
    in *kaizen* reliability training and scorecard
        audit, 238–240, 241, 242
    machine basic reliability, 48, 51–53
    manpower basic reliability, 48, 49–51,
        54–56
    materials basic reliability, 48, 53–54
    methods basic reliability, 48, 54
    production-flow scorecard, 241, 242
Batch-building boxes, 159–161, 169–171, 255,
    308
Beer Distribution Game, 153
Beer Game, 247–249
Bending cells, 18
Bill of materials, 117–118
Binning, 213
Border of line, 73–82
    advantages of using small containers, 74–76
    arrangement of parts, 81–82
    concept of small container, 73–74, 82
    defined, 38, 73
    flow containers, 79–81
    location of parts and containers, 77–78
    nature of, 59–60
    production-flow actions, 284
    single feed, 81–82
    types of, 76–77

Border-of-line supermarkets, 122–123, 144
Bosch, 56
Bosch Production System, 56
Broken-case handling, 179–181, 204
Bulk containers, 198, 199, 200, 201
Bullwhip effect, 151–154
Buying plans, 24

Call-off orders, 112–113, 165
Capacity adjustment, 168
Capacity planning, 164–165
Cause-and-effect diagrams, 53
Chaku chaku line design, 61–62, 70, 86–87, 102
Change:
    old *versus* new paradigms, 4–6, 25–26
    resistance to, 5, 54–56
Change capability, 45–46
Changeover suppliers, 100–101
Changeover (CO) time, 11, 47, 58, 95
    gradual reduction, 101
    one-container quick changeover capability, 138
Christopher Columbus model, 14
Churchill, Winston, 14
Columbus, Christopher, 14
Commonality of parts, 164
Company A, 17–26, 275–288
    continuous improvement (CI), 24–26
    described, 17
    finished goods assembly lines, 19–24, 278–283
    kaizen pull-flow planning and implementation, 276–288
    key performance indicators (KPIs), 275–276
    process improvement, 18–19
    results and ongoing strategy, 287–288
    subprojects, 284–287
    supply chain and logistics loops, 19–24
        assembly of finished goods, 21–23

Company A, supply chain and logistics loops (*Cont.*):
        buying components from external suppliers, 24
        picking and delivery of finished goods, 20–21
        preassembly and internal manufacturing, 23
Computer numerical control (CNC), 104–105
Continuous improvement (CI), 3, 24–26. See also Toyota Production System (TPS) and entries beginning with "Kaizen"
Continuous material movement, 58
Continuous supply. See Kanban (continuous supply)
Cross-dock distribution centers, 193–194, 195, 217
Cross-dock hubs, 193
Cross-docking, 191, 193
Current-state analysis, 229–250
    action plan, 230, 263–274
    building teams and setting challenges, 230–232
    defining main KPIs of current state, 249–250
    gemba walk in, 232–238
    of information flow, 236–237
    kaizen reliability training and scorecard audit, 56, 238–249
    of material flow, 233–235
    preparing, 232–233
    value-stream design (VSD), 230–232, 251–262
    value-stream mapping (VSM), 229–238
    waste observation and awareness exercises, 237–238
Customer call-off, 224
Customer demand data, 237
Customer packaging requirements, 179–181
Customer-service policies, 190–192
Customer-service-level data, 237
Cycle time, 64–66, 68, 252

Daisy-line design, 69, 252
Data reliability, 172
Data types, in information-flow map, 237
Delivery flows, 176–177, 211–219
    basic warehouse operations, 212
    delivery side and, 14
    elements of delivery flow strategy, 218–219
    external logistics flow and, 39, 173–174,
        176–177, 211–219
    factors in creating, 211–212
    flow warehouse operations, 181–182, 212,
        213–218
        large and awkward parts, 216
        medium-sized parts, 216–218
        small parts, 218
    nature of, 173–174
    production-flow actions, 286
    in value-stream design, 231, 258–259
Delivery in full and on time (DIFOT), 21
Demand amplification effect, 220
Demand seasonality, 167–168
Demand spikes, inventory to offset, 168
Discovering the Future (Barker), 5
Dunning/dunnage, 75, 81
Dweck, Carol S., 4
Dysfunctional inventory, 112

Economic order quantity (EOQ) model,
    96–97
Effective utilization time, 52
Efficiency:
    efficiency-at-any-cost paradigm, 98
    OEE (overall equipment effectiveness of
        key equipment), 51–53, 267
Engineering department, in value-stream
    design, 231
Enterprise resource planning (ERP), 22–24,
    34–35, 112
EOQ model, 96–97
EPEI concept, 117, 150–151
Equipment operating time, 51–53

Ergo packs, 81, 130
Ergonomic factors, in using small containers,
    76
ERP (enterprise resource planning), 22–24,
    34–35, 112
Escher, Mauritz Cornelis, 29–30
Every product every interval (EPEI), 117,
    150–151
Execution planning, 165–167
External *junjo* containers, 198–201
External logistics flow, 37, 171–225
    categories in, 39
    delivery flows, 39, 173–174, 176–177,
        211–219
    external logistics subprojects, 272
    improving, 39
    introduction, 171–178
    in *kaizen* reliability training and scorecard
        audit, 245–249
    logistics pull planning, 39, 177–178, 207,
        219–225
    milk runs, 39, 175, 176, 189–196
    production-flow scorecard, 248, 249
    source flows, 173–174, 175–176, 197–209
    storage and warehouse design, 39,
        174–175, 178–187
    subprojects, 272, 286–287
    traditional approach compared with,
        172–173
External transportation, 219

Far milk runs, 194–195, 196
Final customer order, 20–21
Finished goods assembly lines:
    in no *kaizen*, no pull-flow company, 19–24
    planning strategy, 162–164
    production flow concepts in, 278–283
Finished goods picking, 31–33, 34
Finished goods production, 33
Finished goods strategy, 162–164
Finished goods warehouses, 179, 180

First-in, first-out (FIFO) principle, 77, 78, 118, 119, 121, 132, 143, 160, 170
Five *S*s (5S), 55
Five whys technique, 53
5S Game, 240
Fixed location (FL), 187
Fixed mindsets, 4
Flexible layout, 186
Flow:
 defined, 27
 pull-flow *versus* push-flow supply chains, 4–6, 25–26, 221
 types, 27–28
Flow containers, size standards, 79–81
Flow service contracts, 191
Flow-rack supermarkets, 120–121
Focused changeover improvement group, 100–101
Ford, Henry, 57, 59
Forecast orders, 112–113, 172
Forklifts, 23, 115, 128–131
Forrester, J., 153
Four *M*s of basic reliability, 40, 48–56. *See also* Manpower basic reliability
 machine basic reliability, 48, 51–53
 materials basic reliability, 48, 53–54
 methods basic reliability, 48, 54
Front supply, 77, 146
Functional layout, 62–66

Galileo, 5
Gemba kaizen, 46, 219. *See also* Current-state analysis
Gemba Kaizen (Imai), 3
Gemba kaizen workshop, 8, 13, 40, 52–53, 264–269
 kobetsu, 267, 268
 line-design, 267–269
 SMED, 264–266
 standard work, 266–267
Gemba orientation, 7–8, 114–115, 116, 232–238

Gembutsu (real things), 8
Goods ready to be sold, 220–222
 finished goods warehouses, 179, 180
 logistics pull planning, 220–221
Graupp, Patrick, 50
Ground storage on wheels, 120–121
Growth mindsets, 4–6

Hanedashi, 106
Harris, F. W., 96
Heijunka (leveling), 117, 149. *See also* Leveling
Heinunka (leveling) boxes, 132, 158
High runners, 163

Imai, Masaaki, 3
Implementation. *See* Action plans
Inbound operations flows, 31, 198–205, 219
 external logistics flow and, 39
 muda elimination, 204–205
 supply logistics, 202–204
 traditional, 198–202
Inbound warehouse operations, 31
Information flow, 109, 236–237
Information-flow map, 236–237, 259
Intermodal containers, 190
Internal *junjo* containers, 198, 199, 200, 201
Internal logistics flow, 37, 109–170
 categories in, 39
 defined, 119
 improving, 38–39
 in *kaizen* reliability training and scorecard audit, 244–245, 246, 247
 leveling, 110, 117, 149–161
 mizusumashi, 39, 109, 115–116, 127–136, 144–147
 production-flow scorecard, 246, 247
 production-pull planning, 39, 110, 117–118, 162–170
 in pull-flow supply chains, 254–255
 supermarkets, 39, 109, 114–115, 118–126, 144–147

Internal logistics flow (*Cont.*):
  synchronization, 39, 110, 112, 116–117, 136–147
  traditional supply *versus* flow supply, 110–114, 221
Internal transport system, 204
Inventory accumulation, 10
Inventory coverage, 21
Inventory management:
  finished-goods strategy, 162–164
  first-in, first-out (FIFO) principle, 77, 78, 118, 119, 121, 132, 143, 160, 170
  goods ready to be sold, 179, 180, 220–222
  to offset demand spikes, 168
  replenishment signal, 142, 145, 211–212
  safety stock, 153–154, 172
  vendor-managed inventory (VMI), 178, 219
  in waste reduction, 28–30
  work in process (WIP), 23, 47, 59, 62–63, 84
Ishikawa diagrams, 53

Jidoka, 70
Job Instruction (JI), 50, 88, 273, 283
Job-shop layout, 62
Jobs, Steve, 7
Jones, Dan, 229–230
Junjo (sequenced supply), 34, 74, 76–77, 116–117, 124, 131–133, 134, 136, 141–144, 146–147, 176, 198–201, 252, 280, 283
Junjo cards, 142
Junjo loops, 116–117, 141–144
Junjo supermarkets, 122–123
Just-in-sequence delivery. *See Junjo* (sequenced supply)

Kaizen (Imai), 3
Kaizen clouds, 260, 261

Kaizen Institute, 3–4, 8, 40, 46, 55–56, 98
Kaizen management system (KMS), 55–56
Kaizen mindset, 46
Kaizen pull-flow principles, 5, 6–16, 113–114, 263–264. *See also* Pull-flow supply chains
  adopting, 13
  at Company A, 275–288
  concept of, 3–4
  gemba orientation, 7–8, 114–115, 116, 232–238
  implementing, 3–4, 276–288. *See also* Toyota Production System (TPS)
  models of pull flow, 169–170
  people development, 10–11
  process and results, 11–12
  pull-flow thinking, 12–13
  quality first, 7, 18–19, 70, 75
  steps for leveling, 154
  structure in logistics and supply chains, 14–16
  supply chains. *See* Pull-flow supply chains
  sustaining, 13–14
  visual standards, 11
  waste elimination, 8–10
Kanban (continuous supply), 34, 74, 76–77, 115–117, 122–125, 131–133, 146–147, 252, 283
  converting orders into *kanban* cards, 155–156, 162–163
  production loops, 139–140, 301–311
    production-batch, 140, 308–311
    production-flow, 139, 301–305
    production-signal, 140, 305–308
  replenishment logistics loop, 136–139
  transport loops, 139, 291–299
    transport-delivery, 139, 291–293
    transport-internal, 139, 297–299
    transport-source, 139, 294–296
  types of *kanban* loops, 136, 139–141, 291–299, 301–311

Kanban cards, 116, 128, 136–137, 138, 140, 149–150, 154, 155–156, 158, 159, 162, 169–170, 271, 291, 296
Kanban mizusumashi, 132, 133
Karakuri, 72, 102
Key performance indicators (KPIs), 84
    defining current state, 249–250
    examples of, 18, 64–65
Kitting, 123–124, 146–147
Kitting supermarkets, 123–124
Kobetsu:
    defined, 267
    gemba kaizen kobetsu workshop, 267, 268
KPIs. *See* Key performance indicators (KPIs)

Large containers, 198, 199, 200, 201, 203
    ergo packs, 81, 130
    size standards, 81
    supermarket, 121
Layout and line design. *See* Line and layout design
Layout vision map, 259
Lead time:
    calculating, 257
    categories of, 138
    estimating, 47
    nature of, 15, 28
    reducing, 222
    supply, 224
    total lead time within the pull logistics loops, 47
Lean transformation. *See also* Toyota Production System (TPS) *and entries beginning with "Kaizen"*
    Christopher Columbus model in, 14
    tools of, 19
Learning by doing, 45–46
Learning organizations, 45–46
Learning to See (Rother et al.), 229–230, 233
Leveling, 149–161
    bullwhip effect, 151–154

Leveling (*Cont.*):
    format design, 150
    internal logistics flow and, 39, 110
    line sequencing, 155–159
    nature of, 110, 117
    process of, 149–150
    production-flow actions, 285–286
    standard leveling model, 159–161
    Toyota definition, 150–151, 152
Leveling (*heinunka*) boxes, 132, 158
Life-cycle time, 69
Limit of current paradigm, 5
Line and layout design, 38, 58–59, 62–72
    functional layout, 62–66
    gemba kaizen line-design workshop, 267–269
    information-flow map in, 259
    key principles, 71–72
    layout vision map in, 259
    lean line-design features, 69–71
    line balancing, 67–69
    mockups in, 71
    nature of, 58–59
    optimized one-piece flow line, 70
    process graphs, 66–68
    process layout, 62–64
    production-flow actions, 284
    production-flow scorecard, 243, 244
    simple profiling, 66–69
Line balancing, 67–69
Line sequencing, 155–160
Line-haul transport, 190
Local distribution centers, 179, 180
Local milk runs, 193–194, 196
Local-far milk runs, 194, 195
Logistical flow, 118–119
Logistics and supply chains, 14–16, 34–35, 40–41
    external logistics flow. *See* External logistics flow
    internal logistics flow. *See* Internal logistics flow

Logistics and supply chains (*Cont.*):
  logistics domains. *See* Logistics domains
      overview, 37
  paradoxes of, 30–31
  production flow. *See* Production flow
      system for *kaizen*, 28
Logistics boxes, 156–157
Logistics cells, 121–122
Logistics department, in value-stream
      design, 231
Logistics domains:
  leveling, 110, 117
  logistics implementation subprojects,
      270–271
  mizusumashi, 109, 115–116, 127–136,
      144–147
  production pull planning, 39, 110, 117–118,
      162–170
  supermarkets, 39, 109, 114–115, 118–126,
      144–147
  synchronization, 39, 110, 112, 116–117,
      136–147
  traditional *versus* flow supply, 110–114
Logistics loops (LLs), 19–24
  assembly of finished goods, 21–23
  buying components from external
      suppliers, 24
  chain of, 34–35, 36
  picking and delivering finished goods,
      20–21
  preassembly and internal manufacturing,
      23
  supply chain, 34–35, 36
  theory of pull, 31–34
Logistics pull planning, 177–178, 207,
      219–225
  algorithms for, 313–314
  external logistics flow and, 39, 177–178,
      207, 219–225
  goods ready to be sold, 220–222
  order pull planning, 223–225

Logistics pull planning (*Cont.*):
  production-flow actions, 287
  steps in, 222–223
Logistics unit output, 175
Losses time, 52
Low runners, 163
Low-cost automation (LCA), 61–62,
      101–108
  automation levels, 102–104
  comparison with conventional
      automation, 101
  design guidelines, 107–108
  examples of LCA devices, 104–107
  nature of, 38, 61–62
  production-flow actions, 284

Machine basic reliability, 48, 51–53
Machine CO time, 47
Main distribution centers, 179, 180
Maintenance department, in value-stream
      design, 231
Make to order (MTO), 33, 113, 117–118,
      162–170, 176, 281
  capacity planning, 164–165
  demand seasonality, 167–168
  execution planning, 165–167
  finished-goods strategy, 162–164
  inventory to offset demand spikes, 168
  models of pull flow, 169–170
  parts-supply strategy, 164
Make to stock (MTS), 33, 113, 117–118,
      162–170, 178, 281. *See also*
      Stock-keeping units (SKUs)
  capacity planning, 164–165
  demand seasonality, 167–168
  execution planning, 165–167
  finished-goods strategy, 162–164
  inventory to offset demand spikes,
      168
  models of pull flow, 169–170
  parts-supply strategy, 164

Manpower basic reliability, 48, 49–51
    absenteeism, 49
    people development, 10–11
    punctuality, 49
    resistance to change, 54–56
    standardize, do, check, and act (SDCA),
        49–51
Market in principle, 7
Master production schedule, 281
Material waiting quantities, 237
Material-flow map, 233–235
Materials basic reliability, 48, 53–54
Materials requirements planning (MRP), 25,
    34–35, 112, 172, 202, 256–257, 281
Medium containers:
    size standards, 80–81
    supermarket, 121
Methods basic reliability, 48, 54
Methods-time measurement (MTM), 23
Milk runs, 189–196
    customer-service policies, 190–192
    external logistics flow and, 39, 175, 176
    nature of, 141, 175, 189, 192
    production-flow actions, 286
    Toyota City, 190
    types, 192–195
    using different types, 196
Mindset (Dweck), 4
Mixed production, 97, 117
Mixed-model lines, 68
Mizusumashi, 127–136
    assembly-line supply, 131–133
    characteristics of, 127–128
    designing a *mizusumashi* line, 134–136
    examples, 144–147
    implementing, 270–271, 283
    internal logistics flow and, 39, 109,
        115–116, 127–136, 144–147
    nature of, 109, 115–116, 127
    production-flow actions, 285
    standard work, 133, 135

Mizusumashi (*Cont.*):
    traditional forklift supply versus
        mizusumashi supply, 128–131
Mock-ups, 71, 259
Model T Ford, 59
Monthly plans, 22
Movable location (ML), 187
MRP (materials requirements planning), 25,
    34–35, 112, 172, 202, 256–257, 281
MTO. *See* Make to order (MTO)
MTS. *See* Make to stock (MTS)
Muda (waste), 5, 8–10, 25
    identifying critical variables, 46–48
    inventory accumulation, 10, 28–30
    material moving, 10, 28
    material waiting, 9, 12, 28
    synchronization of supply chain, 204–206
        defining container size, 204
        defining internal transport system, 204
        inbound operations flow, 204–205
        repacking, 205, 207
        returnable packaging, 205–206, 207
    targets for minimizing, 181
    types of, 28, 29
    waste observation and awareness exercises,
        237–238
Mura (variability), 8–9, 68–69, 154
Muri (difficulty), 8–9, 104

Nagara switches, 106
Next-day delivery, 223
Next-day service, 191
Nonfunctional inventory, 21

OEE (overall equipment effectiveness of key
    equipment), 51–53, 267
Ohno, Taiichi, 3–4, 8, 12, 27–28, 45–46, 57,
    64–65, 95–97, 114–115, 259
One-piece flow, 5, 18, 30–31, 57, 63–70, 253
One-piece mixed flow, 97
One-small-container flow, 109

Operations data, 237

Operations types, 27–28

Optimal inventory level (OIP), 225

Order pull planning, 223–225

Order size, 224, 294–296

Outbound operations flows, 39, 219

Outbound warehouse operations, 31

Overall equipment effectiveness of key
    equipment (OEE), 51–53, 267

Pacemaker lines, 52, 154, 155, 158

Paradigms:
    change and, 4–5, 54–56
    defined, 4
    fixed mindsets, 4
    growth mindsets, 4–6
    limit of current paradigm, 5
    new, 5
    pull-flow *versus* push-flow supply chains,
        4–6, 25–26, 221

Paradoxes, 28–31

Parts-supply strategy, 164

PDC (production distribution center), 19–24,
    28–30, 280–283

PDCA (plan, do, check, act) cycle, 53, 55, 267

People development, 10–11

Pick to order, 113

Picking alley, 122

Pitch time, 116, 156, 254

Plan, do, check, act (PDCA) cycle, 53, 55, 267

Plug Game, 242–244

Poka yoke devices, 70, 102, 105–107, 159,
    186–187

PQ (Parts Quantities or Pareto) analysis, 66,
    174

Primary location, 185

Primary (supermarket) storage, 209

Process analysis sheet, 233–235

Process and results, 11–12

Process graphs, 66–68

Process improvement, 18–19

Process layout, 62–64

Product distribution center (PDC), 19–24,
    28–30, 280–283

Product out principle, 7

Production department, in value-stream
    design, 231

Production flow, 37, 57–108. *See also* Total
    Flow Management (TFM) model
    border of line, 59–60, 73–82
    categories in, 38
    finished goods assembly line, 278–283
    improvement projects, 38
    internal logistics flow, 109–170
    in *kaizen* reliability training and scorecard
        audit, 240–244
    line and layout design, 38, 58–59, 62–72
    low-cost automation, 61–62, 101–108
    single-minute exchange of dies (SMED),
        60–61, 95–101
    standard work, 11, 60, 82–94
    subprojects for Company A, 284–286
    summary, 69–72
    targets of, 57, 58
    traditional supply *versus* flow supply, 4–6,
        25–26, 110–114, 221
    in value-stream future maps, 251–253

Production *kanban* loops, 139–140, 301–311
    production-batch, 140, 308–311
    production-flow, 139, 301–305
    production-signal, 140, 305–308

Production parts picking, 34

Production planning department, in value-
    stream design, 231

Production pull planning, 162–170
    algorithms for, 314–316
    capacity adjustment, 168
    capacity planning, 164–165
    dealing with demand seasonality,
        167–168
    deciding planning strategy, 162–164
    execution planning, 165–167

Production pull planning (*Cont.*):
    finished goods pull planning and leveling,
        280–283
    internal logistics flow and, 39, 110,
        117–118, 162–170
    inventory to offset demand spikes, 168
    models of pull flow, 169–170
    nature of, 110, 117–118
    production-flow actions, 286
    pull planning subprojects, 271–272
    in pull-flow supply chains, 255–256
Production-flow pillar, 58, 284–287
Production-logistics contracts, 156–157
Product-quantity (PQ) analysis, 66, 174
Pull logistics loops, 31–34
    FGs picking, 31–33
    FGs production, 33
    production parts picking, 34
Pull planning. *See* Logistics pull planning;
        Production pull planning
Pull-deliver strategy, 288
Pull-flow supply chains, 4, 12–13, 28, 41,
        110–114, 221, 251–262
    creating delivery-flow strategy, 258–259
    creating source-flow strategy, 256–258
    identifying internal logistics loops,
        254–255
    misunderstanding, 25
    production pull planning, 255–256
    push-flow supply chains *versus*, 4–6,
        25–26, 110–114, 221
    supply chain design strategy, 259–262
        defining vision, 259
        mock-ups, 259
        putting it into practice, 260–262
    total pull flow, 35–41
    value-stream future map, 251–254
        creating production flow, 251–253
        fine-tuning, 253–254
Pull-make strategy, 288
Pull-Plug Game, 245

Pull-source strategy, 288
Punctuality, 19
Purchasing, 24
Push-flow systems, 4–6, 25–26, 110–114, 221

Quality, cost, and delivery (QCD), 7
Quality first, 7, 18–19, 70, 75
Quality improvement, 18–19

R Game, 240
Raw material and components warehouses,
        179, 180
Reality orientation, 7–8
Rear supply, 77–78, 146
Regional distribution centers, 179, 180
Repacking, 205, 207
Replenishment signal, 142, 145, 211–212
Reserve storage, 209
Return on investment (ROI), 64, 260–262
Returnable packaging, 205–206, 207
Revolution in Manufacturing, A (Shingo), 95
Roller bases, 115
Rolling forecast, 165
Rother, Mike, 229–230

Safety stock, 153–154, 172
Same-day delivery, 223
Same-day service for orders received until
        10 a.m., 191
Same-day service, self pickup, 190, 223
SDCA (standardize, do, check, act), 49–51
Secondary location, 185
Seiketsu, 55
Seiri, 55
Seiso, 55
Seiton, 55
Self-pickup, 190, 223
Sequenced supply. *See Junjo* (sequenced
        supply)
Sequencers, 142–144, 155–160
Shingo, Shigeo, 27–28, 59, 95, 100, 105–107

Shitsuke, 55
Shojinka, 65–66, 69, 252
Shook, John, 229–230
Sigma, 52
Simple profiling, 66–69
Simulation games:
    5S Game, 240
    Beer Game, 247–249
    Plug Game, 242–244
    Pull-Plug Game, 245
    R Game, 240
Single-minute exchange of dies (SMED), 38,
    95–101, 151, 240, 252
    conflicting targets in, 97–98
    gemba kaizen workshops, 264–266
    impact on capacity, flexibility, and flow,
        96–97
    nature of, 38, 60–61
    origins of, 95–96
    production-flow actions, 284
    SMED process, 98–101
SKUs (stock-keeping units), 19, 178, 182, 185,
    212. *See also* Make to stock (MTS)
Small containers, 198, 199, 200, 201, 203
    advantages of using, 74–76
    autonomy of, 74
    concept of, 73–74, 82
    defined, 82, 120
    location of parts and containers, 77–78
    one-small-container flow, 109
    paradox of using, 30
    standard for flow containers, 79–80, 82
    in supermarkets, 120–121
SMED. *See* Single-minute exchange of dies
    (SMED)
SMED effect, 96
Source flows, 175–176, 197–209
    elements of source-flow strategy, 206–209
    eliminating *muda* through
        synchronization of supply chain,
        204–206

Source flows (*Cont.*):
    external logistics flow and, 173–174,
        175–176, 197–209
    inbound supply logistics, 202–204
    nature of, 173–174
    production-flow actions, 286
    source side and, 14
    traditional inbound operations flows,
        198–202
    traditional *versus* flow paradigms, 197, 221
    in value-stream design, 231, 256–257
Spaghetti charts, 40
    specific *junjo*, 132–133
Standard leveling model, 159–161
Standard work, 11, 34, 38, 82–94
    gemba kaizen workshop, 266–267
    mizusumashi line, 128, 135
    nature of, 60
    production-flow actions, 284
    role of containers in design of, 88–94
Standard work improvement process, 84–88
    consolidating work, 87–88
    defining target for improvement, 84
    improving work, 86
    observing work, 85–86
    standardizing work, 86–87
    steps in, 85
Standard work sheet (SWS), 86–87, 135, 245
Standardize, do, check, and act (SDCA),
    49–51
Stock review, 224
Stock-keeping units (SKUs), 19, 178, 182, 185,
    212. *See also* Make to stock (MTS)
Storage and warehouse design, 178–187, 219
    customer packaging requirements,
        179–181
    external logistics flow and, 39, 174–175,
        178–187
    nature of, 174–175
    organization and availability, 178–179
    production-flow actions, 286

Storage and warehouse design (*Cont.*):
  traditional *versus* flow warehouses,
    181–182
  warehouse flow principles, 183–187
    fewer abnormalities, 186–187
    flexible layout, 186
    product stored by type and turnover,
      183–185
    product-specific storage location for
      each part by part number, 185
    storage of delivery packages is
      accommodated, 186
    visual management, 186
  warehouse paradigms, 181–182
  warehouse types, 179, 180, 209
*Study of the Toyota Production System: From
  an Industrial Engineering Viewpoint, A*
  (Shingo), 27–28, 95, 105–107
Subassembly cells, 18, 23
Subprojects, 272, 286–287
Supermarket size simulation, 125–126
Supermarkets, 118–126
  border-of-line, 122–123, 144
  deciding size of, 124–126
  examples, 144–146
  flow racks, 120–121
  ground storage on wheels, 120–121
  implementing, 270, 283
  internal logistics flow and, 39, 109,
    114–115, 118–126, 144–147
  kitting, 123–124
  logistics cells, 118, 121–122
  nature of, 109, 114–115
  production-flow actions, 285
  rules of, 118
Supplier frequency of shipment, 224
Supply chains:
  as chain of logistics loops, 34–35, 36
  pull-flow systems. *See* Pull-flow supply
    chains
  push-flow systems, 4–6, 25–26, 110–114, 221

Supply chains (*Cont.*):
  structure in, 14–16
  supply-chain design, 38, 40–41, 230–232,
    251–262
Supply lead time, 224
Sustainability, 13–14
Swap-trailer far milk runs, 194–195
Synchronization, 136–147, 254–255
  examples, 144–147
  importance of, 25
  internal logistics flow and, 39, 110, 112,
    116–117, 136–147
  junjo logistics loops, 141–144
  kanban replenishment logistics loop,
    136–139
  muda elimination through supply chain,
    204–206
  nature of, 110, 116–117, 136
  production-flow actions, 285
  types of *kanban* loops, 139–141
Synchronization domain, 136
Synchronization effectiveness, 142

Takt time, 28, 51–53, 59, 109
TFM. *See* Total Flow Management (TFM)
  model
Time factors:
  time-saving devices, 102
  in using small containers, 76
Total Flow Management (TFM) model, 4,
  12–13, 28, 34, 38, 39–41, 142–144
  basic model, 15
  basic reliability, 40, 45–56
    change capability, 45–46
    creating *kaizen* mindset, 46
    four *M*s, 40, 48–56
    identifying critical *muda* variables,
      46–48
  external logistics flow, 37, 171–225
    delivery flows, 173–174, 176–177,
      211–219

Total Flow Management (TFM) model,
external logistics flow (*Cont.*):
introduction, 171–178
logistics pull planning, 39, 177–178,
207, 219–225
milk runs, 39, 175, 176, 189–196
source flows, 173–174, 175–176,
197–209
storage and warehouse design, 39,
174–175, 178–187
internal logistics flow, 37, 109–170
leveling, 110, 117, 149–161
logistics domains. *See* Logistics domains
mizusumashi, 109, 115–116, 127–136,
144–147
production-pull planning, 39, 110,
117–118, 162–170
supermarkets, 39, 109, 114–115,
118–126, 144–147
synchronization, 39, 110, 112, 116–117,
136–147
traditional supply *versus* flow supply,
110–114, 221
logistics and supply chains in, 14–16,
34–35, 40–41
overview, 38
production flow, 37, 38, 57–108
border of line, 59–60, 73–82
line and layout design, 38, 58–59, 62–72
low-cost automation, 61–62, 101–108
standard work, 11, 60, 82–94
pull-flow supply chains in. *See* Pull-flow
supply chains
scorecards, 317–341
SMED (single-minute exchange of dies),
38, 60–61, 95–101, 151
total pull flow in, 35–41
Total lead time within the pull logistics
loops, 47
Total pull flow, 35–41
Toyoda family, 12

Toyota Motor Corporation, 3–4, 6–16, 27–28,
40, 50, 60, 88–89, 95, 96, 177, 273
kitting system, 147
Koromo plant, 64–65
Toyota Production System (TPS), 3–4, 12–13,
30, 56, 83, 95, 98
leveling, 150–151, 152
Toyota's journey to lean distribution, 187
Toyota Sewing System (TSS), 89
Toyota Supply-Chain System. *See* Total Flow
Management (TFM) model; Toyota
Production System (TPS)
TPM prepared line, 70
Training Within Industry (TWI) training
programs, 50, 88, 273, 283
Transport. *See* External logistics flow; Internal
logistics flow
Transport hubs, 191
Transport *kanban* loops, 139, 291–299
transport-delivery, 139, 291–293
transport-internal, 139, 297–299
transport-source, 139, 294–296
Trigger points, 125
TWI Workbook (Graupp and Wrona), 50
Two-bin systems, 18, 24
Two-day delivery, 223

Unit batches. *See* One-piece flow
U.S. Army, 273
U.S. Department of War, War Manpower
Commission, 273
Unloading time, 102, 106–107
Upstream improvement, 7

Valeo, 56
Valeo Production System, 56
Value-added operations, 59, 69
Value-stream design (VSD), 230–232
building teams and setting challenges,
230–232
defined, 230

Value-stream design (VSD) (*Cont.*):
  departments involved in, 231
  number of people, 231
  pull-flow supply chains in, 251–262
    delivery-flow strategy, 231, 258–259
    finalizing design strategy, 259–262
    internal logistics loops, 254–255
    production pull planning, 255–256
    source-flow strategy, 256–257
    value-stream future maps, 251–254
Value-stream future maps, 251–254
  creating production flow, 251–253
  fine-tuning, 253–254
Value-stream mapping (VSM), 229–238
  defined, 229–230
  of information flow, 236–237
  of material flow, 233–235
  overview, 199
  in supply-chain design, 40
Vendor-managed inventory (VMI), 178,
  219
Very small containers, 198, 199, 200
Vibrator bowls, 81
Vision, in supply-chain design strategy,
  259–262
Visual management, 115, 186
Visual standards, 11

Warehouse management system (WMS), 217

Warehouses. *See also* Storage and warehouse
    design
  basic operations, 212
  inbound *versus* outbound operations, 31
  nature of, 24, 31
  paradigms, 181–182
  storage principles, 213–216
  types of, 179–181
  types of logistics units, 212–213
Waste elimination. *See also Muda* (waste)
  three *Ms*, 8–10
  types of waste, 8
Water spider. *See Mizusumashi*
Waterfall (Escher), 29–30
Weekly plans, 22
Whiplash effect, 222
Wilson model, 96, 97–98, 138
Wilson, R. H., 96, 97–98
Womack, James, 229–230
Work in process (WIP), 23, 47, 59, 62–63, 84
Work-content load, 154
Workplace Management (Ohno), 45
World class business management system, 9
World War II, 3, 50, 273
Wrona, Robert J., 50

Yamazumi charts, 68

Zero setup, 61

ABOUT THE KAIZEN INSTITUTE

Founded by Masaaki Imai in 1985, the Kaizen Institute is the pioneer and global leader in promoting the spirit and practice of *kaizen*. Its global team of professionals is dedicated to building a world where it is possible for everyone, everywhere, every day, to improve their work and themselves.

The Kaizen Institute guides organizations to achieve higher levels of performance in the global marketplace—easier, faster, better, and cheaper. The Kaizen Institute's *sensei* challenge clients to help develop leaders capable of sustaining continuous improvement in all aspects of their enterprise. The Kaizen Institute creates a worldwide community of practice in *kaizen*.

The major services of the Kaizen Institute include

- Consulting and implementation
  - Partnering with clients for long-term *kaizen* implementation
  - Operating-system design and deployment
  - Breakthrough projects and turnarounds
- Education and training
  - Business training and academic and online training curriculum design
  - *Kaizen* practitioner, coach, and manager level certification
  - On-site training, workshops, and seminars
- Tours and benchmarking
  - *Kaikaku* benchmark to best-in-class organizations in Japan and worldwide
  - Building peer-to-peer learning and tour exchange network

Visit www.kaizen.com to learn more about *kaizen* and the world-changing purpose of the Kaizen Institute.

KAIZEN INSTITUTE CONSULTING GROUP

AMERICAS

United States

Kaizen Institute
7137 East Rancho Vista Drive, B-11
Scottsdale, AZ 85251 USA
Tel: +1 480 320 3476
Fax: +1 480 320 3479
Email: usa@kaizen.com

México

Kaizen Institute
Av. Chapultepec 408
Int. 3 Colinas del Parque
78260 México
Tel: +52 444 1518585
Email: mx@kaizen.com

Brazil

Kaizen Institute
Al. dos Jurupis, 452 – Torre A – 2º
Andar 04088-001
São Paulo – SP Brazil
Tel: +55 (11) 5052 6681
Fax: +55 (11) 5052 6681
Email: br@kaizen.com

Chile

Kaizen Institute
Av. Providencia 1998 of. 203
Providencia, Santiago, Chile
Tel: +52 (0) 2-231-1450
Email: cl@kaizen.com

ASIA PACIFIC

Japan

Kaizen Institute
2-9 Kagurazaka
Shinjuku, Tokyo
162-0825
Tel: +81 (0) 3 6909 8320
Fax: +81 (0) 3 6909 8321
Email: jp@kaizen.com

China

Kaizen Institute
1027 Chang Ning Road, Suite 2206
Shanghai, China
Tel: +86 (0) 21 6248 2365
Email: cn@kaizen.com

Singapore

Kaizen Institute
20 Cecil Street
#14-01 Equity Plaza
Singapore 049705
Tel: +65 (0) 6305 2410
Email: sg@kaizen.com

New Zealand
Kaizen Institute
15a Vestey Drive, Mt Wellington
Auckland 1060 New Zealand
Tel: +64 (09) 588 5184
Email: nz@kaizen.com

India
Kaizen Institute
Office No. 1A, Second Floor
Sunshree Woods Commercial Complex
NIBM Road
Kondhwa 411 048 Pune, India
Tel: +91 92255 27911
Email: in@kaizen.com

EUROPE, MIDDLE EAST, and AFRICA

Germany
Kaizen Institute
Werner-Reimers-Strasse 2–4
D-61352 Bad Homburg, Germany
Tel: +49 (0) 6172 888 55 0
Fax: +49 (0) 6172 888 55 55
Email: de@kaizen.com

France
Kaizen Institute
Techn'Hom 3
15 Rue Sophie Germain
F-90000 Belfort, France
Tel: +33 145356644
Fax +33 145356564
Email: fr@kaizen.com

United Kingdom
Kaizen Institute
Regus House
Herald Way
Pegasus Business Park
Castle Donington DE74 2TZ UK
Tel: +44 (0) 1332 6381 14
Email: uk@kaizen.com

Netherlands
Kaizen Institute
Bruistensingel 208
5232 AD, 's-Hertogenbosch
Netherlands
Tel: +31 (0)73 700 3440
Email: nl@kaizen.com

Spain
Kaizen Institute
Ribera del Loira, 46 Edificio 2
28042 Madrid, Spain
Tel: +34 91 503 00 19
Fax: +34 91 503 00 99
Email: es@kaizen.com

Switzerland
Kaizen Institute
Bahnhofplatz
Zug 6300 Switzerland
Tel: +41 (0) 41 725 42 80
Fax: +41 (0) 41 725 42 89
Email: ch@kaizen.com

Portugal
Kaizen Institute
Rua Manuel Alves Moreira, 207
4405-520 V.N.Gaia, Portugal
Tel: +351 22 372 2886
Fax: +351 22 372 2887
Email: pt@kaizen.com

Italy
Kaizen Institute
Piazza dell'Unità, 12 40128
Bologna, Italy
Tel: +39 051 587 67 44
Fax: +39 051 587 67 73
Email: italy@kaizen-institute.it

Kenya
Kaizen Institute
c/o KAM – Kenya Association of
    Manufacturers
3 Mwanzi Road, Opp Nakumatt Westgate
Westlands
Nairobi, Kenya
Tel: +254722201368
Email: afr@kaizen.com

Additional Kaizen Institute locations
Austria, Czech Republic, Finland, Hungary, Malaysia, Poland, Romania, Russia

Website
www.kaizen.com

Online training
www.GembaAcademy.com

Blog
www.gembapantarei.com